Involuntary Motion

Involuntary Motion contributes to the study of refugee flight by using movement as a lens to explore problems in refugee performance and understand the experience of bodies in motion.

Drawing from somatics, movement analysis, and dance praxis, the chapters explore forces that set bodies in motion; the spaces in which forced movement occurs; the movement of refugee identity arcs; the monstrosity of refugee performance; and the relationship between writing and body culture. How does forced movement impact identity? What are the philosophical implications of robbing individuals of agency over motion? What performances does involuntary motion necessitate? These questions are important as the world confronts the threat of a return of the horrors of the twentieth century.

Bringing together debates in migration studies and movement studies, the book argues that refugees are akin to dancers performing on disappearing stages not of their choosing. This book will be of great interest to students and scholars of performance, dance, and politics.

Jeff Kaplan is Assistant Professor of Dance & Theatre at Manhattanville College, USA.

Involuntary Motion

The Somatics of Refugee Performance

Jeff Kaplan

Routledge
Taylor & Francis Group
LONDON AND NEW YORK

First published 2021
by Routledge
2 Park Square, Milton Park, Abingdon, Oxon OX14 4RN

and by Routledge
52 Vanderbilt Avenue, New York, NY 10017

Routledge is an imprint of the Taylor & Francis Group, an informa business

British Library Cataloguing-in-Publication Data
A catalogue record for this book is available from the British Library

Library of Congress Cataloging-in-Publication Data
A catalog record has been requested for this book

ISBN: 978-0-367-49004-1 (hbk)
ISBN: 978-1-003-09706-8 (ebk)

Typeset in Times New Roman
by Newgen Publishing UK

To my elementary school librarian, who told stories wonderfully. I don't remember her name, but I do recall promising myself if I ever wrote a book, I would dedicate it to her.

Contents

Figures

Acknowledgments

I would like to give special thanks to all of those who helped in the process of drawing forth this book from whatever ether such things emerge. Contrary to images of writers toiling away in garrets by candlelight in the dead hours, with piles of teabags leaving indelible stains on chipped saucers, writing does not (usually) happen that way. Most books manifest via collaborative effort. This one is no exception.

Consequently…

Special thanks to everyone at Routledge, including Ben Piggott, Laura Hussey, Swati Hindwan, Grant Schatzman, and the book's production team, led by Lekshmi Priya S., and Luke Finley for his virtuosic copyediting. Like a live performance, a book's audience sees the final product. I would love to show you the magic that happens backstage. Thanks also to whoever the anonymous peer reviewer was, who knew my subject better than I did.

Special thanks to Provost Louis Feroe and Dean of Arts and Sciences Christine Dehne at Manhattanville College for funding, support, and encouragement. Thanks also to everyone in the department of Dance & Theatre for their ongoing collegiality.

Special thanks to the organizers, activists, and photographers with whom I interfaced, and who forgave my clumsiness as I barged into their worlds. These individuals also validated the fact of my work. They felt that scholarship constitutes its own form of activism, which was encouraging beyond words.

Special thanks to my daughter for her forbearance, as well as her "tough love" in keeping me on track for chapter deadlines. You are my entire world, Arianna.

Finally, thank you to everyone who does something to ameliorate the plight of the tens of millions of displaced persons. Every act of kindness matters. As a metaphor, in Jewish cemeteries, visitors carry on a tradition of placing pebbles on tombstones. Time moves earth around, disturbing remains. By replacing small stones, passersby participate in *tikkum olam*, or "healing the world." In the same way, artists, activists, and scholars engage in acts of healing of immense potency. Something as mundane as making eye contact with another person restores a piece of humanity. Hopefully this book adds to this growing pile of effort. Thanks to all I forgot to mention.

Introduction

We stand witness to a catastrophe of global proportions. According to the UN High Commissioner for Refugees (UNHCR), violence has displaced 70.8 million people from their homes, approximately one out of every 112 people in the world. As of this writing, 57% of displaced persons come from three countries: Syria, South Sudan, and Afghanistan, which illustrates the unequal distribution of the costs of the crisis. On the other hand, 43% of refugees do not come from these regions, indicating a phenomenon that transcends any one conflict ("Figures at a Glance" 2019). To give a sense of scale, World War II rendered somewhere between seven and eleven million persons without homes. Although any one person's life is as valuable as an entire world, to paraphrase the Talmud, we should also reflect on the fact that the number of refugees in the aggregate is now ten times that of seven decades ago, when Europe lay in ashes. Wanderers have struck forth since 1945, but the presence of the foreign in numbers has engendered a resurgent nationalism that evokes the horrors of the twentieth century. Specters the past, never entirely banished, utter shibboleths with a brazenness that chills.

The act of writing about a phenomenon of such a scale itself risks dehumanization. With the most open of intentions, we distance the people we seek to empower. In a study of displaced Liberians in America, Bernadette Ludwig found that the word "refugee" stigmatizes either through victimization or beneficence (or both). As one of her subjects related, "When I hear that ['refugee'] I feel like an outcast, like somebody that had nothing." Naming people as "refugees" can make them feel as if their history has slipped through their fingers, "Like you're putting somebody down" (Ludwig 2016, p.12). One could respond, "but refugees *are* victims," and a stream of stories involving drowning, suffocating, and languishing would seem to bear out this judgment. Nevertheless, not only does such rhetoric fail to recognize that a refugee is more than a backpack and a blanket, or that many refugee stories do end well, but it reinforces a "politics of fear" that makes political action less likely (Bleiker et al. 2013). Artists, scholars, activists, and concerned citizens thus find themselves in a quandary over how to reconcile the need to *do* something, or to *write* something, without re-rehearsing familiar isms. How can we speak about the migrant "crisis" without reducing persons to numbers? How

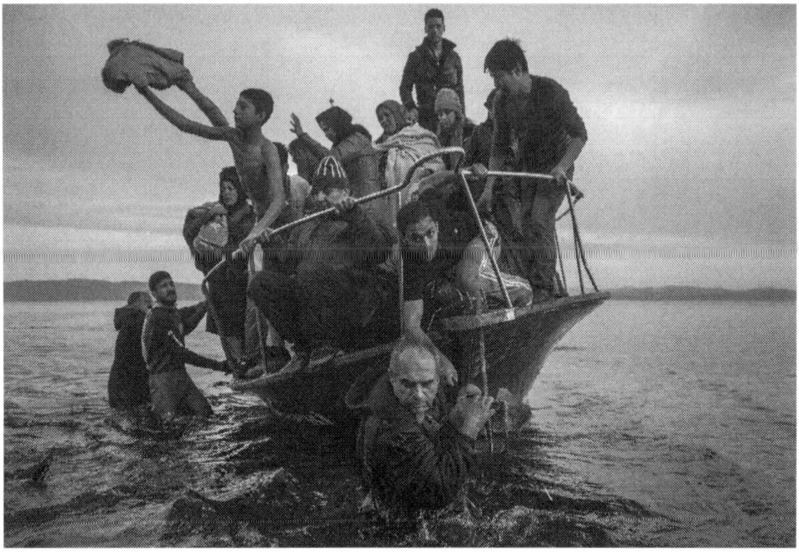

Figure 0.1 Migrants arrive on a Turkish boat near the village of Skala in Greece. Photo © Sergey Ponomarev.

might we empathize with refugees on a human level, and in such a way that avoids imposing labels on subjects for whom we advocate? This book offers one pathway forward, by affirming the centrality of movement to refugees' experiences.

The body in motion

This book begins with the observation that refugees are, in essence, bodies in motion. This quality makes them akin to dancers, which in turn reframes conversations about peoples on the move. Recent trends in scholarship would seem to create space for such a body-centric approach. In particular, so-called "mobility studies" rejects frozen representations of cultures, like the maps that adorn schoolrooms with solid blocks of color within national borders (e.g., the French live in France and speak French). Rather, mobility studies emphasize movement as the defining characteristic of society. As such, anything from traffic lights to trending tweets offers insight into how people live. On the other hand, mobility permits nuance. Tim Creswell, in helping lay out the foundations of the subject, called for an "entanglement of movement, representation, and practice." The world is more complicated than moving and not-moving, and "constellations of mobility" have histories (Cresswell 2010).

As with any field, origin stories emerge after a process of institutionalization. Today's mobility studies practitioners find foreshadowing for their work in neo-Kantian sociologist Georg Simmel, for instance (Sheller and

Urry 2006).[1] Regardless of provenance, the field took on momentum in the 1990s, perhaps not coincidently with the rise of cognitivist/network models in psychology, with the growth of the internet, and then with the ubiquity of smartphones following the millennium. At first, mobility studies constellated around the social sciences, and with a group of sociologists out of the University of Lancaster. Then, Mimi Sheller and John Urry coined the field's name in 2006. From there, mobility studies have taken on the trappings of academic legitimacy, with institutions such as journals, conferences, and research consortia.

As one might expect, migration appears as a frequent object of study within mobility studies, though the forced movement of peoples provides a shared concern across disciplines. Legal scholars, economists, political scientists, and geographers approach the same subjects as critical theorists. Performance scholars take an interest in borders, gender-based violence, refugee camps, and urbanization, which overlaps with the work of NGOs (non-governmental organizations), think tanks, and aid agencies. Single-author works on migration, like Mae Ngai's *Impossible Subjects*, about the construction of race in America through its history of immigration, have become classics across disciplines, while academic meccas like Freie Universität Berlin, Oxford University, University of Copenhagen, Yale University, and a dozen others devote resources to bringing researchers together to produce works on migration (Ngai 2014). Migration literature has matured to the point where publishing houses have released multi-edition tomes that anthologize across subject and region (e.g. Gold and Nawyn 2019; Fiddian-Qasmiyeh et al. 2014).

As time passes, mobility, migration studies, and allied fields seem destined to broaden their purviews, offering more tools with which to approach the problem of writing about refugees. Disciplinary expansion entails risk, as claiming anything that moves as an object of study could shift the field away from a well-defined subject and towards something more like an approach to research. A cynic might note that a "Department of Mobilities" has the same diffuse quality as a "Department of Empiricism," say. However, we would expect that additional perspectives make for more robust conversations. Peter Merriman and Lynne Pearce embrace this view when they argue that mobility studies has traditionally taken a too-literal definition of movement. They suggest that

> mobilities scholarship has, at times, demonstrated a tendency to adopt rather conservative, limited and indeed "realist" framings of mobility and movement, where movement is either that of discrete objects or subjectified, feeling, experience and governed bodies who generate distinctive effects, affects and meanings.
>
> (Merriman and Pearce 2018, p.5)

To invoke a visual metaphor, culture is more than the interacting pathways of billiard balls.

Using the term "kin-aesthetics" as a catchall, Merriman and Pearce celebrate arts and humanities-based inclusions to mobility, in particular the intuitive synergy between movers and movement, as well as the debates that these approaches ignite. At the same time, the editors caution that such approaches tend to become wooly. The arts and humanities are not the social sciences, and as a result, these studies "might not translate into a clear methodology, hypothesis, set of intentions, body of data, or set of conclusions," Merriman and Pearce warn (p.6). They characterize dance contributions to mobilities in particular as, at times, untethered, relying on the weight of historical precedent from Delsarte forward in lieu of, at times, clarity in research paradigm. Merriman and Pearce therefore pose a dilemma: How might a mobilities approach use the arts and humanities as a research tool for people on the move, while maintaining, if not the rigor of quantitative approaches—the arts and humanities offer embodied subjectivity as a unique value—something that feels systematic? How can we avoid objectifying refugees, while also extrapolating beyond the level of anecdote? How might we (and to whom does that first-person plural pronoun refer?) validate the embodied experiences of refugees, create kinesthetic empathy with them, giving them voice, all the while translating corporeal experience into writing?

With humility, *Involuntary Motion* responds to these challenges by applying the ways dancers, movement analysts, and other somatic practitioners have been accumulating for the past century-and-a-half to think about the body—that, I would argue, avoid the kind of idiosyncrasy against which Merriman and Pearce caution—to the study of refugees (and therefore migration and mobility studies). Again, refugees are bodies in motion, so applying the past century-and-a-half's accumulated wisdom of how movers describe movement seems justified. In fact, this approach has precedent. For instance, Gabrielle Brandstetter and Holger Hartung anthologize the ways that movement across borders changes the mover, reinforces borders through their performance, and creates impediments for crossings (2013). In a similar vein, Naomi Jackson and Thoni Shapiro-Phim use dance as a lens for exploring the relationship(s) between dance, human rights, and social justice, which entails intercultural movement (2008). Jackson and Shapiro-Phim's anthology emphasizes movement's healing qualities, the way it can, as the subtitle suggests, restore dignity to those whom dislocation has dehumanized.

Although these, and similar works that I will discuss shortly, represent significant landmarks, to my knowledge no one has approached refugee performance specifically from a somatic (body) performance perspective. I would like to move conversations about bodies in involuntary motion forward by using dance, somatics, and movement analysis as a lens to explore key questions in refugee performance and performativity: How does forced movement impact identity? What are the consequences of robbing individuals of agency over movement? What performances does involuntary motion necessitate? This book, then, seeks to build bridges between bodies of knowledge whose purviews include bodies in motion, in order to address one of the defining crises of the moment.

Choreographic "tools"

As an artist-scholar who works at the intersection of dance, theater, and performance studies, I take an expansive view of "refugees," "refugee performance," and performance generally. On a legal level, *refugees* constitute a subcategory of displaced persons, along with "asylum seekers," "internally displaced persons," "economic migrants," "illegal immigrants," and "undocumented persons," among other headings. For example, at the time of this writing more than half of the world's nearly 80 million bodies in motion fall under the category "internally displaced persons" (a term replete with visceral, choreographic intuition), meaning they are on the move within their own national borders. Many more wait in camps and other holding centers. Each of the terms for displaced persons depends on legal processes, and, after basic survival, status determination often forms the central conflict in displaced persons' experiences. Strictly speaking, a *refugee* is someone who qualifies for asylum under the 1951 United Nations Convention Relating to the Status of Refugees (which came into force in 1954). Deriving from the Universal Declaration of Human Rights (1948), Article 14, which covers peoples fleeing from persecution, of the 1951 treaty defines as a refugee anyone who,

> As a result of events occurring before 1 January 1951 and owing to well-founded fear of being persecuted for reasons of race, religion, nationality, membership of a particular social group or political opinion, is outside the country of his nationality and is unable or, owing to such fear, is unwilling to avail himself of the protection of that country; or who, not having a nationality and being outside the country of his former habitual residence as a result of such events, is unable or, owing to such fear, is unwilling to return to it.
>
> (Art. 1.A.2.)

A follow-on treaty in 1967 broadened *refugees* to include persons who became displaced after World War II, as well as territories outside of Europe. On the other hand, not all countries have signed the 1951/1967 treaties, or other relevant agreements. Also, signatories pursue their differing interpretations of their responsibilities based on (perceived) national interest. On a policy level, the treaty builders designed the system for the survivors of a decimated Europe, and the 1951 apparatus has proven insufficient to handle today's global crisis. On a rhetorical level, terms like "asylum seekers," "internally displaced persons," "economic migrants," "illegal immigrants," or "undocumented persons" carry non-legal connotations based on context—and these are only some of the words for displaced persons, in English.

With the preceding caveats in mind, this book makes the conscious choice to use "refugee" to refer to all displaced persons, since this is the only common term that contains a sense of motion (from the Latin *fugere*, "to flee," as in, "one who seeks refuge"), and as a strategy to reappropriate a term that, for many, has become pejorative, veering in meaning towards its cognate, "fugitive." Refugee-ness is not what people in motion *are* but what they *do* or *have done*. They flee not from legality but from danger. "Refugee," in the way I conceive it, is verb-like, a lexeme that indicates action, involves a subject, and includes a way of describing context. The traditional sense of "refugee" tends to imply that all vectors are interchangeable. They are not. A refugee fleeing the political disintegration of Venezuela does not have the same experience as one of the million or so ethnically Turkish Uyghurs that the Chinese government has put under intense surveillance and in reeducation camps, nor does one Uyghur have the same experience as the next. Temporal, national, ethnic, linguistic, tribal, racial, religious, gender, and sexuality differences between groups, and between individuals within groups, matter. At the same time, all displaced persons are in motion, by definition: a motion against their will. This book begins with this premise.

Likewise, *Involuntary Motion* adopts a broad understanding of "refugee performance." Positing a precise definition of what constitutes refugee performance risks predetermining the study's conclusions. In his anthology *Refugee Performance: Encounters with Alterity*, Michael Balfour cautions, "[t]oo often in refugee performance work it is the well-intentioned practitioner/agency that unravels a social dynamic and leaves behind scar tissue, hidden behind silent, polite smiles. All too often I have learnt what not *to say*, and what not *to do*" (Balfour 2013, p.xxii; italics in original). Therefore, Balfour calls the title of his book a "paradox," and means for the text to serve as a space in which artists, academics, refugees, and those in combinations of these roles, "who have sought out performance as a tactic in their work" provide a cross-sectional snapshot of the ways that performance intervenes in refugee politics (p.xxii). Balfour's insistence on creating a space for dialogue rather than providing categorical boundaries seems wise.

However, I also take as a point of departure Alison Jeffers, who, in *Refugees, Theatre and Crisis: Performing Global Identities*, observes that the refugee treaty system puts the onus on asylum seekers to provide documentary evidence for the danger that caused their flight, as well as the threat that awaits their return (2012). Since in most cases the powers who could provide such testimony are the ones who pose the threat, those who flee their homes with nothing are unlikely to be able to meet this threshold. Consequently, Jeffers coins the term "bureaucratic performance" to refer to the liminal space in which displaced persons become "conventional refugees" (a verbal play on "refugee conventions"), which is to say, "those who conform to cultural expectations of refugees, particularly in relation to suffering" (p.17). A shopkeeper from Kabul has to negotiate the complexities—and vagaries—of international law from a displaced person's camp in Germany, after having crossed the Mediterranean on their way to Sweden, for instance. A choreographer, playwright, or applied theater practitioner might add additional layers in fashioning work about the shopkeeper, for the benefit of a specific audience. Following Jeffers, *Involuntary Motion* uses embodied experience as a critical lens to investigate the performances refugees enact, and the performances refugees and/or outsiders make about migration across dance, theatre, and mediatized imagery. Peggy Phelan argues that disappearance is a precondition of performance (1993). Refugees, then, are akin to unwilling dancers, on stages not of their choosing. Such a multivariate performance requires a multicomponent analytic to parse, a suite of tools rather than a single screwdriver.

In order to engage with case studies in refugee performance, this project adopts somatics, dance studies, and movement praxis as a three-level "toolbox." Somatics (from the Greek *σῶμα*, "body") refers to a structured movement system that incorporates reflexivity during its execution. In 1976, Thomas Hanna defined "somatics" as "the field which studies the *soma*: namely the *body* as perceived from within by first-person perspective" (1991, p. 31; italics in original). For Hanna, humans can perceive one another's bodies, but the use of proprioception ("self-sensing") gains purchase on the *soma*, the schema or patterning that undergirds our corporeal identity (1991, p.31). Any exercise can become mindful, according to Hanna's definition, although the term most comfortably refers to forms like Alexander, Feldenkreis, Pilates, body–mind centering, and also yoga, Tai Chi, and Chi Kung, or massage, whose precepts involve the union of inner attention and corporeality. These practices yield training effects, including increased range of motion, lowered blood pressure, improved circulation, balance, and so forth. They also "pattern" the body through mindful practice. Breathing, visualization, and repetition help to establish connections between and among body parts. A yoga practitioner begins to look like someone who practices yoga. In somatic terms, a regular practice produces "movement integration."

In studio, "somatics" often involves a set of floor exercises that German-to-American immigrant Irmgard Bartenieff (1900–81) formulated as part of her work in movement as a therapeutic modality. For example, in one of the "Bartenieff Fundamentals," participants lie down in a "big X" and dorsiflex the right foot sharply, so that pulses of momentum travel up the leg, across the torso, through the left shoulder and out through the fingers of the left hand (they then repeat this sequence for the other side). Teachers help participants identify breaks in the movement flow, which indicate psycho-physical discontinuities that could have resulted from injury, predisposition, or childhood experiences. Babies develop "cross-lateral" connectivity by crawling on the ground in gleeful pursuit of chaos, but when parents keep children in restraining furniture, or, increasingly, put glowing devices in the hands of their screaming charges in order to quiet them, they (the babies) miss out on developmental patterning. The foot-flexing exercise, over time, restores diagonal connections, such as you would need for a crawl-stroke in the pool, or making spirals in choreography.

In addition to its healing potential, Bartenieff Fundamentals has served as a kind of postmodern "floor *barre*," and the basis of so-called "release technique." Exemplars of this style reject the vocabulary of ballet and traditional modern dance idioms, and can instead flow in and out of the ground like water, execute seamless transitions, perform seemingly unconstrained movements in unison, and propel movement initiations with a level of detail perhaps unprecedented in Western concert dance. Release technique dovetails with an overall post-Merce Cunningham dance ideology that eschews master narratives, includes dancers in the creation of dances, and above all, emphasizes creative process over product. Emerging from a group of dancers that cohered at Judson Church in New York in the 1970s, these artists sought to formulate a rejection of modernism, and flesh out what a postmodernism might mean for dance.

Giving voice to this spirit of movement-for-its-own-sake, Yvonne Rainer wrote the anthemic "No Manifesto" (1965):

> No to spectacle.
> No to virtuosity.
> No to transformations and magic and make-believe.
> No to the glamour and transcendency of the star image.
> No to the heroic.
> No to the anti-heroic.
> No to trash imagery.
> No to involvement of performer or spectator.
> No to style.
> No to camp.
> No to seduction of spectator by the wiles of the performer.
> No to eccentricity.
> No to moving or being moved.
>
> (see Banes 1987, pp.41–56)

Nevertheless, somatics-based dance does possess an aesthetic. Modeled after Cunningham's philosophy of dance as a process-based rather than theater art, the form has come to dominate dance in higher education. The "postmodern" style has brought a democratizing effect. Performers (in theory) need not have perfect turn-out of the hips, possess an extreme ectomorphic body type, and/or starve themselves, and can take part in the process of making dances. At the same time, release technique often embraces anti-theatricality, and values movement efficiency to the point of anti-athleticism. In its disavowing of narrative, character, and fetishizing floorwork to the abandonment of vertical space, audiences can at times find this work self-absorbed, repetitive, and boring. Dance communities are already beginning to self-correct, however, as choreographers, always restless for the next "step" (in every sense), begin to rediscover the theatrical elements of their art.

Somatics, which is to say, mindfulness in movement, plays a key role in our sense of the world, and in our ability to empathize with others, and is therefore a key to this study. Movement analyst Peggy Hackney notes that,

> As we move, whether in dance, theater, sports or simply in being with others *we want to connect*. In order to do this we need to find means to connect inwardly, both to what we want to say and to how all parts of the body relate to each other to support our statement and purpose.
>
> (2002, p.vii; italics in original)

Similarly, dance philosopher Sondra Fraleigh remarks, "Experience arises from the doings of consciously undertaken movement and can arrive as embodied knowledge" (2015, p.xxiii). As the similarity between the words "movement" and "emotion," which share the Latin root *movere*, suggests, an embodied understanding of refugee performance can enable us to empathize without essentializing, and can give refugee-artists/scholars a tool to articulate their humanity. Fraleigh's use of italics emphasizes that although consciousness movement *can* produce new embodied knowledge, not all somatic approaches *do*—a distinction that the following chapters will hold firmly in view.

The second shelf of tools, movement analysis, or Laban movement analysis, refers to a body of work that, as the name implies, analyzes movement. Its originator, Rudolf von Laban (1879–1958), was a movement practitioner from a high-ranking military family in the Austro-Hungarian Empire. He lived in Bosnia-Herzegovina, studied in Paris, and worked in Munich. During the interwar years, Laban performed, choreographed, and set work for "movement choirs" while establishing eponymous schools. His approach to embodied performance emerged out of the same physical culture impulse as François Delsarte's work on gestures, Émile Jaques-Dalcroze's eurythmics, Eugene Sandow's proto-body building, Swedish gymnastics, and *tableaux vivants*.[2] Laban had a direct influence on German expressionist dancer Mary Wigman, as well as choreographer Kurt Jooss, whose anti-war ballet *The Green Table* exists in repertories to this day. Escaping Nazism for Britain, he institutionalized his work in the United Kingdom and, through his followers, the United States, and worldwide.

As happens with any continuation of knowledge from a "guru," Laban's students codified his theories according to their interests and interpretations. Today, certification-granting institutes include the Trinity Laban Conservatoire of Music and Dance in London (a fusion of the Trinity College of Music and the former Laban Centre for Movement), the Laban/Bartenieff Institute of Movement Studies in New York, and Integrated Movement Studies in Santa Barbara, California, as well as coursework and modules in larger university dance programs. movement analysis overlaps with dance, but certified analysts also work with athletes, the film industry, and corporate professionals, in addition to private clients. Leaders of certification programs continue to refine the system through each iteration of teaching it, and those who bring facility in writing, such as Peggy Hackney, have contributed textual touchstones (2002).[3] This shelf draws primarily from the Laban → Bartenieff → Hackney line, which organizes movement into Body, Effort, Shape, and Space, categories that individual chapters will define in turn.

The third level, dance praxis, alludes to the inherited wisdom of practitioners who fashion movement-based art. This cultural knowledge might serve as the most practical of the three "shelves" but also, and ironically, the least accessible. As dance educator Penelope Hanstein notes, dance makers make a habit of slipping into "shop talk" when speaking among themselves (2003, pp.23–7). Although all professions carry their own jargon, dancer talk can become a habit, as any non-dancer guest who has attended a social gathering of dancers and can follow none of the conversation knows first-hand. Within academia, choreography is growing in popularity as a critical lens. For example, philosopher Richard Shusterman has called for a revision of the way we understand lived experience, based largely on his reading of dance phenomenologists (2008, 2012). As this trend hopefully continues, the importance of recruiting dancer/scholars to help translate among disciplinary worlds will become increasingly important.

The metaphor of "tools" suggests something mechanical, although I also use the term here in the compositional sense: as a kit of choreographic resources with which to fashion work, as the following example illustrates.[4] Gabriele Brandstetter, Gerko Egert, and Holger Hartung's recent anthology, *Moments of Interweaving: Dance and Corporality in Times of Travel and Migration*, suggests resonances between dance and travel (2019). Brandstetter and her collaborators bring together perspectives from senior scholars, along with new voices in dance studies, under Erika Fischer-Lichte's use of the controlling metaphor of "interweaving." Drawing from (one could say "interweaving") Barthes' notion of the generative nature of tissue, Derrida's understanding of "quasi-metaphor" as an "ambivalent movement between literal and figurative meaning," and Deleuze and Guattari's under-earth model of intertangling rhizomes, *Moments of Interweaving* posits intercultural travel as a process of tapestry-making, of forming knots from pathways across borders. The anthology encompasses all types of travel, not just refugee experiences, but the collection itself makes a powerful statement that movement practitioners have joined the conversation about a phenomenon that is, or is largely, kinesthetic.

The image of "interweaving" calls to my mind choreographer Alwin Nikolais' dance masterwork *Tensile Involvement* (1953). A visionary of the *Gesamtkunstwerk*, Nikolais crafted pieces based on concepts around which he built theatricality by composing his own sound scores, fashioning costumes that extended or abstracted dancers' forms, and making (then) non-digital projections. *Tensile Involvement* begins with eight dancers running onstage across the upstage-right to downstage-left and the upright-left to downstage-right diagonals, carrying elastic ribbons that extend to attachments near the top of the proscenium arch offstage, stage right and left. Lighting renders the ribbons purple and red, and a branching, red, tree-shaped design on the torso of the dancers' unitards echo the spatial design. The dancers position themselves in such a way as to wrap bands across their ankles, so that the lines make an "X" across the entire stage from the audience's vantage point, with horizontal lines running along the bottom, parallel to the ground.

As the piece progresses, the performers become entangled in the ensuing cat's cradles their movement creates. Wrapped up in ribbons, which also act as visualizations of "spatial pulls," alternating soloists execute circular *ronde de jambe* movements of the legs, *battement* kicks, and swivels of the hips, ensnared in center stage. During ensemble phrases, the performers become models of the stage in miniature, as they position the ribbons so as to make boxes around themselves and cross-lateral patterns. Bodies shift in unison, now prone, now turning, interacting with the interweaving lines to form larger patterns. Just before the end of the piece, the dancers let go of their ribbons—yet the tent-like pattern stands freely—and run back and forth underneath the ribbons' weave. In the final moment, eight dancers stand in lines downstage-to-upstage, facing forward just onstage of the wings, four apiece on either side of the stage. They take hold of and then release the ribbons as a central figure thrusts her arms back, a statue drawing the spell to a close, summoning a sudden blackout.

Tensile Involvement could produce varying meanings, or stand as an abstract work in its own right. In this conversation, I would suggest that the piece provides a visual metaphor for the interweaving that movements of people causes across the stage of the world. The entangling ribbons are a four-dimensional recording of our travels, and also an indication of how we become caught up in the systems that enable our movement (economic, carbon, political). Once ensnared, we cannot escape. Every time we turn on a light, eat a store-bought vegetable, or travel somewhere, we participate in a global system that produces disparities of wealth, and ultimately displacement. In fact, the more we move, the more actions we take, the more caught up we become in patterns that we cannot see from inside of our webs. We stand in the center of our own stage in the presentation of ourselves, but networks have no center. Our story may cut across the map, but the ensuing interweaving is too great for any one person to parse. Ariadne's thread has become a spider's trap. We may exert agency over the parts of our lives we do control, as if making a dance or writing a book were like swinging a leg or bending at the hips. The only escape, the dance suggests, would be for everyone to release (say, carbon), all at once, although the dance cannot predict the outcome of such an action. The solitary figure could represent an angel whose dance ends in fire. The piece ends in a sudden blackout at the release of the ribbons. To pass beyond our networks is to also void our webs of signification, so we cannot know what a new world would mean until we take a leap of faith across the void of dark unknowing.

The preceding interpretation of *Tensile Involvement* serves as a parable for crossings, and also functions as an example of a kind of kinesthetic reading of philosophical issues from which projects in dance studies ironically—but typically—shy away. Dance philosophy has tended to emphasize logocentric modalities, such as semiotics, intertextuality, and—despite its focus on sensed experience—the wordiness of phenomenology. Jeffers provides the kind of body-focused critique of migration I have in mind, as an example, when she asks us to *turn away* for a moment from the albeit worthy debate on the ethics of *face-to-face* encounters with refugees during refugee-based performance, and instead explore the utopian performatives that can occur within audiences when audience members stand *shoulder-to-shoulder* (Jeffers 2013, pp.299–308). Dancers and movement analysts have developed systems for describing spatial relationships like the one Jeffers intuits, and I would like to adapt this work as a frame for approaching the problem of refugee performance.

"Somatics" appears in the subtitle of this book because kinesthetic empathy serves as the goal of this project, but somatics, movement analysis, and insights from dance praxis offer tools with which to interweave a plait of case studies from dance, theater, and mediatized images. The intersections of these readings form patterns that cohere in juxtaposition. The book follows individual examples that run where they run, but that taken as a whole, illume underlying structures in refugee performance. As an interweaving, interdisciplinary project, *Involuntary Motion* could be of interest for scholars, scholar/practitioners, and students in theater, performance studies, dance, cultural studies, and refugee and migration studies, or for anyone who takes an interest in the global immigration crisis, and suggests that the conceptual framework of the preceding century-and-a-half that students of movement have built provides a warehouse of ideas for scholars in allied fields.

Creative constraints

As the reader may surmise, a three-part methodology offers three times the potential insights, but also a triple helping of creative constraints, to which we can also add a paradox. As a first problem, tension would seem to exist between somatics and movement analysis. The former involves subjective perception, whereas the latter objectifies, by definition. Put another way, somatics emphasizes "inner" experiences, whereas movement analysis charts observable characteristics of bodies in space, time, and energy. The two modes intertwine in productive ways, and practitioners rely on the differences between both "inside-out" and "outside-in" approaches. For example, an actor can develop the inner life of a character and also do a vocal warm-up. A yoga instructor can pause class in order to clarify correct alignment in a posture. A ballet dancer can take an occasional glance at a mirror. In the same way that inner and outer perceptions may differ, somatic and movement analysis lenses may result in readings of case studies that might seem to work against one another.

I will point out such dissonances in the chapters, keeping in mind that (up to a point), divergences represent different parts of the proverbial elephant.

Second, the problem of authorial permission deserves mention. As with any disquisition on the "subaltern," who may speak for "them"? That is to say, who may write this book? Do I need to be a refugee who *flees*? An artist who *makes*? A dramaturg who *assists*? An applied theater or dance artist/scholar who *facilitates*? Do I need to conduct "fieldwork" for each case study, or can I glean information from afar? Does scholarly integrity require ethnographic-level engagement with every subject? If so, are single-author books that canvass the facets of refugee experiences possible? I think so, but I also come to this project from the vantage of my biography. I self-identify as an American artist/scholar with academic and artistic credentials in both dance and theater, who makes trans-disciplinary work, and writes in an interdisciplinary way—a professional indeterminacy analogous to Gloria Anzaldúa's "Borderlands," the experience of having feet in two or more worlds, yet full membership in neither or none (1987). Aside from a Judaic heritage (the "Wandering People"), I am not myself a refugee. However, having spent my adult career as—as one department chair put it—a disciplinary "ampersand," I understand in my own way the idea of crossing borders, and approach this work from the mindset of building conceptual bridges. The practitioners and activists with whom I interfaced praise my critical distance, and have helped encourage me to see my scholarship as a form of activism, but I still worry about my role and responsibilities.

Third, combining subjects raises problems in reconciling technical language. Given that the thrust of this project involves bringing bodies of movement knowledge to bear on a range of case studies in refugee performance and performativity, for the benefit of scholars, scholar/artists, and academically interested artists, I endeavor to write as plainly as possible. This choice dovetails with my ongoing interest in approaching scholarship as a problem of creative nonfiction. I see scholarship and writing as related, but distinct skill sets, and apprentice myself to both. Although my scholarly empyrean expands with my daily reading practice, and as brilliant as much of this work is, I sometimes wonder for whom we scholars pen our wares. If I could write like anyone I would choose Joan Didion or James Baldwin, and I endeavor to do so to the extent my facility allows. For specialists who find this book's avoidance of a certain style of cadence, syntax, and terminology off-putting, I beg forbearance and humbly offer that accessibility in academic writing requires *more* rigor, not less.

Finally, perhaps the most trenchant problem lies in the fact that for those of us who have committed our lives to dance and/or its allied disciplines, the idea that movement can do anything but bestow benefit will be challenging. Dancers love movement: this joy is why we dance. Somatic practices begin with the assumption that movement leads to good things, and that the more movement we experience, the more we actualize as humans. (Although, does this logic compel its inverse, that those who have movement restrictions, such as differently abled bodies, are therefore less human?) An overwhelming scientific consensus demonstrates how even a minimal amount of exercise can cut the incidence of dread diseases by half or more. Particularly in advantaged nations, whose citizens chase after fad diets and magic pills (dietary supplements will achieve a global market value of $195 billion by 2025), movement acolytes persevere as proselytes.

Yet not all movement is salubrious. Jumping off a tall building or stepping in front of an oncoming train does not, in the main, promote movement integration. In addition to the urgency of its subject, a deep conversation about the involuntary motion of refugees stands as an exercise in self-reflexivity with which to grapple. Movement to excess can cause injury—although no statement is more typical of a young dancer than something along the lines of, "Of course I didn't go to a doctor—we still had more shows that weekend." Herein lies the paradox: for refugees, movement itself robs movers of their personhood, a fact that runs counter to the mentality driving every plié, hip isolation, time step, sun salutation, and floor exercise dancers execute every day in the studio.

With these challenges in mind, each of the chapters that follow begins with a selection of tools from somatics, movement analysis, or dance praxis that serve as methodological frames. Using these instruments, the chapters make close readings of case studies in dance, theater, performance art, and visual poetics, in order to survey as wide a register of refugee performance and performativity as possible. Having discussed motion throughout, the book concludes with a meditation on stillness as a human right.

The structure of the book

Chapter 1, "Movement initiation—Dance and refugee performance," begins with beginnings. It introduces the idea of "movement initiation," which within dance practice specifies a point in the body where a movement ("kinetic chain") originates. The chapter examines the forces that set refugees in motion, as well as the effects that movement initiations have on individual experience. It then makes a close reading of Canadian choreographer Crystal Pite's work *Flight Pattern* (2017), for the Royal Ballet in London. Pite speaks with eloquence about the impulse that led her to make a work about refugees, and movement initiations on a body level stand out as a defining feature of her choreography. The chapter concludes with New York City-based Battery Dance, an organization that has taken its "Dancing to Connect" program to over sixty countries. A five-year multi-agency grant is allowing the company to send Dancing to Connect facilitators to seventeen cities across Germany to engage in refugee integration workshops. Battery's organizational movement initiation results in kinetic chains of dance activity among refugee communities.

Chapter 2, "Body—Undocumented zombies and sea creatures," connects language from movement analysis regarding shape and movement qualities ("movement efforts") to recent work in the performativity of monstrosity, such as Michael Chemers' analysis of the work monsters perform by standing in for "others." Specifically, the chapter examines the perversion of two basic forms of locomotion: walking and swimming. The first part of the chapter, "Undocumented zombies," looks at ways the US television series *The Walking Dead* uses zombie hordes as racist code for overland Mexican immigrants. The second part, "Creatures from the deep," discusses the dangers (physical, legal, mythological) of crossing water in the Mediterranean region, especially in the surreal context of international maritime law. Chapter 2 culminates in a reading of images of a drowned Syrian toddler, Alan Kurdi, and the ways that Chinese dissident Artist Ai Weiwei's use of shape-matching in his enactment of the boy's body cut through monstrous transformation by creating kinesthetic empathy.

Chapter 3, "Space—Revisiting Arendt and a trip to *The Jungle*," focuses on the spaces in which refugees move. Although the chapter touches on Jacque Rancière's/Alain Badiou's ideas about public space, and Michael Warner's work on "counter-publics," the bulk of the chapter applies movement analysis concepts of space in revisiting Hannah Arendt's "space of appearance." For Arendt, such spaces occur whenever individuals come together to disclose their identities in speech-driven, ephemeral moments. The chapter theorizes the inverse idea of motion-driven "spaces of disappearance," which suppress personhood. The chapter applies neo-Arendtian and movement analysis rubrics of space to Joe Robertson and Joe Murphy's play *The Jungle* (2017), an immersive work about the imminent destruction of a refugee camp in Calais, France, based on their applied theater initiatives that rely on creating theatrical spaces within temporary, geodesic structures.

Chapter 4, "Trace forms—The non-hero's journey," maps movement patterns onto storytelling. A "floor pattern" is a pathway a moving body makes on a surface as seen from overhead. Likewise, a "trace form" is the line a body part makes as it travels through three-dimensional space. The chapter examines how interpreting dramatic structure in terms of trace forms and floor patterns enriches our understanding of characterization. It first establishes the idea of the "non-hero's journey," wherein a person fulfills the requirements of Joseph Campbell's classic construct of the hero's journey, but does not enjoy the hero's status. The chapter then theorizes from my own "text and movement" performance of *Iftu's Story*, in which I narrate (while dancing) an Ethiopian teenager's account of his close escape from smugglers. The chapter then follows trace forms of the character archetypes in al-Hakawati, a multi-nation storytelling project based on traditional folktales Syrian refugees told one another during their refugee journeys.

Finally, Chapter 5, "Labanotation—Writing and/on/of refugee bodies," connects refugee studies to body culture using embodiment, while adapting "motif writing" as an alternative approach to "close readings" of visual images. In particular, it investigates two instances of writing on clothing: the message "I DON'T REALLY CARE, DO U?" on the Zara jacket that First Lady Melania Trump wore to visit a children's detention center in McAllen,

Texas, and the words "Being Human" on the back of an African immigrant's tee-shirt while waiting on the deck of a patrol boat in the harbor of Malta's capital city Valletta. The chapter considers the problems of writing on the corporeal, writing about the corporeal, and symbol-based systems of recording movement.

The dancing species

As a final introductory thought, the refugee crisis contains a tragic irony in that to be human is to be in motion. From our initial meanderings around the savannah, *Homo sapiens sapiens* loped upright throughout the world. With respect to Thomas Hobbes, neither archaeological evidence nor comparison with extant traditional cultures suggests that a nomadic life was "nasty, mean, brutish, and short." Rather, meandering tribes of gatherer-hunters maintained motion as an organizing pattern spanning perhaps two hundred thousand years. In a foundational text of "economic anthropology," Marshall Sahlins estimates that traditional cultures spent around three to five hours a day engaged in activities that we would recognize as "work" (2017). Our peripatetic ancestors may not merit idealization, as Ur-Disney types who knew not strife and sang to birds. However, the current xeno-nativist recoil from mass migration today may have to do with an anti-movement bias that perhaps extends back to the time in which populations ceased their ramblings.

A litany of anti-body tropes suggests a shift in attitudes towards movement. The West has long harbored a fear of the body that Elizabeth Grosz calls "a profound somatophobia" (1994, p.1). Traveling players had no place in Christian graveyards. Dancers occupied a social role bordering on that of prostitutes. Stowaways on trains were "hobos." To be "homeless" is now an obscenity, a by-product of urbanization, a suggestion of mental disease, drug use, and an implied moral failing. Moreover, movement has come to signify death. American settlers drove native populations on a genocidal "Trail of Tears." The Ottoman Turks murdered 1.5 million Armenians, many through death marches into the mountains and deserts. The Nazis tried to exterminate all Jews and Romani by transporting them on trains to death camps. When the "Great Migration" brought millions of African Americans north, "White Flight" established American suburbia as a racist response. Chairman Mao emerged from his "Long March" to power, and the subsequent deaths of untold millions of his citizens. Stalin murdered as many as or more people than Hitler, with secret police knocking at doors to take away the doomed to gulags, secret prisons, or unmarked graves.

On the other extreme, perhaps due to its taboo quality, movement takes on a whiff of romanticism. Marco Polo's tales dazzled his contemporaries. The Silk Road shimmers with heat waves lifting from dusty trails that lead into myth. Cowboys ride off into the sunset. Young people backpack across Europe. Religious pilgrims undertake peregrinations, such as the pillar of faith for all Muslims, both Shia and Sunni, to undertake a *Hajj* to Mecca during their lifetimes. Shamans undertake spirit journeys in order to heal the sick and patients with life-threatening illnesses. The automobile symbolizes freedom for Americans, an unending dream of the open road so intoxicating that the ground speeds past their carbon footprints. Revolutions happen in "movements." Communists in capitalist Gomorrahs referred to one another as "fellow travelers." Immigrants living on the outskirts of Paris vent their rage by running, leaping over obstacles as they present themselves.

However, these yearnings are the stuff of dreams, and as dreams (to conflate Lorca and Shakespeare), end such that "all is mended." The hero returns at the end of the journey. The desperado settles down, at least until the sequel. The young adult completes her gap year and enrolls in Accounting. The dancer retires in his early thirties. The movie fades to black, as an afterimage of a white picket fence burns into the retina. Life goes on. Conversations about migration must confront the conflict between our locomotive origins and our sedentary present. We moderns have built our civilization around the model of ownership of property, and trespassers evoke uncomfortable echoes of our remote past. The current imbroglio over those in involuntary motion follows the classic loathing/longing binary. Maybe part of the outcry has to do with the ways refugees remind the rest of us of the birthright of motion we have relinquished in the sedentary, "developed" world. As in any critique that seeks to shift power, we must find elements within ourselves that resonate with the experience of others in order to cease to think of them as others. Since we all have bodies, we have common ground on which to build.

Notes

1 Simmel took inspiration from the same sources as the Futurists, such as cities, technology, and acceleration, but his insistence on the centrality of the human provides a contrast.

2 For a fascinating view into the world of physical culture, through a performance/performativity lens, see Preston (2014). A certain approach to the body permeated all areas of Victorian life, and challenges stereotypes of that period.

3 Although, as both Bartenieff and Hackney would (and do) say, experiencing movement analysis in a studio setting is preferable to reading about it.

4 Admittedly, this characterization somewhat misses the entire postmodern critique of power in the creative process, but in my view, choreographers have thrown the choreographic baby out with the bathwater. Student choreographers should still have access to audience-friendly dancemaking techniques like those of Louis Horst, Doris Humphrey, and Alwin Nikolais. Non-dancers knew who Martha Graham was, in part, because her dances told stories.

References

Anzaldúa, Gloria. *Borderlands: La Frontera*. San Francisco: Aunt Lute Books, 1987.

Balfour, Michael, ed. *Refugee Performance: Encounters with Alterity*. Bristol, UK & Chicago: Intellect, 2013.

Banes, Sally. *Terpsichore in Sneakers: Post-Modern Dance*. Middletown, CT: Wesleyan UP, 1987.

Bleiker, Roland, David Campbell, Emma Hutchison, and Xzarina Nicholson. "The Visual Dehumanization of Refugees." *Australian Journal of Political Science* 48, no. 4 (2013): 398–416.

Brandstetter, Gabrielle, and Holger Hartung, eds. *Moving (across) Borders: Performing Translation, Intervention, Participation*. Bielefeld: transcript Verlag, 2013.

Brandstetter, Gabriele, Gerko Egert, and Holger Hartung, eds. *Moments of Interweaving: Dance and Corporeality in Times of Travel and Migration*. Abington, Oxon, UK and New York: Routledge, 2019.

Cresswell, Tim. "Towards a Politics of Mobility." *Environment and Planning D: Society and Space* 28, no. 1 (2010): 17–31.

Fiddian-Qasmiyeh, Elena, Gil Loescher, Katy Long, and Nando Sigona, eds. *The Oxford Handbook of Refugee and Forced Migration Studies*. London: Oxford UP, 2014.

"Figures at a Glance." United Nations High Commissioner for Refugees (UNHCR), 2019.

Fraleigh, Sondra, ed. *Moving Consciously: Somatic Transformations through Dance, Yoga, and Touch*. Urbana: University of Illinois Press, 2015.

Gold, Steven J., and Stephanie J. Nawyn, eds. *Routledge International Handbook of Migration Studies*, 2nd ed. New York & London, 2019.

Grosz, Elizabeth A. *Volatile Bodies: Toward a Corporeal Feminism*. Bloomington: Indiana UP, 1994.

Hackney, Peggy. *Making Connections: Total Body Integration through Bartenieff Fundamentals*. London & New York: Routledge, 2002.

Hanna, Thomas. "What is Somatics?" *Journal of Behavioral Optometry* 2, no. 2 (1991): 31–35.

Hanstein, Penelope. "Researching Choreography." *Choreologia* 26 (2003): 23–7.

Jackson, Naomi, and Thoni Shapiro-Phim, eds. *Dance, Human Rights, and Social Justice: Dignity in Motion*. Plymouth, UK: The Scarecrow Press, 2008.

Jeffers, Alison. *Refugees, Theatre and Crisis: Performing Global Identities*. New York: Palgrave Macmillan, 2012.

Jeffers, Alison. "Hospitable Stages and Civil Listening: Being an Audience for Participatory Refugee Theatre." In *Refugee Performance: Encounters with Alterity*, edited by Michael Balfour, 297–316. Bristol, UK & Chicago: Intellect, 2013.

Ludwig, Bernadette. "'Wiping the Refugee Dust from My Feet': Advantages and Burdens of Refugee Status and the Refugee Label." *International Migration* 54, no. 1 (2016): 5–18.

Merriman, Peter, and Lynne Pearce. "Mobility in the Humanities." In *Mobility and the Humanities*, edited by Peter Merriman and Lynne Pearce, 1–16. London & New York: Routledge, 2018.

Ngai, Mae M. *Impossible Subjects: Illegal Aliens and the Making of Modern America*, updated ed. Princeton, NJ: Princeton UP, 2014.

Phelan, Peggy. *Unmarked: The Politics of Performance*. London: Routledge, 1993.

Preston, Carrie J. *Modernism's Mythic Pose: Gender, Genre, Solo Performance*. London: Oxford UP, 2014.

Sahlins, Marshall. *Stone Age Economics*. London & New York: Routledge, 2017.

Sheller, Mimi, and John Urry. "The New Mobilities Paradigm." *Environment and Planning A* 38, no.2 (2006): 207–26.

Shusterman, Richard. *Body Consciousness: A Philosophy of Mindfulness and Somaesthetics*. Cambridge, UK: Cambridge UP, 2008.

Shusterman, Richard. *Thinking through the Body: Essays in Somaesthetics*. Cambridge, UK: Cambridge UP, 2012.

1 Movement initiation

Dance and refugee performance

Chapter 1 begins with beginnings. Whereas the preceding introduction established the rationale for reading refugees as bodies in unwilling motion, this chapter introduces the idea of "movement initiation," which within dance practice specifies a point in the body where a movement originates. After establishing movement initiation as an analytic, it examines the forces that set refugees in motion and then turns to dance, the form of expression that takes movement as its medium. The chapter makes a close reading of Canadian choreographer Crystal Pite's *Flight Pattern* (2017), a dance response to the migration crisis that derives its power in part from the choreographer's emphasis on granularity in movement initiation on a body level, as well as her eloquence in describing the emotions that propelled her to make a work about unwilling movement.

The chapter then explores the ways that dance-based refugee initiatives spread through the body politic, just as movement initiations propel "kinetic chains" through the body. In particular, the narrative shifts to the New York City-based company Battery Dance, and its award-winning "Dancing to Connect" program, which it is currently using in support of German chancellor Angela Merkel's controversial refugee integration policy. In addition to the power of the workshops themselves, Dancing to Connect workshop alums are now fashioning their own initiatives across Europe, Africa, and the Middle East. The chapter concludes by highlighting the parallels in movement initiation on the body, organizational, and migratory levels.

Movement initiation

All movement has origins, and all living things move. The impulse for locomotion begins with inception, from the movements of intertwining lovers (or laboratories) to the commingling of chromosomes. As long as life lasts, the body changes place. Our hearts beat in three-part meter, whereas the lungs oscillate between inhalation and exhalation. From the first cry in oxygenated air, we ride a three-against-two polyrhythm, a syncopation that pulls us into the following phrase. Yet against this measure we seek rest, or at least regularity. Our bodies maintain homeostasis. We mark our days against recurrence—the

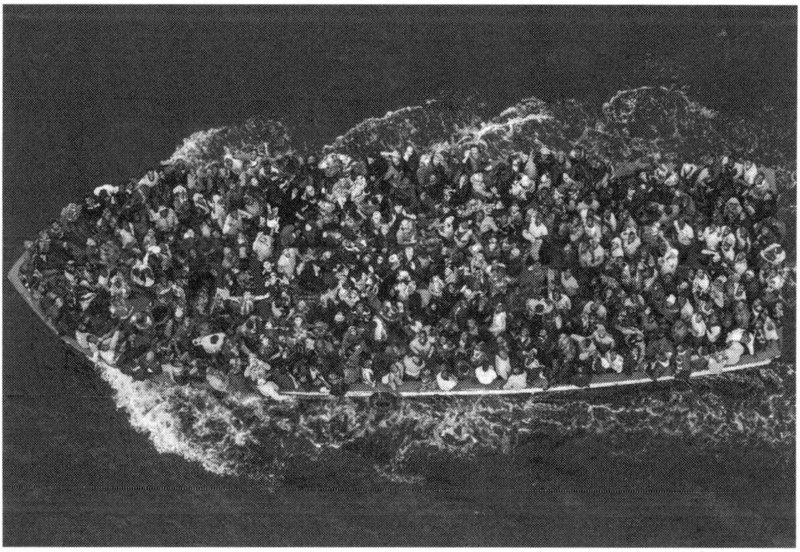

Figure 1.1 Operation Mare Nostrum: a Bergamini frigate of the Italian navy rescues a boat of 500 migrants off the coast of Libya. Photo © Massimo Sestini.

sun, the moon, or mechanical modes of time-telling. Systems of meditation seek to calm the "vibrations of the mindstuff."[1] Alternatively, we dampen the ripples of our thoughts with the glow of screens, or through chemicals.[2] In general, we seek a home, a family, a bed in which to sleep. A clear calculus must underlie a decision to overcome inertia. In the best of circumstances, uprooting causes stress. The decision to drop everything and flee implies an elevated threshold. What precipitates such motion? How might dance express the desperation that refugee flight requires? How does "involuntary motion" start, and where does this momentum go?

In dance, a *movement initiation* refers to the point in the body from where a movement begins, and this concept will serve as a metaphor for the case studies to come. In Laban movement analysis, a movement initiation describes the initial impulse of a body translating position in space, time, and energy (Fernandez 2015, p.100). Usually, the initiating movement continues from this point of anatomy into a kinetic chain of body events ("sequencing").[3] As shorthand, movement analysts place impulses into categories based on anatomical regions, such as "core," "mid-limb," or "distal," but movement ideas can start anywhere in the body (p.101). For example, a dancer might initiate a rippling movement from her scapula that travels through her shoulder, down her arm, and through her fingers. A choreographer might demonstrate a spiraling step, explaining, "you see, it starts from the head." A ballet dancer begins the sweep of a *grade battement* at the barre from the brush of his foot along the floor, evoking a mental image of "initiating" the leg kick with a *tendu*, although in terms of body mechanics, hip flexors like the iliopsoas do the brunt of the work. Just as a decision to communicate precedes a speech act, a movement initiation marks a kinetic choice, and commits a dancer to a course of action.

Movement analyst and practitioner Peggy Hackney articulates a model for movement in which any movement phrase subdivides into "inner preparation (intent), the moment of the initiation (a beginning of movement in the body), the main action (exertion), a follow-through, and recuperation." Intent can take place through any of the four main areas of movement analysis (Body, Shape, Effort, Space)—i.e., I can plan to move my leg, intend to make a certain shape, set out to move in a fluid way, or choose to travel in spirals towards the corner of a room. Movement initiation marks this moment of decision, "The moment of initiation determines the entire process and path the movement will take … *Once the movement is initiated, the action fulfills itself*," Hackney writes (2002, p.50; italics in original). Preparation establishes a plan. Initiation sets movement in motion. The follow-through involves filling out the form of the phrase, and recuperation provides a return to neutral, long enough to begin the cycle anew. Initiation determines a movement's sense of attack.

In addition to their anatomical landmarks, and kinetic pathways based on neuromuscular patterning, movement initiations can occur at various points within a movement phrase. Although varieties of phrasing extend without limit, in practice, dividing them into three proves helpful. Propulsion can occur at the beginning, middle, or end of a movement. A dancer can initiate movement using "impulse" phrasing, with an accent on the start of the phrase, like a firework burst with a legato trailing energy. Energy might reach its peak midway, or the dancer can accelerate into a binding quality at the end of the movement—a common feature in urban dance forms like hip hop or pop-locking, for example. Practitioners across somatic forms work hard to pattern their bodies to move in certain ways that their physical instruments carry into movement vocabularies, so all they have to do is provide initiations.

The idea of movement initiation resonates with findings in quantitative fields like sociology, political science, and economics. Since the turn of the millennium, social scientists have been studying the threshold at which people become willing to tear themselves away from employment, social networks, extended family, child support, education, places of worship, entertainment, and the familiar. These research lines do not speak with one voice within subdisciplines, let alone more widely, regarding the causes of refugee flows. Also, social scientists take pains to make circumspect claims based on discrete data sets. However, over the past twenty years some generalizations have coalesced.

In general, empirical models take a balance-sheet approach to the study of human decision-making. In simplest terms, if staying produces a lower cost than leaving when danger looms, people will remain where they are, and if it is higher, they will leave. Intuitively, violence weighs the scales towards flight. In a widely cited article, economist Eric Neumayer determined how economic hardship/discrimination, when combined with minoritarian identity, provoked flight to Western Europe as of 2005, as well as, "political oppression, human rights abuse, violent conflict and state failure" (2005, p.389). Neumayer found that natural disasters and famines do not impact sustained patterns of migration, given their punctuated occurrence (p.300).

From this point, decision trees bifurcate. Neumayer's survey includes ciphers that add or subtract from the balance sheet: living standards; employment; laws impacting family reunification; restrictions on freedom of assembly, speech, ability to hold political office; assassination of dissidents; threats from government and dissident groups; and poverty impact inertia. Additional factors that affect the cost of migration include historical pathways to other countries; linguistic similarity; aid; geographical proximity; and the welfare policies of host countries. Neumayer concludes that economic conditions cannot alone account for so-called economic migrancy. For that matter, we cannot exclude financial motivations as part of political flight (Neumayer 2005 pp.405–6). In all scenarios, analyses like Neumayer's assume that people under stress approach decision-making based on a rational, game-theory approach.

Neumayer considered the then-available models based on empirical data that existed when formulating his approach. Other dynamics have since gained currency. Researchers appear to agree that destination plays a role in the decision to initiate movement, but debates arise regarding the factors that determine the flow along specific pathways. For example, Seraina Rüegger and Heidrun Bohnet summarize four "pull" categories around which current research congregates: personal agency (the ability to negotiate flight), political factors (stability and its attendant dynamics in both source and target regions), economic/ecological factors (relative wages, standard of living), and social networks (2018, p.67). Neumayer's data did not suggest that religious affiliation influences migratory pathways, whereas Rüegger and Bohnet find that ethnic kinship in neighboring countries, as well as histories of accepting co-ethnic refugees, do.

Social scientists have also learned to differentiate vectors. "Refugee" as a universal singular noun flattens the range of experience displaced persons possess; similarities in trajectories may mask differing initiations. Extending Neumayer's critique, David Scott FitzGerald and Rawan Arar (2018) point out the fallacy of dividing peoples on the move into "refugees" and "migrants," and argue for models that focus on the interaction of economic and political dynamics. Also, although Neumayer's data, from the vantage of 2005, did not suggest that ecological events affected refugee flow, climate change may begin to produce environmental refugees, with estimates ranging from distribution models predicting tens of millions displaced to apocalyptic visions of one billion persons on the move by 2050.[4]

Once in motion, refugees' routes are not random. Geography influences transit; refugees, as well as potential refugees, might perceive some destinations as more desirable than others; and other factors help predetermine pathways.

Rüegger and Bohnet plot out how ethnic affiliation, which does not always correspond to national boundaries, offers predictive roadmaps for migration (2018, pp.68–70). They also imply that refugee treks do not constitute singular phenomena, but break down into steps: flee the immediate danger; secure passage from nearby way station to a transfer point; negotiate a potential series of intermediary steps, smugglers, refugee camps; pursue legal processes once in a host country (and the possibility of deportation back to the origin country). Refugees may not have a plan when they first depart, beyond reaching a border. They tack due to exigency along the way. Each step requires a decision. Moments of recuperation separate one impulse from the next.

The ways in which movement initiation works in dance map well onto results from the social sciences. The decision to move must precede the mechanics of doing so. Movement from rest, or changing direction, is harder than adding momentum. Once motion begins, movement follows preexisting pathways. Whereas some refugees follow kinship maps, for dancers, energy transverses kinetic chains of pre-patterned neuronal pathways. Refugees travel along some branches of decision trees and not others. Ballet dancers train their bodies to jump and land through the heel-ball-toe of the foot, along with a plié of the feet and knees. Postmodern dancers roll around on the floor, engraining "head–tail," "cross-lateral," and "body half" developmental patterns. As Rüegger and Bohnet show, pulls draw refugees along vectors. In movement analysis, "spatial pulls" may draw parts of the body towards fixed points in space, a topic that Chapter 3 will cover in more detail. Refugees encounter multiple decision points. Likewise, dancers can drive movements in sequence (e.g., knee, then arm, then head). In its execution, a movement initiation in the body politic works in many of the same ways that it does in a dancing body.

Perhaps most importantly, for both dancers and refugees, the nature of a movement initiation predetermines the quality of the motion that follows. To reiterate Peggy Hackney's point, once a dancer commits to a kinetic chain, only an equal and opposite impulse can balance the resulting inertia. Thus, a brush of the leg and a translation of potential to kinetic energy in the standing leg turns into a soaring *grand jété*. A lateral thrust of the hips becomes a sultry jazz isolation. Dance steps can and do go awry mid-execution, but generally the audience sees a movement with a certain quality in lag time. The dancer has already made a movement decision and the step itself is a follow-through.

Likewise, the nature of an initiation influences, if not predetermines, the quality of the subsequent movement of peoples. A refugee's movement initiation bestows a change in self-concept—a citizen perhaps *becomes* a refugee at and because of this choice, at least in terms of personhood if not in a legal sense. A person traversing a mountain pass over the Caucasus because they seek higher wages does not share the same experience as someone for whom a stray anti-aircraft missile destroyed their home, or for whom global warming has caused crops to fail, even if the three walk in step. Peregrinations differ in ways that visual inspection may not reveal, so we must look towards initiations to analyze involuntary motion.

As visual hyperbole to demonstrate the role of cause in determining the quality of movement experience, consider the following thought experiment. The first mental image takes place indoors, on a smooth surface, with signage directing the flow and figures coming towards the lens. The second occurs outdoors, on a natural surface, with no directional information and with people walking away from the spectator. Assume that the first venue includes travelers in a modern airport, whereas those in the second are Syrian refugees. In both instances, travelers walk, rolling suitcases with one hand and carrying luggage via straps. Adults guide children, or carry them. Without context, we could switch the two groups while maintaining plausibility. Their locomotion through space matches. Yet the two experiences could not carry more disparate meanings. One set of travelers engages in movement via choice, and the other because war destroyed their homes. Their movements pair, but their movement initiations—and therefore what their experiences *mean*—oppose.

Using the term "movement initiation" to understand refugee flight opens up a set of vocabulary from dance and movement analysis in the subsequent case studies. I also like the term because it bestows the additional resonance of initiation as a rite, and therefore a means of reframing refugee identity. That is to say, movement initiations produce movement initiates, or ones who answer a calling through spiritual and usually physical motion. In Marcia Eliade's classic conception of shamanic initiation, elders may indoctrinate a supplicant through the revelation of mysteries (2004). The seeker's indoctrination may involve privation, isolation, starvation, hallucinogens, and above all a physical *journey* to a sacred place, where spirit animals may rend the body before bequeathing their magic. At the moment of induction, the acolyte transforms into an initiate. After surviving the journey, the initiate may graduate to pyschopomp and mediate the worlds of life, death, and spirit for the benefit of the group. Moreover, the term "shaman," from the Manchu-Tungus language family, means "one who knows" (Karafistan 2003, p.151). To describe refugees as "movement initiates" rather than "displaced persons," "migrants," or "undocumented" evokes the sense of pilgrimage in service to gods with inscrutable desires. Therefore, "refugee" does not share synonymy with words like "criminal" or "victim." Rather, refugees are movement initiates whose bodies in motion set them apart from "those who do *not* know."

Taking flight

Ballet might seem an unexpected place to begin an investigation of the somatics of refugee performance. In fact, the ballet world has embraced the politics of refugees. The Copenhagen Royal Theatre, for instance, presented *Uropa—An Asylum-Seeker's Ballet* (2016), under Christian Lollike's direction, which included six refugees in the cast whose deportation status remained uncertain up to and at opening curtain. The Netherlands-based ballet dancer Ahmad

Joudeh has created buzz as a self-taught prodigy who grew up in a Palestinian refugee camp in Damascus.

Above all, a recent dance work commands consideration: Canadian choreographer Crystal Pite's commission for London's Royal Ballet, *Flight Pattern* (2017). Pite (1970–) enjoys recognition as one of the leading artists in ballet. She joined the Frankfurt Ballet under William Forsythe in 1996, who identified her choreographic talent and assumed a mentoring role. Pite took over the direction of the Les Ballet Jazz de Montreal from 2001 to 2004, while establishing her own company, Kidd Pivot, in 2002, and has been producing works that rank as paragons of dance composition ever since.

Pite collaborated with her husband, writer and actor Jonathan Young, on their two-hour *Bettroffenheit* (2015), a dance/theater work about post-trauma. Pite's *Polaris* (2015) explores the potentialities of shape with a cast of sixty, to a score that calls for seventy-five instrumentalists. Leading dance companies have commissioned Pite, including Nederlands Dans Theater, Cullburg Ballet, the National Ballet of Canada, the Paris Opera Ballet, and the Royal Ballet, among others. As the cast size of *Polaris* indicates, Pite takes an interest in large-scale composition. On the level of movement vocabulary, Pite's dance steps tend tends towards the sinewy, meticulous, and sequential. Choreographically, Pite attends to *mise-en-scène*, which lends her movement a sense of theatricality.

The Royal Ballet commissioned Pite to set a work in 2017. She chose refugees as her theme, and created a ballet for thirty-six dancers. Her long-standing collaborators supplied production values. Jay Gower Taylor designed a set, Nancy Bryant contributed the costumes, and Tom Visser the lighting. *Flight Pattern* enjoyed immediate recognition. *The Guardian* gave Pite's ballet five stars (out of five), and called it "a somber and deeply affecting work" (Jennings 2017). *The Independent* praised the work for its "immense scale and ambition" (Anderson 2017). *The Telegraph* highlighted Pite's connection to the dancers, whose collaboration created a "heart-rending but extraordinarily beautiful emotional odyssey," the critic felt (Monahan 2017). *Flight Pattern* won the 2018 Olivier Award for Best New Dance Production. The Royal Ballet last presented the work towards the end of their 2018–19 season and released the work on DVD in 2020 (Orchestra of the Royal Opera House 2020).

Pite's artistic impulse for *Flight Pattern* began in an emotional place, an initiation the choreographer has articulated across interviews. For instance, Pite told the BBC that the piece functioned as, for her, "a way of coping with the world at the moment." Expressing a feeling of helplessness, Pite said, "I feel overwhelmed. I feel powerless and I feel frustrated. I feel angry" watching the world fail to adequately respond to an ever-growing humanitarian crisis. Pite does not know to what extent ballet can effect change, but despite self-doubts, she also feels, "if I'm going to talk about something that is so important to me, then it had better be through dance." Using art as a way to release artistic response in some regards bespeaks a sense of privilege, or at least centers the emotional lens on the observers—and beneficiaries—of globalization. ("Can Art Effect Change?" 2017). Having recourse to the universality of the language of embodiment, Pite intends her work to promote kinesthetic empathy. She tells writer Sarah Crompton, "Refugees embody the collapse of order. What has pushed them to leave their homes and risk their lives are forces that are beyond our capacity to imagine or control. It is easy for us to give in to fear, but I think that art can help to keep pathways open to the humane" (Crompton [2017]). A dancer, Pite uses dance to express her response to the plight of people on the move.

From this impulse, Pite began her choreographic process with music, which the performance reflects. *Flight Pattern* begins with the conductor mounting the podium in the pit, asking the orchestra to rise, shaking the first violinist's hand, and then bowing to the stage. The lights go out, the musicians sit, and all eyes turn to the opening drone of the bass. The stage lights stay dark. Preludes constitute a standard invocation for ballet, but the ritual mirrors the impulse that initiated Pite's creative process. Kite chose the thirty-minute first movement of Henryk Górecki's Symphony No. 3, Opus 36 (1976–77), "Symphony of Sorrowful Songs." Górecki wrote the powerful, three-movement composition according to medieval modes, using text that deals with a mother's mourning for a child. The first movement incorporates a fifteenth-century Polish lamentation of Mary for Jesus, the second the graffiti of a prisoner in a Gestapo prison, and the third the words of a mother whose son died during the Silesian uprisings of 1919–21. For whatever constellation of reasons, *Symphony of Sorrowful Songs* resonated with the Zeitgeist of the 1990s. Electra Nonesuch's CD issue of the London Sinfonietta's 1977 recording has sold a genre-defying 1,000,000 copies since its 1992 release (no one quite knows why).

In the movement, a double-bass drone precedes a long crescendo, akin to Ralph Vaughan Williams' *Fantasia on a Theme by Thomas Tallis* or Ravel's *Bolero*, lending the work an inexorable quality, like a single brushstroke through time. The chiaroscuro of Górecki's composition evokes the shadows of a Gothic cathedral. Hauntings of the Holocaust also accompany the piece into the theater. Although the composer denied this connection throughout his lifetime, the dark industrial costumes in *Flight Pattern* evoke the possibility of concentration camps. At one point, the dancers remove their light jackets to reveal light gray sleeves and tank tops. They place their jackets in piles, referencing the piles of clothing curators have left in front of the gas chambers in Auschwitz for visitors to see. However, the setting stops short of periodization. In a program insert for the audience, music critic Paul Kilbey cites the fiftieth anniversary of World War II, the Bosnian War, and famine in Africa, in addition to the refugee crisis, making the melancholy of the Górecki's first movement, "uncanny, the sort of direct expression of emotion that loses little relevance over time, at once overwhelmingly broad and piercingly specific" (Kilbey [2017]). A tangle of references, the music sets the tone of a history that turns back on itself with regularity, but never repeats.

The dance itself begins with the dancers in three rows of twelve. The lines rock back and forth, the lighting arrayed in such a way as to cause the dancers' faces to glow, while the darkness of their clothing against the black dance floor and black backdrop makes their bodies blur into the gloom. The rocking motion has the quality of ocean waves, and each row executes unison movements that emphasize the faces, like passengers on a long journey. Pite then introduces compositional variation. The dancers in the front row look up while they rock back and forth. The second row crouch and then rise. The front row look out at the audience and then bend their upper backs forward. The back row look stage right, then stage left, then they disappear in a forward bend. This opening sequence evokes passage, and brings me back to a recent memory of riding on a train in Hamburg. A group of young Roma women in traditional dress and headscarves came through the compartment to beg. One of the women, maybe eighteen, took both of my hands in hers, and kissed my knuckles. I don't recall if I gave her money, but I will always remember her face.

From the opening leitmotif of rocking lines, Pite develops her chess pieces. The rows alternate raising their sternums to the sky, rocking horizontally, rounding forward. A male dancer bends over, an asylum-seeking Thespis stepping out of the chorus. His neighbor puts a hand on his back. The dancers expand their facings, emphasizing upstage left, a subgroup now peeling off in a spiral. The shape grows more complex. The ensemble coalesces into a tableau, hands touch backs, a water hydra of gray. The back line of travelers against the cyclorama opens a crack, emitting a diagonal of light just stage left of the edge of the mass of dancers, a border, a limit.

The dance then evolves in sections, now a writhing mass, then a tender duet suggesting motherhood, a final duet reminiscent of lovers looking back in time. *Flight Pattern* climaxes with a slow rain of material dropping from the top of the stage in a conical light special, representing winter, or human ash. Curtains close on the scene on the final *pas de deux*, leaving a vertical slit for us to glimpse the white snow of the past, establishing a "fifth wall" beyond the fourth. From our (the audience's, and the final two performers') perspective, we can look through the doorway that the curtains make of the vast verticality of the Opera House stage. The final tableau seems intended as a multi-layered visual metaphor, but maybe the act of watching the dancers watching the past impugns us in a collective act of negligence, reminding us that we are forsaking our oaths of "never again."

In making the work about the experience of others, Pite maintains cognizance of her position, and takes ownership of empathy as her art's goal. Rather than impact policy, which she doubts her art can do, she uses language like, "What I want is that we come together in the theater," that her work allows her to speak "clearly and truthfully about something," for it "to open up those channels to the humane" and allow audiences "to have a conversation" ("Can Art Effect Change?" 2017). Pite's comments evoke Jill Dolan's notion of "utopian performatives," moments in a theater in which audiences share a glimpse of a better world, "one full of hope and reanimated by a new, more radical humanism" (Dolan 2010, p.2). Live performance can offer glimpses of future timelines in which we fulfill our obligations. *Flight Pattern* calls attention to refugees, but the dance's final lamentation seems to be a call to action. Future generations will look back and judge us for our choices.

From a practitioner's perspective, the Royal Ballet dancers' facility with movement vocabulary beyond ballet is astonishing. In prepared remarks for the Olivier ceremony, Pite extended thanks to her dancers, whom she described as "masterful, generous, and brave" ("Best New Dance Production—Flight Pattern" 2018). We should also add "capable." Both English and European ballet companies own classical and modern pieces in their repertoire, especially the larger companies. European companies tend not to draw as much of a distinction between "modern dance" and "ballet" as their American counterparts, but often set contemporary works on ballet-trained dancers. Even so, the Royal Ballet dancers exhibit a degree of comfort with Pite's movement vocabulary, as well as her theatricality, that previous incarnations of the company would not likely have been able to demonstrate. The twenty-minute work contains perhaps two instances of ballet "steps" that have names in French. For artists steeped in a dance form that recognizes five possible positions of the feet, the Royal Ballet dancers seemed like native movers in a piece that would test modern dancers.

Flight Pattern reflects the impulse Pite felt in her awareness of the world around her. On a body level, Pite's choreographic approach relies heavily on movement initiation. In an extended BBC interview, Pite allowed the cameras to roll while she worked with six of the dancers on in-progress phrase work in the piece ("Crystal Pite Rehearses Her New Piece with The Royal Ballet" 2017). Starting with her legs in a wide stance with feet parallel, hands on either side of the ears, Pite tells the dancers, "First of all, we're leading with the head, yeah? And after that, we're leading with the arm." Demonstrating as she speaks, Pite pivots her left knee inward and drops almost to the ground. Her head drops in a circular motion into the negative space within the crook of her right elbow, so that her body ends up facing towards stage right, her left arm out to the side, and her right arm bent. The dancers trace the shapes of their heads with their hands, like cats washing. From here, Kite specifies initiations. The dancers incline their torsos to the right in a deep turned-out, second-position *plié*, against a pushing movement of their hands towards their left knees. She asks them to show their eyes as they travel and turn stage left, so that they are "erasing their features" in a wiping motion across their faces. Now facing stage right, they leave their right hands open-palmed, facing up, and move their heads away from their hands as they lean back, their hand moving in opposition towards the floor.

Clarifying details, Pite tells the dancers where she wants movements to begin in their bodies: "think of doing this more with your shoulder blades rather than your elbow," she says. "This leg wants to go a little further." She wants a "shearing action" that the right ear leads; for the dancers to cantilever the torso over each leg even though a forced metatarsal arch would seem to make the shifts come from the lower body. She starts another correction with a compliment: "you're doing a great job moving your head, but I think we can actually pull through the ribs a little bit more ... yes, exactly!" Pite explains the connection between movement initiation and kinetic chains, showing how lifting and propelling her left shoulder blade causes her left arm to spiral inward, whereas the ballet dancers' instincts tell them to lead with the fingers. The left thumb then pulls the left arm down the left lower thigh, generating momentum as the back of the hand passes the back of the knee. Pite asks the dancers to use this moment as a chance to "take a risk," as the trailing hand becomes a spiral across the upper torso and then initiation transfers to the right foot, which next pulls the right leg, causing a wave to flow through the upper body into a layout.

If you have never seen a dance rehearsal, you will likely find yourself unprepared for the level of specificity to which the artists attend. In this section of the video, Pite rehearses nine-and-a-half counts of eight, or around forty-five seconds of choreography—that the dancers already know—for twenty-three minutes of studio time. For concert dance, especially for featured dancers in one of the world's leading ballet companies, learning a new masterwork from a leading choreographer, this kind of detail matters. Moreover, for Pite's work, which relies on granularity in texture in non-unison phrases, the dancers must achieve razor precision, as well as a hive consciousness, lest the work turn to mush. Some of this intensity is normal. Dancers share a common shorthand. Choreographers push in rehearsals because they never have enough time to achieve the impossible perfection they seek. Even so, Pite's reliance on movement initiation requires an attention to detail that elevates the focus of dancers at the peak of their field. Moving an arm from the elbow is not the same as moving it from the scapula. Starting a layout by pulling an extended leg forward from the big toe is not the same as arching back from the thoracic vertebrae. Dancers—these dancers—doing this choreographer's work, need to know the difference.

Connecting through dance

New York City-based Battery Dance runs its global operations out of a fifth-floor walk-up in Tribeca. Slightly out of breath after ascending the wide, wooden staircases, I step over the gazelle-like bodies of dancers in the narrow hallway on either end of two small, light-filled studios, the kind in which decades of dancers doing *demi-pliés* produces afterimages that time will never fully erase. Doubling back, I enter the one-room office in which Battery's half-dozen or so personnel have coordinated programming in over sixty-two countries. The room buzzes with unflustered, productive commotion, while negotiating the same spatial problem-solving as New York restaurants whose kitchens have no room for a second garbage can. The desiderata of office life seem secondary to a sense of mission. Since we are not far from the Lower

East Side, at least geographically, I allow the Yiddish word *mishpokha* to come to mind to describe what I am seeing: "family."

Waiting in the office, I chat for a moment with Alyx, a delightful conversationalist who has turquoise hair and dual master's degrees from NYU in museum education and ancient Egyptian linguistics. Among other tasks, Alyx acts as Battery's interface with the labyrinthine New York City school system (deciphering hieroglyphics might be the more straightforward task). At a conference table in the center of a sea of papers, Battery's chief operating officer, Emad Salem, is trying to wrap up a conversation having something to do with insurance. Salem holds two bachelor's degrees from American University in Washington, DC, and a master's from Columbia University's School of International and Public Affairs. A *Wunderkind*, Salem seems like he could be a policy advisor for a progressive Democratic senator, someone who fellow staffers would want to meet in Georgetown to decompress after a Senate subcommittee hearing. Overall, the caliber of Battery's people falls in line with my impressions when researching the case studies throughout this book. Despite pejorative stereotypes about the emerging generations, a cadre of "the best and the brightest" exists, its members bring sophistication that leverages shoestring budgets, and they are choosing the arts as a venue for effecting social change.

A few minutes later, Jonathan Hollander arrives, wearing an elegant posture and a fedora. Mr. Hollander was originally a visual artist but came to New York on choreographer Merce Cunningham's invitation. Something about Mr. Hollander recalls Cunningham, maybe a certain mien, attenuated frame, or intellectual sharpness. Hollander founded Battery Dance Company in 1976 at the age of twenty-four. He has directed the company ever since, putting Battery in the company of a very small number of dance organizations in New York City with similar staying power. Battery's annual summer dance festival is the longest-running event of its kind. At lunch in a neighborhood trattoria, Mr. Hollander talks about Battery's upcoming return visit to India, and his concern with Prime Minister Narendra Modi's virulent Hindu nationalism. Mr. Salem has ideas about how to facilitate country visits among refugees who have gone through Battery's programming, which would piggyback on social media community-building, which is already happening organically.

Hollander is an award-winning choreographer, and Battery continues to perform original work. However, outreach takes much of the organization's focus. After having worked with supposedly "lost" public high school students in year-long dance programs since 1984, Battery found itself short on funding and started doing one-week intensives. Hollander found that the goal-oriented, time-constrained format unleashed creativity. In 2006, the company formally inaugurated the "Dancing to Connect" program. Battery dancers and Battery-trained facilitators use Dancing to Connect workshopping under rubrics such as "Inclusion/Exclusion," "Conflict Resolution and Prevention," "Empowering the Less Advantaged," "Gender-based Violence and Human Trafficking," and "The Disabled," as well as academic content areas. I asked Mr. Hollander how Battery accomplishes so much with so little. He replied, "I guess it's just passion, commitment, an unwillingness to be defeated [laughter], what else can I tell you … we just won't stop" (Hollander 2020). Battery's "unwillingness to stop our stubbornness" now carries them forward into the heart of the refugee crisis.

In 2016, Battery Dance won a five-year program contract to adapt Dancing to Connect to the problem of refugee integration across seventeen cities in Germany. Funding comes from the European Recovery Program Transatlantic Fund (the successor to the Marshall Plan), *Bundesministerium für Wirtshaft und Energy* (the German Federal Ministry for the Economy and Energy), the US Embassy in Berlin, Qatar Foundation International, and *Schöpflin Stiftung* (a German non-profit), as well as additional sources. The German government provided impetus through Chancellor Angela Merkel's larger project of refugee integration. In 2015, Syrians fleeing civil war accounted for the largest group of foreigners in Germany. Committed to an open, post-War central Europe capable of assimilating the influx, Merkel told her people, *Wir shaffen das* ("We can do this"), a clarion redolent of US President Barack Obama's campaign slogan, "Yes, we can!"

Specifically, Merkel's administration launched a national-, regional-, and local-level push to integrate refugees into German society, particularly through vocational training. In the 1960s, Germany brought in hundreds of thousands of Turkish "guest workers" in response to a labor shortage, but without support programs. As a result, to this day Turks in Germany constellate in segregated communities with high unemployment rates. Merkel wanted to avoid the mistakes of Germany's recent past (Hindy 2018; see also Chandler 2019). Tragically, the Syrian experiment has fueled ultranationalist right-wing populism. Nazism had never gone away—the Freedom Party of Austria's strength during the 1980s comes to mind, for instance. However, with the perception of the government's encouragement of foreigners in numbers, neo-Nazism has exploded into the public arena in Germany with movements like the anti-Islamic Pegida or the anti-EU, xenophobic party Alternative für Deutschland. Neo-Nazis conduct marches and have perpetrated thousands of attacks against foreigners, refugees, Jews, and others, and a neo-Nazi won the mayoralty of a town in Hesse.

Faced with growing Euroscepticism, at best, and a *volte-face* to fascism at worst, Chancellor Merkel battles to reconcile her commitment to an open post-War Germany with centrifugal forces that could rend her nation apart. How she deals with the presence of refugees in Germany serves as a test case, and a potential detonation wire, for government policy, and perhaps the future of a democratic German state. Perhaps not realizing the aptness of the synecdoche, during the summer of 2019, the German tabloid *Das Bild* ran stories that called attention to instances of Merkel trembling in public (Thurau 2019). The features sought to raise questions about Germany's privacy laws concerning the health of German public officials, but the sight of crowds marching against what they call the pollution of the foreigners should make the entire body politic shake.

Despite, and deliberately oblivious to, such incendiary rhetoric, Battery Dance's refugee integration workshops have proven a runaway success. Something about the immediacy of solving problems in the studio has the effect of equalizing participants—which is the idea. Although circumstances shift by location, Battery facilitators generally lead one-week workshops of four to five hours a day, for groups ranging in age from about fourteen to early twenties, split evenly between German and refugee youth. Traveling in one-month assignments, the teaching artists facilitate the creation of five-to-eight-minute dance works, which they then aggregate into concerts that the students perform along with the professional dancers. The German government provides nexus points, such as schools, cultural centers, and found spaces, but the Battery facilitators, like any type of creative artist, work with the conditions they find at hand. The experience proves transformative for all involved.

I speak over the phone with Dancing to Connect teaching artist Sarah Housepian, a lithe, powerful dancer (Housepian 2020). Housepian developed a relationship with Hollander and Battery dancers through unrelated projects, and then joined the company two-and-a-half years ago. I ask half-jokingly if when Battery signed her, they asked if she had a current passport. She said yes, that actually was the first question. Housepian has been leading workshops for the refugee integration project for the past two-and-a-half years. She speaks about the challenges, but is emphatic in her claim that her work is a "dream job for me." She is calling in from San Diego Airport, and will be heading back overseas in a week for the company.

Dancing to Connect workshops create creative provocations. Although the Germans provide translators, refugees who have been in-country for less than a month may not benefit from English-to-German translation, or English-to-Arabic either. Housepian relates, "you have to be on the fly. These tools are very adjustable, but every group is different." For example, one Battery dancer felt so struck by the number of countries participants had crossed that she recorded the refugees saying the country names, and helped them make solo word phrases; both elements then appeared in the final dance. Another facilitator used pushpins on a map to create floor patterns based on the refugees' trajectories, pausing in stage locations that corresponded to their flight patterns (e.g. "three seconds for three years.") Housepian herself prompted one of her groups to pick ten things they liked about their city and ten they disliked. The participants felt safe voicing their fears. One German student said, "sometimes I don't like the refugees because my parents say to not go out at night." Housepian helped the students translate their feelings into movement, asking, for example, "if you think of being scared, what would you do?" From sitting in a circle, they then built standing phrases, which then evolved into choreography.

On a human level, the workshops live up to their title, connecting through dance. Housepian tells me about Abraham, a sixteen-year-old refugee who

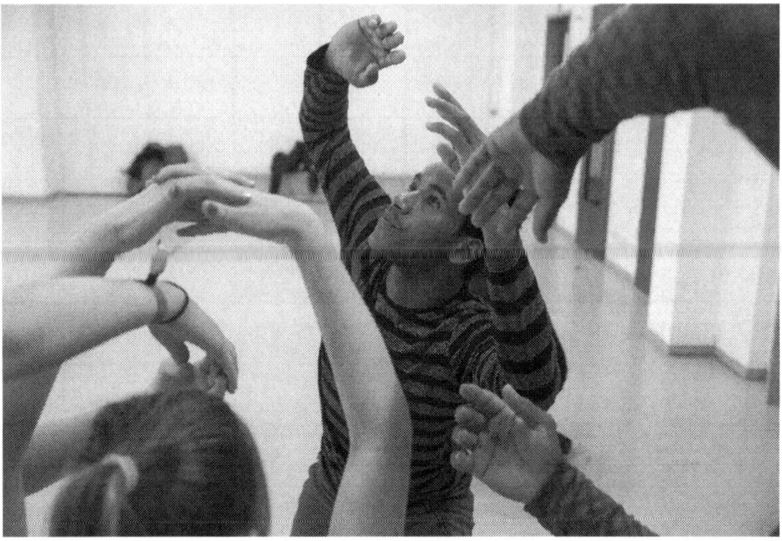

Figure 1.2 Dancing to Connect workshop, Brandenburg. Photo © Christian Jungeblodt.

lost his brother and both parents during his travels to Germany, where he lives with German students his age. In a workshop with eleven languages bounding around the room, Abraham stood out. " 'I have never seen him so happy,' his teacher said. He was the first one up, so encouraging, and so excited, and he just jumps up, 'Oh, we're back from lunch.' " The refugees usually have no dance training (neither do most of the German students). Nevertheless, the workshops empower them: "they're making friendships … they've just performed on a professional stage with professional dancers and they're like, 'look what I can do now,' " Housepian relates. Whatever reservations manifested on the first day are generally gone by the performance at the end of the week, as tear-filled photos evidence.

I asked Hollander why refugees invariably appear happy in the workshops. Regardless of gender, place of origin, religion, encultured attitudes towards dancing bodies, laughter abounds. He suspects that the specificity of the challenge drives the healing power of the workshops. "I think you have to go more basic than that [cultural factors] in human nature and think about what these refugees are dealing with on a daily basis … and they get into a dance workshop and it's not so hard," Hollander says. "All of a sudden they might be top of the class. Something gets unlocked there, a *joie de vivre* that's natural for any young person that's been beaten out of them because they've grown up way too soon, but it's still there." Hollander notes that at times the refugees find responding to open-ended prompts easier than their German co-participants do. After enduring problems beyond their control during their journeys, refugees find the workshop's creative prompts solvable and attack them with abandon.

In my interview with Housepian, I pose the same question. Are such results typical? She relates that like students anywhere, many feel trepidation at first, but fear transmutes into joy as they sink into the work. As for the stated goal of making connections, Housepian says, "it is has never not worked, that's our job, you have to make it work." On a personal level, Housepian says that she has learned, "so much more as a human than I would say even as an artist. It has opened my eyes to so many different stories and so many different ways of life." An old saw claims that a dancer's dancing life is short, yet these kinds of applications seem like a life's work.

Dancing to Connect exemplifies the idea of movement initiation and kinetic follow-through. Jonathan Hollander added a movement pulse to the New York dance world forty-four years ago. Battery Dance's extraordinary trajectory confounded whatever expectations he might have had. Hollander says,

> Nothing has been master-planned or mapped out ... just the way you make a dance piece, it comes out of scratch, and it comes out of the interaction between you and your dancers, and nobody knows how it happened once it's done, at least that's my way. I've never said, "I'm going to make a dance about this subject, and it's going to have three movements, and it's going to be in ¾ time signature," you know what I mean? It just evolves, and that's the way the programs at Battery Dance have evolved, by trial and error.

A reliance on choreographic process mirrors organizational growth, and also serves as a life metaphor.

The refugee integration workshops produce a similar momentum. Workshop graduates stay in touch over social media, and Mr. Salem hopes to generate additional programming out emerging networks. Dancing to Connect facilitators hear from their students, who send testimonials crediting their dance experience with helping them integrate, pursue advanced education, even fall in love. Hollander hopes to expand the German initiative into a "Dancing for Trust" initiative that would broaden the German workshops to include topics like anti-Semitism and xenophobia, in addition to refugee integration. Battery has trained Syrian refugee dancers to teach workshops in Germany, and Greek professional dancers to conduct programming in Greece. At home in New York, Battery dancer Hussein Smko, an Arab-Kurdish Iraqi immigrant, premiered his contemporary/hip hop piece *Ballade: The Rain Song* on a platform overlooking the Statue of Liberty as part of the 2017 Battery Dance Festival, featuring spoken word poetry by Iraqi American refugee journalist Riyadh Mohammed (Bauer 2020). From well-placed movement initiations, kinetic chains branch out in spiderweb patterns.

Similar kinetic chains are propagating globally. For example, Congolese choreographer Fabrice don de Dieu Bwabulamutima began his own organization Refugees on the Move in the Democratic Republic of the Congo in 2015, around when Dancing to Connect conducted programming in Kinshasa. Bwabulamutima possesses prowess in organization and fundraising, in addition to artistry. With his group Kongo Drama Company, he entered into global partnerships with the UNHCR, the Clinton Foundation, and others to create dance spaces in refugee camps, for refugees, and by refugees (e.g. Turner and Kirchof 2018). Bwabulamutima's workshop participants are finding choreographic voices, and so the energy continues.

The ballet world is not sitting still, either. At the time of this writing, architect and director Kibwe Tavares is presenting *Aisha and Abhaya* (lit., "Prosperous" and "Fearless") for the Rambert ballet company at the Royal Opera House, which features movement by Israeli choreographer Sharon Eyal, costumes by Russian artist and photographer Uldus Bakhtionzina, and film animation. A collaboration between the Royal Ballet, Rambert, and BBC Films, the multimedia, interdisciplinary hour-long work reinterprets Hans Christian Andersen's classic, "The Little Match Girl" in terms of the refugee crisis. When I asked the Royal Ballet about the impetus for this new work, they indicated that artists are driving socially aware work, which they support. Artistic administrator Rachel Hollings emailed, "Narratives that can express the world we live in, and help to make sense of it, make for particularly resonant, rich and meaningful topics for our programming" (personal communications, Feb. 17, 2020). The energy that movers like Pite and Hollander propelled into the dance world continues to travel.

Refugees are those who move against their will, but all motion begins from prior movement. For the ancients, the only truly stationary object in the universe is that which does not move and therefore creates everything else, or Aristotle's "unmoved mover."[5] In dance, a movement initiation begins with a shift in thought. A mover makes a commitment to move, and that decision initiates a kinetic chain of events along pre-patterned pathways in the body. Through art-making, dancers use dance to repattern the kinetic chains that movement initiates follow within global body politics. As Crystal Pite's *Flight Pattern* and Battery Dance's Dancing to Connect program show, movement impulses follow pathways that sculpt over time, like rainwater.

Notes

1 A rough translation of Patanja's second sutra, *Yogas chitta vritti nirodhah*: "Yoga stills the vibrations of the mindstuff." For a complete commentary and translation, see Bryant (2015).

2 The brain exhibits less activity in front of a television screen than during sleep. Television also impairs cognition and verbal memory. See, e.g., Fancourt and Steptoe (2019).

3 A kinetic chain is a neuromuscular pathway—i.e., a sequence that repetition ingrains. Although anatomy may suggest certain kinetic chains over others, culture,

training, and individual movement preferences predispose sequences. A baseball player commits thousands of hours to perfecting a specific kind of foot-to-wrist spiral that he hopes will result in a .300 batting average, for instance.

4 The future of climate refugees is a contentious subject with many unknown variables. Tacoli (2009) is an older but influential piece.

5 ὃ οὐ κινούμενον κινεῖ or *primum movens*.

References

Anderson, Zoë. "Flight Pattern, The Royal Ballet, Royal Opera House, London, Review: It has Immense Scale and Ambition." *The Independent*, March 19, 2017.

Bauer, Claudia. "Coming to America: What It's Like to Create Dance as an Immigrant in America. *Dance Magazine*, April 2020.

"Best New Dance Production—Flight Pattern." Olivier Awards, April 9, 2018.

Bryant, Edwin F. *The Yoga Sutras of Patanjali: A New Edition, Translation, and Commentary*. New York: Farrar, Straus, and Giroux, 2015.

"Can Art Affect Change? Kirsty Wark Meets Choreographer Crystal Pite." BBC Newsnight, April 26, 2017.

Chandler, Caitlin. "Integration and Its Discontents: Germany's Bold Experiment." *The New York Review of Books*, December 12, 2019.

Crompton, Sarah. "Outside Time and Place." Program insert, Royal Opera House, n.p., n.d. [2017].

"Crystal Pite Rehearses Her New Piece with The Royal Ballet." BBC, February 9, 2017.

Dolan, Jill. *Utopia in Performance: Finding Hope at the Theater*. Ann Arbor: University of Michigan Press, 2010.

Eliade, Mircea. *Shamanism: Archaic Techniques of Ecstasy*. Princeton, NJ: Princeton UP, 2004.

Fancourt, Daisy, and Andrew Steptoe. "Television Viewing and Cognitive Decline in Older Age: Findings from the English Longitudinal Study of Ageing." *Scientific Reports* 9, no.1 (2019): 1–8.

Fernandez, Ciane. *The Moving Researcher: Laban/Bartenieff Movement Analysis in Performing Arts Education and Creative Arts Therapies*. London & Philadelphia: Jessica Kingsley Publishers, 2015.

FitzGerald, David Scott, and Rawan Arar. "The Sociology of Refugee Migration." *Annual Review of Sociology* 44 (2018): 387–406.

Hackney, Peggy. *Making Connections: Total Body Integration through Bartenieff Fundamentals*. London & New York: Routledge, 2002.

Hindy, Lily. "Germany's Syrian Refugee Integration Experiment." The Century Foundation, September 16, 2018.

Hollander, Jonathan. Personal interview with the author, February 10, 2020.

Housepian, Sarah. Personal interview with the author, February 19, 2020.

Jennings, Luke. "Royal Ballet Triple Bill Review—Five Stars for Crystal Pite." *The Observer*, March 19, 2017.

Karafistan, Rachel. "'The Spirits Wouldn't Let Me Be Anything Else': Shamanic Dimensions in Theatre Practice Today." *New Theatre Quarterly* 74, no. 19, part 2 (2003): 150–68.

Kilbey, Paul. "Sorrowing with Górecki's Songs." Program insert, Royal Opera House, n.p., n.d. [2017].

Monahan, Mark. "Crystal Pite's Flight Pattern Is an Emotional Odyssey that Passes in the Blink of an Eye—Royal Ballet Mixed Bill, Review." *The Telegraph*, March 17, 2017.

Neumayer, Eric. "Bogus Refugees? The Determinants of Asylum Migration to Western Europe." *International Studies Quarterly* 49, no. 3 (2005): 389–409.

Orchestra of the Royal Opera House. *Vivaldi & Bosso: Within the Golden Hour; Purcell: Medusa; Gorecki: Flight Pattern*. Directed by Christopher Wheeldon and Crystal Pite. BBC/Opus Arte, 2020. DVD.

Rüegger, Seraina, and Heidrun Bohnet. "The Ethnicity of Refugees (ER): A New Dataset for Understanding Flight Patterns." *Conflict Management and Peace Science* 35, no. 1 (2018): 65–88.

Tacoli, Cecilia. "Crisis or Adaptation? Migration and Climate Change in a Context of High Mobility." *Environment and Urbanization* 21, no. 2 (2009): 513–25.

Thurau, Jens. "Angela Merkel's Shaking Changes How Germany's Leaders Discuss Their Health." *Deutsche Welle*, July 11, 2019.

Turner, Vania, and Andreas Kirchof, "Congo Dance Project Helps Refugees Take Steps Towards Rebuilding Lives." UNHCR, March 12, 2018.

2 Body

Undocumented zombies and sea creatures

Chapter 1 began this book's application of somatics, movement analysis, and dance to problems in refugee performance with the idea of movement initiations, and the ways that energy travels along kinesthetic chains. Movement analysis typically divides Rudolf von Laban's sprawling corpus into "Body," "Effort," "Space," and "Shape." In practice, the four areas interrelate, since bodies form shapes as they move through space with perceptible movement qualities. Chapter 2 groups the Body, Effort, and Shape categories, as together they provide a vocabulary for discussing embodiment in refugee performance.

In particular, Chapter 2 explains Laban's concepts of "Shape" and "movement efforts" as ways of describing bodies, and uses this terminology to understand the basis of racist tropes that characterize refugees as monsters. After surveying Laban's system of Effort/Shape, and the role shaping plays in the performativity of monstrosity, the chapter looks at two case studies of refugees-as-monsters based on a perversion of two basic forms of locomotion: walking and swimming. The first study interprets how the zombie hit TV show *The Walking Dead* resonates with racially coded politics of immigration from Mexico to the United States. The second reads refugee flight over water in the context of sea monsters, within the liminal space of international maritime law. The latter section concludes with a close reading of Chinese dissident artist Ai Weiwei's shape-matching performance of Alan Kurdi, a three-year-old Syrian refugee who drowned in the Mediterranean Sea, which highlights tensions between theories of abjection and kinesthetic empathy.

The Effort/Shape of monsters

Shape can inform our understanding of monstrosity in terms of the work refugees perform as bogeymen for societies in the throes of xenophobic racism. The following analyses draw inspiration from work by theater historians like Michael Chemers, who provide grounding for understanding the performativity of monsters. For Chemers, bestial archetypes serve as scapegoats, avatars whose identities shift over time, depending on the waxing and waning of imagined communities. Monsters act as surrogates, providing "relief" for theater audiences by assuring them of a world that "would be perfect and harmonious if it were not for the outliers, aliens, traitors, subversives, or monsters" that invade their imaginations (2018, p.15). Monster stories that stay within accepted narratives fail as vehicles for catharsis, however. When audiences reenter their daily lives, the adrenaline rush of vicariously vanquishing evil beasts fades against the clarifying dullness of reality. Outsiders remain, whose flesh and blood merge with the cultural form of monsters as the cause of a society's self-perceived ills, and who therefore qualify as potential ritual victims. Every generation must reboot monster tropes in terms that make sense to them, and in relation to the outsiders they find in their midst.

Chemers makes a major contribution to "monster studies" by taking the beasts of our nightmares from the semiotic realms of literature and cinema into that of the corporeal bodies of live theater. I would like to summon monsters further into the visceral with a discussion of how somatics can contribute to the approach that Chemers exemplifies.

By way of preliminary definitions: "shape" in *choreography* refers to the arrangement of bodies in positive and negative space. "Positive space" constitutes the shape that the "inside" of a dancer's outline makes, whereas "negative space" describes the space around her outline, a distinction that corresponds to figure and ground. Dancers can make shapes with each other, operating with one another's positive space (they touch), or form shapes by highlighting one another's negative spaces (they form shapes around one another without touching). Dancers may make symmetrical or asymmetrical shapes along an axis, and also form shapes on different vertical levels. Alternatively, "Shape" in Irmgard Bartenieff's interpretation of Laban refers to how bodies change during movement. Based on force of habit, bodies can conform to "shape forms" such as "Wall," "Ball," or "Pin," quasi-Platonic solids that carry emotional connotation, or describe personality types. In motion, Shape can shift in terms of itself ("shape flow"), take "directional" movement ("arcing" in curves or "spoking" in lines), or "carve" space through three dimensions. Shapes can relate to specific points, and shapes in motion convey relational qualities (e.g., "rising," "spreading," "enclosing," "advancing"). "Shape flow support" describes how the shape of the torso relates to the rest of the body.

If we think of shapes as "nouns," and shapes (i.e. bodies) in motion as "verbs," then "movement efforts" act as "adverbs," or the movement quality of shapes as they shift through space.

Movement analysts refer to both shapes and the sensible qualities of shapes as they travel under the rubric "Effort/Shape." The "Effort graph," which will become significant in the following discussions of monstrous refugee performance, charts movement qualities along four factors: *space* (direct versus indirect); *weight* (strong vs light); *time* (sudden versus sustained); and *flow* (bound versus free). The fluidity of Tai Chi demonstrates purity in

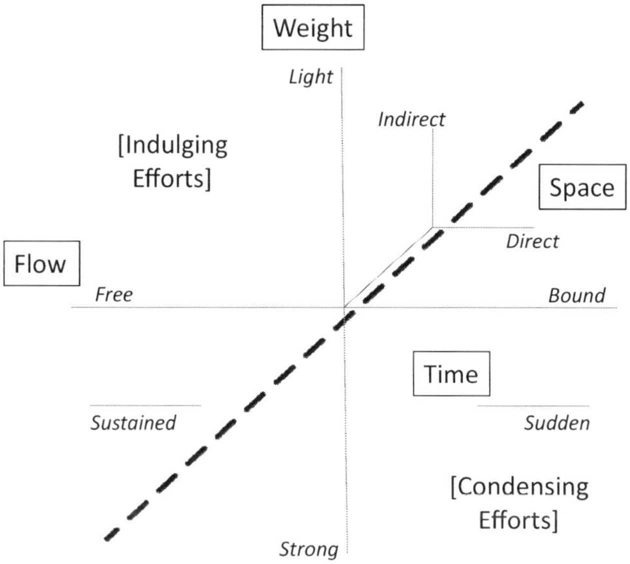

Figure 2.1 The Effort/Shape graph.

sustainment, for example, whereas an Olympic-level archer takes direct focus to an extreme. Semester-long courses teach students to embody Effort factors, and actors have found movement efforts helpful for characterization, both individually and in combination (e.g. "punch" = direct + sudden + strong + bound; "float" = indirect + sustained + light + free).[1]

Before turning to case studies, I would like to argue that monstrosity involves operations on morphology that achieve a performative effect through embodiment. Distortions in shape can make monsters monstrous in multiple ways, including (but not limited to) the following:

- Magnification (*Godzilla*, *King Kong*—even to the point of camp, as in *Attack of the 50 Foot Woman*)
- Multiplication (*The Birds*, *Invasion of the Body Snatchers*, swarms, insects)
- Pastiche (*Frankenstein*, composite beasts like hippogriffs, the Sphinx, satyrs)
- Metonymy (*Jaws*, i.e., the dorsal fin stands in for the shark, which accentuates the fear of the unseen)
- Exaggeration (gargoyles, especially when drawing attention to sexual organs and viscera, which becomes the basis of Bakhtin's notion of the grotesque (Bakhtin 1984), vampires' elongated teeth, "My, Grandmother, what large eyes you have," etc.)
- Transparency/invisibility (*Poltergeist*, ghosts)

Shape distortion is a convention of monstrosity, not its cause, as Chemers shows. However, these operations serve as signs, signals that something monstrous is afoot. We know that King Kong is a monster (a performative creature that embeds layers of psycho-social signification) because he is so big. Alfred Hitchcock's movie *The Birds* terrifies because although individual birds are fragile, as a swarm they can peck a person to death. Consequently, refugees have multiple ways of transforming into monsters in mediatized images and political rhetoric: through signals in "choreographic" shapes in space, by representations of movement efforts, and with distortion of shapes, depending on context.

The shape flow of blobs

When speaking in generalities, right-wing politicians evoke immigrants in terms of shape flow. In this trope, immigrants are an amorphous blob, unrelenting, an inexorable ooze overtaking the system. For example, to take one of Donald Trump's stream-of-consciousness statements at a press conference more or less at random:

> I say, and this is our new statement, the system is full. We can't take you anymore. Whether it is asylum or anything you want, illegal immigration, we can't take you anymore. Our country is full. Our area is full. The sector is full. We can't take you anymore. Sorry, can't happen. So turn around, that's the way it is. If you look at our southern border, the number of people and the amount of drugs and human trafficking. Human trafficking is something that nobody used to talk about. It's a terrible thing. It is ancient and it is never been bigger than it is modern. Human trafficking, a terrible thing. They come into these areas where you don't have the wall. They come into areas where you don't have the wall. Then they make a left or they make a right and they come right into the country. Loaded up with people in many cases, and it is pretty sad.
>
> (Apr. 5, 2019)

To say that President Trump's remarks are incoherent/racist/xenophobic lands as too easy a critique. Whatever its cause, Trump's vagary has a messaging effect that we ignore at a cost: immigrants are a self-contained, unthinking globule. Like an amoeba, "immigrants" (i.e., a catchphrase for brown-skinned incomers, legal non-white immigrants, and terrorists—also normatively non-white, despite the uptick in white nationalist violence) constitutes a single-celled organism that lacks an internal structure that might differentiate one part from the next ("whether it is asylum or anything you want") This entity has penetrated unprotected openings, clogging up the works ("the system is full"). Insufficient protections have allowed the invading being to enter into the American body politic ("they make a left or they make a right and they come right [in]"), where the mass will spread. Issues like drugs and human trafficking blend together like flavors in a toxic stew. All immigrants are part of an undifferentiated, unthinking mass, which will continue to expand unless something stops it. From this point, such rhetoric comes within reach of the conceptual metaphor of *outsiders as a disease*, which calls for medical cleansing, and a return to the genocides of the twentieth century.[2]

The remedy, Trump's rhetoric argues, is to counter shape with shape. Like a game of Rock Paper Scissors, *Wall* blocks *shape flow*. During the 2016 election and after, Trump's followers responded to his proposal of building a wall along the US–Mexican border with a zeal that perhaps took Trump himself by surprise. Since he is real estate mogul, many took Trump's campaign pledge on face value—that he would build a physical partition and in some unexplained way make the Mexican government pay for the landmark, a just recompense for America's southern neighbor having foisted immigrants/drugs/trafficking on North America, in the eyes of Trump's enthusiasts. Critics levied arguments based on *policy* (the idea is racist, would require the illegal seizure of private lands, would not achieve its stated goals, etc.). However, Trump's critics misunderstood the point. The "Make America Great Again" ("MAGA") community argued that "we" (although a variegated collation, including former Obama voters, a bloc of non-college-educated whites who see academia, coastal states, and urban centers as warrens of arrogant, liberal elites and themselves as victims of multiculturalism) should build a wall, if possible, but more importantly, we must *become* a Wall.

Because of its lack of structure, shape flow lends itself to stoking fear of the creature in the darkness. For example, right-wing French politician Marine le Pen refers to the "imponderable threat" of Islamic extremism, which tends to blend with "savage globalization" and immigration in her rhetoric (Joseph 2017). Likewise, Trump has become a model for would-be strongmen in their calls to end the unspecified threats of outsiders. Slippage occurs, so refugees fleeing violence become its perpetrators. For example, in 2014, a Midland, Texas, county sheriff told the hosts the popular Fox show *Fox and Friends*, without evidence, that his forces had found copies of the Qur'an on the ground on the Mexican side of the US border, apparently a bit of cellular detritus that implies a link between skin color, Mexican immigration, Middle Eastern terrorism, and human trafficking—as well as equating Islam with violence. Shape flow proves effective in the abstract, referring to a "them" who are "out there," waiting to come "in." Shape flow has its place in storytelling. To take an innocuous example, *The Blob*, a 1958 sci-fi/horror movie in which an alien ooze alights on earth, overcoming everything in its path, still has a camp following. In general, however, anti-immigrant racism requires more specificity on the local level. Bogeymen need more detailing, which is where shaping and movement efforts come into play.

Undocumented zombies

On May 16, 2011, the US Centers for Disease Control (CDC) issued an online document, titled "Preparedness 101: Zombie Apocalypse." The tongue-in-cheek survival guide raised the CDC's web traffic by a factor of 100, causing their website to crash. In the same year, the Obama administration deported a then-record 400,000 people from the United States. Zombies have continued to fascinate the public, resulting in hundreds of millions of dollars from movie sales, advertising income, and video games. At the same time, following a global right-wing backlash, immigration has become a rallying point for resurgent xenophobia in America, facilitating Donald Trump's election in 2016. As America continues to polarize, zombies serve as a vehicle for fantasies of white victimization.

"Zombie" has a long history as a monstrous archetype. The creature's contours may shift over time, and its mapping follows Supreme Court Justice Potter Stewart's definition of pornography: "I know it when I see it" (*Jacobellis v. Ohio*, 378 US 184 (1964)). Generally, zombies are creatures of the undead, with a lurching locomotion and a hankering for brains, or flesh in general. In a widely cited text, sociologist Mimi Sheller weighs the evidence that zombies' propensity to eat the living functions as a cannibalistic metaphor for consumerism and colonialism (2003, pp.143–8). Historically, zombies began in the Caribbean with magical traditions, such as Obeah.[3] Although technical definitions exist, Jean Rhys provides the most succinct in her classic novel, *Wide Sargasso Sea*, when she writes, "A zombie is a dead person who seems to be alive or a living person who is dead. A zombie can also be the spirit of a place, usually malignant but sometimes to be propitiated with sacrifices or offerings of flowers or fruit" (2016, p.97). Set off by a spell, zombies animate the husks of former humans. Untiring, they eat, but also infect, the living.

As creatures of the undead go, zombies are not sexy. Vampires, for instance, have always turned up the heat. Bram Stoker's original Count suffers hairy palms, teasing readers with a Victorian token of auto-erotic excess. The *Twilight* book and movie series casts vampires as coming-of-age teens with sexual prowess and personal problems. Veering into the quasi-pornographic, B-movies have long featured lesbian vampires—a trope to which even film auteur Francis Ford Coppola nods in his lush *Dracula* (1992). Although Coppola pitches the movie as a romance between Dracula (Gary Oldman) and Elizabeta (Winona Ryder), a midnight montage climaxes with a kiss between Elizabeta and her cousin Lucy (Sadie Frost) in a downpour. In contrast, with rotting skin, moldering clothes, and awkward gait, zombies lack game.

At the same time, zombies do possess an erotic, although one that burns with racism and sexual violence. Zombies can stand in for the white-woman-hunting "other," stoking a colonial fear of the populations that the imperials have just subjugated (Aizenberg 1999, p.462). For instance, Lizabeth Paravisini-Gebert notes that *White Zombie* (1932), with Bela Lugosi, a tangle involving a love triangle, a plot to bring a white woman back to America as a zombie, and the steamy jungle, came out contemporaneously to the US invasion of Haiti (1915–34) (Paravisini-Gebert 1997). Similarly, in D.W. Griffith's *Birth of a Nation* (1915)—a lamentation for the South (the film ends with the KKK making a self-immolating cavalry charge)—"Gus," a white actor

(Walter Long) in blackface, stalks a white woman (Lillian Gish) to her death. In his music video for "Thriller" (1983), Michael Jackson and his crew of cadaverous dancers heave to the beat. Conflating zombies and werewolves, Jackson's eyes flash yellow as he embraces his girlfriend in the final scene, to a cackle of laughter. Whether in code or in resplendent rot, zombies locomote through American media, stomping across sex and race in alternating steps, signaling a simultaneous loathing and longing characteristic of constructions of the "other."

Associating with decay and dirt, zombies are an earthy inversion of living flesh, which is fine in fiction. Eroticism turns to horror when zombie sexuality emerges from the liminal. The confluence of consumption, sex, and zombies broke into the real in the case of serial killer Jeffrey Dahmer. Dahmer lured seventeen men and boys to his Chicago apartment between 1978 and 1991, where he had sex with them (both while they were alive and after they were dead). He dismembered, stored, and ate body parts, and attempted to create zombies of some of his victims by means of a drill. Perhaps most disturbing, court psychiatrists declared Dahmer legally sane at his trial. In prison, Dahmer's fellow inmates beat him to death on November 28, 1994. On celluloid, zombies can become camp. In the real world, they cross a line, even for other criminals.

In terms of Effort/Shape, the way zombies move makes them distinctive, more so than their moldering appearance. In order of importance: Zombies have bound flow. An actor portraying a zombie should imagine working against internal bands that make moving difficult. Zombie joints do not work smoothly, so every step seems like an exertion against rotted internal mechanisms. A performer playing a zombie should be sweating by the end of a scene, or could tie elastic exercise bands around her or his limbs to get a sense of this quality. Next, zombies are strong. Unlike ghosts, which glide above the grass, we can see zombies push against gravity, dragging themselves along. They have a sense of their own weight, as well as the power to overcome inertia. In terms of time, Zombies have sudden movement, lurching along in moments of micro-acceleration, pistons firing in disjointed bursts. Finally, they have indirect focus. Instead of laser-like directionality, they tend to wander about, projecting an indistinct field of awareness. They can snap into direct focus, though, when the sound of prey triggers them into pursuit mode.

Focus seems key to zombie intent. A diagonal divides the Effort/Shape graph into two sets of traits, with each quality having affinities for the other efforts in its side of the line. The bottom-left efforts relate to one another as "condensing" qualities: bound, direct, strong, sudden. The top right includes "expanding" traits: free, indirect, light, sustained. The condensing efforts can punch through walls, whereas the expanding ones are more like jellyfish floating in the surf. Zombies keep three of their four efforts on the condensing half, and focus acts as a toggle based on the presence of objects of prey. The living need to avoid drawing a zombie's attention, which slides their movement profile into attack mode. Zombies are dangerous at all times, but calling their attention turns them into unrelenting weapons.

As stars of horror stories, zombies have never gone out of fashion since they staggered from Haiti to Hollywood in *White Zombie*, and they have proven successful of late with the Fox television series *The Walking Dead*.[4] Since its inaugural episode on Halloween 2010, the show has boasted the highest viewership in cable television history. The first season averaged 5.4 million viewers, and the show's audience grew to a peak in its fifth season at 14.4 million. *The Walking Dead* has won only two Emmy Awards (nominated for sixteen overall), for best makeup, but dominated all television, cable or broadcast, in the 18–49-year-old demographic for its first three seasons.[5] Although appealing to viewers of all political persuasions, *The Walking Dead* enjoys its greatest popularity in rural areas, especially in South Texas, Kentucky, and across Appalachia, regions that coincide with conservative voting patterns.[6]

The parallels between zombies and xenophobic/racist constructs are not mysterious. Penny Crofts and Anthea Vogel read the zombie movie *World War Z* as a representation of anxieties about postcolonial borders and the failure of containment (2019). For that matter, in an interview with *Forbes* magazine, Jared Kushner, Donald Trump's son-in-law and senior advisor, confided that the Trump campaign used television ratings data as a guide for regional advertising during the 2016 presidential elections: "say, *NCIS* [CBS's 'Naval Criminal Investigative Service'] for anti-Obamacare voters or *The Walking Dead* for people worried about immigration" (Bertoni 2016). A close reading of *The Walking Dead* reveals conservative antipathy towards/longing for immigration, by making zombies avatars for Mexican immigrants.

In Episode 1, we meet the series protagonist, Rick Grimes (Andrew Lincoln), a blue-eyed deputy sheriff in King County, Georgia, a fictitious rural district outside of Atlanta. His friend is fellow officer Shane Walsh (Jon Bernthal), a burly sidekick with black curly hair. In the opening scene, Grimes experiences a hallucination/dream/flashback in which, gas tank in hand and dressed in his brown and beige uniform, he passes overturned cars. Arriving at a gas station, and indulging in lingering camera shots with rasping breath, he sees a young girl finally turn around, who turns out to be a zombie. Rick shoots her in the head. Later, in waking life, Rick and Shane set up a roadblock. Possibly brown-skinned men in flannels speed over the police spikes, which rolls their car. A shootout leaves two of the riders dead. Rick turns to Shane, not seeing a third man crawl out of the car, who shoots Rick in the back.

After a montage of dream images, Rick awakens in a hospital but finds no one there. Debris fills the hallways, blood smears the walls, and rotting hands try to get through a chained door. Rick finds his way out through a back door, where hundreds of body bags lie on a lot near military vehicles. Black helicopters with mysterious markings stand idle. Rick staggers in his hospital garb back to his suburban neighborhood, and shoots a zombie on the street. The sound draws the attention of an African American man and his son, Morgan and Duane, who at first capture Rick but then offer him hospitality. They explain to Rick that "Walkers" have taken over, and are contagious, "One thing I do know, don't you get bit" (Season 1, Episode 1). Morgan remains because his wife has succumbed. After receiving a bite, she died of a fever and then became a Walker—a creature that moans, has no memories of its previous life, drags its feet as it walks, and craves flesh. Rick gives a rifle to Morgan so as to put his wife to rest (which he can't bring himself to do), stops by the station to bathe, dress in a clean uniform, and rearm, and heads to Atlanta. He finds the city overrun with Walkers, and ends up inside a military tank that he finds parked on the street. Glenn (Steven Yeun), an instantly likable Asian American man in a baseball cap, rescues Rick and leads him out of town. They go to Glenn's camp in the countryside, where Rick reunites with his wife Lori (Sarah Wayne Callies), son Shane, and several minor characters.

Despite frequent—and bloody—turnover, characters drive the drama. *The Walking Dead* serves as a "buddy narrative" between Rick and Shane. The initial episodes also try for a love triangle, as Shane has taken up a relationship with Lori, having lied to her about Shane's fate. Subsequent seasons feature Rick and Shane's relationship with Daryl, a wiry, greasy-haired survivalist with an uncannily powerful gravitas (think "noble savage" if Rousseau had hailed from Georgia rather than Geneva: we first meet Daryl in Episode 3, when he emerges from the forest toting a crossbow and a bag of squirrels). Periodically, Rick and/or Shane feel compelled to point weapons at Daryl, but the three also recognize their interdependence with meaningful nods and grunts. Although episodes include swarms of zombies, zombie parts, and humans who succumb to zombie illness, the show is the story of the not yet undead. The ever-present danger of the unwanted immigrant foregrounds the struggle the ever-changing group undertakes to preserve its humanity. An imagined America endures, barely.

To find the link between zombies and immigrants, we need look no further than the show's name for zombies: "Walkers." The zombies do, in fact, walk (when not dragging themselves along the ground, as when cut in half: only direct trauma to the brain seems to finish them). They also bite, hence an occasional reference to "biters." However, the characters most often use the term "Walkers," which evokes tropes of undocumented immigrants from south of the border. *The Walking Dead* target audiences would have little difficulty making the connection. Fox News viewers have heightened concerns regarding immigration and the threat of illegal (walking) border crossings (de Zúñiga et al. 2012). Fox viewers are also predisposed to see immigrants as pollutants (Cisneros 2008). Consequently, a drama series about contagious interlopers who have overrun city centers and pose an existential threat to the existing community would seem familiar.

Walking connects zombies with immigrants, but characters in Season 1 also use the term "geek" for zombies, as in, "There's one *geek* still up on the tank"

(Season 1, Episode 2) or "Shut up! You're gonna bring the *geeks* down on us" (Season 1, Episode 4) (italics added for emphasis). This usage seems confusing. Originally, "geeks" performed acts like biting heads off of chickens—an apt, although obscure, reference.[7] Perhaps the writers intended to imbue the zombies with additional immigrant identities. "Geek," like "nerd," might evoke white stereotypes of Asian Americans as academically overzealous, and "geek" sounds like "gook," a Vietnam War-era racial slur.[8] Christine Quail argues that geekiness conflates race, gender, and sexuality into a "hip/square dialectic," which, she shows, can map onto Asians on TV (2011). More generally, "geek chic" or, using Quail's language, "nerd commodity" would certainly propel the loathing/longing viewers have for the show's monsters. Perhaps the term proved too much of a stretch, as the writers dropped it after the first season.

Whether Walkers incorporate Asian identities or only Mexican, the threat of the interloper solves Southern hatreds. In Episode 2, Rick decides to go back to Atlanta to retrieve his bag of guns. On a rooftop, the group confronts a man shooting zombies, Merle (who, we learn in Episode 3, is Daryl's brother). Merle rails at their admonitions to make less noise, and inveigles them with racist commentary. When Merle beats T-Dog (IronE Singleton), a black member of the party, Rick puts his gun up to Merle's head, disarms him, and handcuffs him to a pipe. Rick then leans in, speaking as one white Southerner to another, "Look here, Merle. Things are different now. There are no niggers anymore. No dumb-as-shit, inbred white-trash fools either. Only dark meat and white meat. There's us and the dead. We survive this by pulling together—not apart" (Season 1, Episode 2). Old divisions wither in the face of a common enemy. Traditional hatreds have become dangerous, and better to lock a holdover to the roof than lose the entire community to the new threat.

Similarly, misogyny no longer passes muster. "Ed" represents an old stereotype, a plain-speaking bore who lords over women while they work. In Episode 3, a group of women in the survivor's camp wash clothes while Ed sits and smokes. When he bullies his wife, Carol (Melissa McBride), the sultry but tough Andrea (Laurie Holden) tells Ed to do his own laundry. When he demurs, saying that such work is not his job, she asks what his job is: "sitting on your ass smoking cigarettes?" He responds, "Well, it sure as hell ain't listening to some uppity smart-mouthed bitch." When Andrea persists, Ed says, "Hey, don't think I won't knock you on your ass just 'cause you're some college-educated cooze [a derogatory term for a woman's genitals], all right? Now you [Carol] come on now or you gonna regret it later." Ed strikes Carol, which causes Shane to jump Ed, leaving his face a pulpy mass. Shane warns Ed, "You put your hands on your wife, your little girl or anybody else in this camp one more time, I will not stop next time" (Season 1, Episode 3). The ever-near presence of the Walkers outside of Atlanta renders *verböten* hobgoblins like racism, misogyny, anti-intellectualism, and sloth.

The first season makes the link between zombies and Mexican immigrants explicit in Episode 4: "*Vatos*" (Spanish for "dudes," near in sound to *gatos* or "cats"). At the end of Episode 3, Rick has led Glenn, Daryl, and T-Dog back to Atlanta to try to rescue Merle from his rooftop, only to find that Merle has cut off his hand and escaped. In Episode 4, the group instead retrieves Rick's weapons bag from the street, when a group of brown-skinned gangsters kidnaps Glenn. At the end of the gang's getaway, Rick and his companions find themselves in possession of Miguel, a teenager. Replete with face and neck tattoos, the *vatos* are meaner than mean. Their leader, Guillermo, a man with a trim goatee and disarming scowl, expresses no interest in bartering for Miguel when Rick and co. come calling at his hideout. Rather, Guillermo will trade Glenn for the guns. The survivor group retreats and then returns, ready for a shootout. At that point, the *vatos* reveal their true character—sort of.

Just as bloodshed seems certain, Guillermo's *abuelita* hobbles between the two sets of firearms and, to Guillermo's consternation, takes Rick by the arm and leads him to the back, as if to feed a misbehaving grandson's friend. As Guillermo's grandmother gives Rick a tour, Rick sees that the *vatos* have taken over an urban clinic and are caring for those who were unable to leave the city. Felipe, a bald gangbanger with bulging biceps, helps an old African American man with an inhaler ("Gilbert is having trouble breathing. He needs his asthma stuff."). The rooms bustle with calm activity, the flowered sheets spotless in full sunlight streaming in through clean windows. The *vatos* want the guns to protect the sick and elderly, whom they cannot transport out of the city in their hot-wired cars. Before the catastrophe, Guillermo worked as the facility's janitor. Rick chastises Guillermo for not being straight with him from the start ("You're the dumbest son of a bitch I ever met"), and, Solomon-like, gives the *vatos* half of the guns. The *vatos* are noble. However. Guillermo confides that others prowl the city with less decorum, "We need the muscle [i.e., the guns]. The people we've encountered since things fell apart, the worst kind of plunderers, the kind that take by force." The guns are not for zombies but for other (presumably brown-skinned) survivors, *walkers* rather than *Walkers*. Thus, conservative media tropes surface: minority-on-minority violence, immigrants overrunning the medical system, "others" dominating city centers, while whites and those who have assimilated into white culture escape to the suburbs. Episode 4, "*Vatos*," is less Hallmark than horror, with zombies playing a supporting role. The exception proves the rule. Brown skin = Mexican = gangs = destruction of white communitas.

The Walking Dead plays on fantasies of white victimhood, especially in rural areas, which tend to have small or nonexistent immigrant populations. The show also nods to a growing distrust of the government—what in the Trump, pro-conspiracy *Umwelt* has become the chimerical "deep state." In addition to the black helicopters in Episode 1, Rick hears helicopter sounds in Episodes 2 and 3. After a band of Walkers kills at least half a dozen characters in Episode 4, Rick leads the remainder to a CDC installation, 100 miles away.

Inside the X-Files-like compound, a lone researcher, Edwin (Noah Meerich), toils away with tissues from his zombified wife. After letting the survivors in, he does not want to release them before the building explodes when it runs out of power. He whispers something to Rick, contributing to the feeling of a government conspiracy. Our final image of Season 1 is that of a white community barely surviving an infectious immigrant onslaught, an invasion immune to the impotence of government response, which might even be part of a conspiracy against white hegemonic values.

The Walking Dead establishes its premise on the perversion of a basic movement pattern: walking. Bipedalism characterizes humans, and it serves as an unusual choice for locomotion, biologically speaking. Humans share their upright manner of traveling with few species, and so we find ourselves in the company of penguins, kangaroo rats, and velociraptors. Walking is controlled falling. As we lope along, our limbs swing in the sagittal plane at the hip, knee, and ankle joints, while the arms sway in opposition to the motion of the legs. The feet are arches, each absorbing up to three-and-a-half times our body weight in force while running. The act of coming down from the trees and ambling about the savannah, sharing space with predators larger, faster, stronger, and better armed than we, must have accrued benefits. For example, one theory holds that early humans engaged in so-called endurance hunting. Although most herd species can outrun humans in a sprint, they have less endurance over distances. After a certain number of dashes, the persistent human may walk up to an exhausted deer and slit its throat. More likely, walking enabled humans to get at more resources closer to the ground: roots, nuts, herbs, nests, insects, materials for tools, and small game. Zombies as "Walkers" therefore perverts a core means of human motion.

Perhaps immigrants-as-zombies resonates as a racist trope because untrammeled bipedalism harks back to a previous age. American history follows, in large degree, the story of European immigrants who "settled" a new world, using genocidal displacement and the importation of slaves (immobilizing them first on boats, then on plantations, and finally within segregated spheres in housing, schools, and public places). In addition to massacring native peoples, "settlers" cleared primeval forests, fenced in prairies, and have been paving the land with asphalt, concrete, and geometry up to the present. America has shifted its posture from walking to sitting, to the point where a sedentary lifestyle has become a public health issue, and a major risk factor.[9] Increasing numbers of Americans sit at home, sit in vehicles, and then sit at their points of destination (work, restaurants, entertainment, even including those who are not differently abled but are sedentary to the point of requiring motorized chairs in order to go shopping). According to the Centers for Disease Control (which also served as a plot device in the series), one in four Americans spend more than eight hours a day sitting (Ussery et al. 2018). Trump and Fox News used repeated images of a so-called "migrant caravan" of Central and South American refugees heading north towards the US–Mexican border as a scare tactic to motivate conservative voters during the 2018 mid-term elections. Perhaps the libel frightened viewers because of depictions of *walking* as much as the perception among certain political demographics of the presence of brown skin as a threat, or maybe due to the combination of ambulation and race.

The difference between shape and Effort/Shape plays a critical role. In terms of positive space (the creatures' outlines), zombies resemble humans. In fact, they *are* people, or were people. In *The Walking Dead*, corpses reanimate via a "resurrection event" after a brief period of deathly immobility. Once reawakened, the zombies do not cease moving until someone does something to destroy the monsters' brains (in a reversal of the trope that zombies savor the contents of the crania of the living). In certain situations, zombies become recognizable *only* through their Effort quality, which sets up moments of drama, and also "jump scares." For example, we last see Morgan in the first episode as he looks through the lens of a sniper rifle, unable to silence the un-life of his zombified wife, who shuffles about their suburban street with the other zombies, blank-eyed and emitting an occasional snarl (in a later episode, a survivor cradles her zombifying sister's head from the moment of death until reanimation, at which point she ends the vigil with a point-blank handgun shot). Similarly, the Southern misogynist Ed sees outlines against his tent he takes to be other survivors but that turn out be his undead comeuppance.

The subtext seems clear: we (white, though also, of late, African American citizens, who preceded the current round of immigrants to this country) must harden our hearts. Undocumented zombies look human, and maybe were people before they started their inexorable march towards our borders. Despite their similarity in shape to us, they are not, or are no longer, human, as their movement quality and the fact of their constant walking reveals. Despite its artistic merits—or perhaps *because* its creative teams so expertly wrought the show—*The Walking Dead* can double as a "fifteen minutes into the future" right-wing parable of what will happen once our unwalled borders fail. At that point, the swarm will spread until resources vanish, and bullets or sickening strikes to the heads of the interlopers will be the only, likely futile, choice left to an increasingly isolated hegemony. Thus, immigrants coming through Mexico, refugees fleeing crushing poverty at best, or people seeking better lives for themselves and their families or escaping political oppression and fear of life and limb, become murderous hordes.

Creatures of the deep

The sea gives and takes life, so we should not be surprised that monsters reside in the oceans as well as on land. I would argue that sea creatures become monsters in part through three of the shape operations that opened this chapter. Firstly, sea creatures become monsters through magnification. The Greek god of the sea, Poseidon, sent the leviathan Cetus to eat Andromeda. In Jules Verne's *20,000 Leagues Under the Sea*, the submarine Nautilus confronts a giant squid. The Old Testament refers to whale-like creatures. Secondly, denizens of the deep may reach monstrous proportions through multiplication, as in a school of flesh-eating piranhas. The sea witch in Disney's film *The Little Mermaid* had an array of octopus-like tentacles. Scylla possessed six heads and twelve arms. Thirdly, sea creatures become monsters through metonymy. The classic sea horror film *Jaws* (1975) created suspense through showing only the dorsal fin of a ravenous shark. The not-seen carries more terror than the visible. Analogous to things going "bump in the night," ripples in the water, appendages poking through the surface, shadows swirling beneath, create more suspense than a reveal of B-movie animatronics. Sea monsters' Effort factors would seem to tend towards strong, direct, sudden, and free. Like zombies, aquatic horrors skew towards condensing efforts (perhaps this is a characteristic of predators generally). Instead of zombie's bound focus, though, sea beasts indulge in freeness. They exhibit a lack of internal resistance, and their litheness, their sinewy movement efficiency, their effortless grace, resemble that of large cats, which makes sea monsters deadly.

Regionally, the Mediterranean Sea and its related waters have housed gods and monsters since antiquity. Poseidon ruled the Greek seas and also served as lord of horses, a source of power in tribal militarism. The *Iliad* posits Oceanus (half bull and half serpent) and his sister Tethys (offspring of the sky and land) as Titan parents of the gods, as did the coupling in Assyrian mythology of Tiamat (saltwater) and Apsu (freshwater). In the *Odyssey*, the eponymous hero plugs the ears of his shipmates with wax while he, tied to the mast, endures the call of the Sirens (XII.165–200). The Hebraic deity started with the sea: "Now the earth was formless and empty, darkness covered the surface of the watery depths, and the Spirit of God was hovering over the surface of the waters" (Genesis 1:2). The God of the Covenant drowned Pharaoh's armies when he released the rage of the Red Sea.

The Mediterranean Sea figures prominently in contemporary refugee flight, since this body of water does what it has always done, which is to say it serves as passage among Africa, the Near East, Southwest Asia, and Europe. Despite its balmy climate, the Middle Sea's depths presage death. Of the three million shipwrecks that litter ocean bottoms, the Mediterranean claims more than its fair share.[10] Today, refugees magnify their exposure to vulnerability when they attempt overwater transit. Between 2015 and 2016, over a million refugees reached Greece. In November 2017, the German daily *Der Tagesspiegel* published the names of the 33,293 people who had drowned trying to reach Europe across the Mediterranean up until that point. The list ran for forty-six pages (Casdorff and Maroldt 2017). Speaking in June 2018, a representative of the UNHCR reported that as many as one in seven drown trying to cross the central Mediterranean (Yaxley 2018). Packed into makeshift boats, attempting runs in secret, trusting to smugglers who often turn out to be predators, avoiding coast guards and hostile patrols, the refugees attempt a journey that all too often leaves a trail of bodies in the water.

In addition to its intrinsic dangers, the sea lends itself to bending body shapes into monstrosity, since water transit puts refugees into the liminal, Alice-in-Wonderland space of maritime law. Legal scholar Richard Barnes characterizes international law relating to search and rescue by way of the understatement "highly unsatisfactory" (2004, p.47). Based on his analysis of the Convention on the Law of the Sea, the International Convention for the Safety of Life at Sea (SOLAS), and the International Convention on Search and Rescue at Sea (SAR Convention), Barnes concludes that although sea rescue stands as "one of the most ancient and fundamental features of the law of the sea," the current apparatus lacks the resiliency for today's refugee crisis. According to Barnes, legal structures fail for multiple reasons. Among other problems, Barnes observes that they mandate rescue but remain unclear as what to do with rescued persons once out of the water; they create conflicts of interest by devolving rescue to private mariners; they do not translate into domestic legal codes; they lack enforcement mechanisms; they fail to address the fact that many boats fly non-signatory flags; they do not specify what constitutes "search and rescue" on the operational level; they run into problems of port passage; and they do not contain provisions for stowaways and migrants.[11] The ocean is up for grabs, an aquatic "Wild West," a place where sea dragons and other leviathans lurk with impunity.

In terms of shaping, reactionary rhetoric assigns shape flow to water-borne migrants as well, with an emphasis on "flow." Embodying the sea, refugees—making illicit passage across the Mediterranean—are a "flood" that threatens "our" shores. In this metaphorical space humanitarians thus seem naïve, holding back the tide of migrants by holding their fingers in the dike. In an analysis of British media coverage of Mediterranean refugee stories, Carole Murphy identified perforation as a theme, with subthemes like "Rivers of Blood" and "Holes," metaphors that allow the conflation of immigration, smuggling, and drug/human trafficking (2018). Refugees pose a threat as a personification of the sea itself. Nativists ascribe more credence to a rising tide of refugees—an embodiment of the aquatic run amok—than they often do to the prospect of actual rising sea levels from climate change.

In addition to the xenophobia of "flood" narratives, the repetition of certain shapes, even in well-meaning media coverage, reinforces monster tropes. In 2017, Public Radio International correspondent Richard Hall rode aboard the rescue vessel *Save the Children* in the Mediterranean Sea near Libya. His report makes the mission seem like naval warfare: "There are no sirens when the call comes in. No alarms or shouting. Just a calm voice over the radio in the darkness of the cabin: 'All stations, all stations'" (Hall 2017). Over the next twelve hours, the three-ship fleet pull 1000 refugees out of the water. The ships contains specialist crew, including "child psychologists, translators and rescuers." A pressure permeates the ship, and "something like relief" ensues once the mission commences.

Their first find occurs with the Libyan coast in view, a "white inflatable boat with a few dozen people on board." Hall mentions that smugglers have started favoring these disposable vessels since they know coast guards scuttle boats once they have cleared their human cargos. The rescue boat lowers a lifeboat with a winch; crews board the inflatable and begin to bring the refugees on board. The transfer carries tension: "The moment the two boats meet is jarring for rescuers and rescued alike," the performance of rehearsed maneuvers for the crews, the end of a journey for the refugees. The crew members are kind, but as in a military rescue mission, anyone apprehended might yet constitute a threat. The rescue boat takes eighty-four people aboard. The initial call sounded at 6am. The process repeats at 9am and continues until the mission terminates, due to threats from the Libyan coast guard, as well as pressure from an Italian prosecutor who believes that the rescue boats collaborate with smugglers.[12]

Reports like Hall's are devastating to hear and show how refugee water paths are nothing short of humanitarian catastrophes. At the same time, reports reinforce monstrous images. One class of *mise-en-scène* arrays refugees in lifejackets, seated in boats. To resort to a cliché, they are "packed like sardines." Dozens of bodies, packed onto a rubber membrane atop the sea-foam can look like a single organism. The entangled limbs, fields of heads, and repeated torsos forming schools of humans slick with brine can also seem like a captured, many-headed hydra. Finally, bobbing in the water or sitting on decks, parts or halves of bodies remain out of view. The quasi-militaristic tone of sea rescue, including the threat of armed encounters, can evoke the machismo of hyper-masculine sea captains, merchant marines, or trawlers.[13] The winches, nets, and cages the boats use to lift lifeboats are like fishers' tools, or crab cages. The boats have netted Nemo's giant squid. The whaling fleet has returned with record cargos. Performance derives from iteration, so as these tropes deepen their imprints, refugees become personifications of the watery monsters from which they flee.

As with overland zombies, images of overwater refugees engender a conflation between victims, perpetrators, and aid agencies. Italian far-right leader Matteo Salvini has characterized NGO rescue boats like the one from which Hall reported as "voracious," and chastised them for "disturbing" and "causing trouble" for the Libyan coast guard. Thus, humanitarians become coconspirators. Refugees transform into monsters. For that matter, rescue boats become sea predators too, insatiable in appetite. NGO boats are leviathans hungry to gobble up smaller creatures, which, within the miasmic world of monstrosity, just makes more monsters. In Salvini's view, rescue boats should leave refugees in the water. Other EU leaders responded in shock to the prospect of leaving people to die, but if you cast refuges as murderous sea creatures, then you are leaving them in their natural habitat. The EU issued statements reaffirming refugees' humanity, but also bowed to Salvini's calls for increased scrutiny of human smuggling operations.

Images of bodies floating in water, and the specter of drowning, underscore the watery force that beckons the unwary. Through repetition of shape, heads, hands, and shoulders that breach the surface, as their owners grip debris or float in oddly artificial-looking water vests, blurring begins to occur. In the eyes of faraway onlookers, riven with fear, refugees start to occupy an uneasy place between Siren and victims. Refugees become personifications of the sea's danger, the allure of sinking. The difference between Siren and stricken mariner becomes unclear. That is, refugees in life jackets awaiting rescue seem monstrous to those predisposed to fear of outsiders. Then, at the moment of actual death, refugees become human again, causing a psychic whiplash that might constitute the most horrific form of monstrosity of all.

A drowned child

The final section of this chapter deals with the death of a child, a three-year-old Kurdish Syrian named Alan Kurdi (initial reports listed him as "Aylan"), which might be upsetting to contemplate—the idea of a drowned toddler *should* be upsetting. As an observer, a parent, and a human, I can only look at pictures of Alan for a few moments at a time. I am including this case study because I feel that we *must* look at the consequences of globalization in instability, as a moral responsibility, and also since we cannot escape participation in the systems that produce suffering. Having said this, the following pages do not contain images of the dead Alan, since the choice to witness horror should reside with the individual. I would encourage the reader to find these images, which are easy to locate online, not as a perverse act of voyeurism but to bear witness. Given the emotional intensity of this example, I would also ask the reader's forbearance regarding the intrusion of details from my own experiences as they relate to the shape of death.

Drowning is a curious way to die. Life began in the oceans, and water comprises 50–65% of the human body. At 0.4% salinity, our bodies correspond with the salt content of the sea. At base, we are sacks of saltwater plodding about on dry land, unable to return to the source. For land mammals, humans are surprisingly decent swimmers due to traits that facilitate locomotion in the water (webbed hands and feet, relative hairlessness, subcutaneous fat). In fact, although it does not command scientific consensus, an "aquatic ape hypothesis," which suggests that facility in the water at some point accrued a survival advantage, persists.[14] Yet when crisis happens in the water, humans panic, holding their breath and flailing about, which causes more panic while using up energy. Apnea causes the body to poison itself. Without oxygen exchange, carbon dioxide builds up in the cells as oxygen depletes. At a certain "breath hold breakpoint," the mouth opens. Water then enters the lungs and stomach, causing suffocation. Ironically, the oceans have plenty of oxygen: seawater contains more than air (34% versus 21%), and the majority of the earth's oxygen comes from submerged plants, a resource our lungs can no longer harvest. Once the body detects an influx of liquid, it responds by slamming the larynx shut, making a seal. The ensuing lack of oxygen begins to kill the brain in about six minutes, and may cause cardiac arrest before then. Cold water can kill within two minutes from shock. As a survival mechanism, the body mounts additional defenses to freezing water, such as cutting the heart rate in half, shunting blood from distal to core areas, and directing blood to the thoracic cavity to prevent the lungs from giving out. However, these strategies themselves cause chemical reactions in the body that can prove fatal.[15]

Alan Kurdi drowned early in the morning on September 2, 2015. He and three family members were attempting to sail from Bodrum, Turkey, to the Greek island of Kos, and thence to relatives in Vancouver, British Columbia, having paid $5860 for their spots. Their inflatable boat contained sixteen people, double its capacity, and sank within five minutes of disembarking. The captain abandoned ship after the engine lost control, while the refugees either had no lifejackets or wore ineffectual vests. Alan's brother Galib and his mother Rehana also died. Alan's father Abdullah survived, and controversy has hovered regarding his potential role as pilot organizing the boat.

Turkish journalist Nilüfer Demir's photographs of the drowned boy exploded into global consciousness. Heads of state made statements. Contributions to relief agencies surged, although images of Alan did not penetrate the United States to the same degree as elsewhere. Despite a rabid anti-gun-control lobby, the ubiquity of violence in movies, and graphic video games, America has had little tolerance for depictions of actual death in its news since the Vietnam War. Since the Kurdis were trying to reach Canadian shores, Alan's specter pervaded the 2015 Canadian federal elections (for a discourse analysis summary, see Wallace 2018).

Demir's images of Alan evoke horror because nothing about the boy's shape belies violence. Alan lies prone in the sand, at the water's edge. He wears blue pants that extend to the knees, a red tee-shirt that has just inched up above his waist, and blue tennis shoes with tan soles. His arms rest down by his sides, palms facing up. His hips are off-center to his right, making his knees, which touch, point towards his left, and his backside stick up a bit. His right big toe touches the underside of the bottom of his left foot. His hair is wet and his head rests such that his right cheek lies in the sand. We can see his closed left eye and left ear. Alan looks like a boy asleep after a long day at the beach, a posture any parent would recognize. Without context, a viewer would assume that after Alan's nap, he will want a snack, and then to play for the rest of the afternoon, preceding a long bath and stories before bed. He looks *cute*, which makes the experience of witnessing the photos images all the more awful. In the final images of Demir's montage, an official wearing black boots, dark slacks, a red, white, and blue vest on top of a khaki shirt with patches, green beret, and white gloves carries Alan off of the beach. Images that made their way over electronic media since then have Alan smiling, scrunching his eyes together and lifting his chin up for the camera.

These pictures of the alive Alan linger as hauntings. At the point of death, the body becomes an object. We see this shift in the astonishing speed with which the corporeal vehicle no longer coincides with the person. Alan's material apparatus transmogrifies from "Alan" into "his body," or "the body," or "the corpse." To make an analogy that hopefully does not come across as crass, the performance of the body at death is like the opposite of how Bert O. States describes objects on stage. For States, audiences perceive props through "binocular vision" of sensoria and semantics. An aluminum chair may stand in for a throne while on stage, but it does not cease to exist as a chair (States 1983). After Alan passed through the curtain of death, his body stopped counting as a person, monster, or refugee. It became a husk. The magical carriage has reverted to a pumpkin, the aluminum chair is once again just a chair, the body dust lying atop the dust from which it came. The show is over. The phenomenological thus rips away from the semiotic with the force of fission. We recoil out of a sense of violation—the death of a child is horrifying. Yet additional dynamics are at play. A body lies on the beach to haunt our fears, while Alan-ness endures as disembodied posts on social media of his smiling face.

Resonances of Alan's death emerge through an act of shape-matching by Chinese dissident artist Ai Weiwei (艾未未). Himself a refugee, Ai displays virtuosity in enacting performances that use images of his body's shape (atemporal) to tell stories (temporal).[16] In the photographic tryptic *Dropping a Han Dynasty Urn* (1995), Ai destroys a priceless 2000-year old vase. In the first frame, Ai holds the vessel between his fingertips; in the second, his hands have moved apart; in the third, his hands have moved back towards his centerline slightly, while the vase lies in pieces on the ground. In all three stages, his body maintains an identical shape against the same background: standing with legs past hip-width apart, head barely tilted, eyes forward, a tuft of hair rising on the right. His fingers splay and wrists bend. The only shift appears to be from the elbows down, like a gesture from Tai Chi or Chi Kung, "Ai destroys the vase." Ai provides the viewer with still shapes, and the viewer's mind fills in the intervening motion.

Similarly, Ai published a self-portrait (2009) on Twitter following surgery for brain hemorrhage, after Chinese government police beat him. In his Munich hospital room, Ai stands in a white hospital gown, the left sleeve draping open like that of a traditional robe. He sports matching white bandages on his right wrist and left temple. He looks up while pointing a camera straight ahead in his left hand, presumably at the mirror (visually, *we* stand in for the mirror, at which he is *not* looking). His right hand holds a transparent surgical bag containing red fluid that Ai's doctors removed from his skull. Tubes trail both from the bag and from underneath the bandage on his temple, while the black camera strap hangs down from between Ai's fourth and fifth fingers. In a small amount of space, and without recourse to movement in space, time, and energy, Ai calls into question Maoist repression, China's relationship to its past, and the consumption of art. In the second image, Ai manages to impugn the Chinese leadership, highlight the cost of free speech, and question the motives of those who spectate at his suffering yet remain silent, by means of a snapshot with an ordinary consumer camera.

On January 31, 2016, Ai gave an interview to journalist Rohit Chawla for a feature in *India Today*, one of India's largest news publications (Chawla 2016).[17] Chawla met Ai on the Greek island of Lesbos, where Ai was engaged in his refugee film project *Human Flow* (2017), which would later enjoy widespread acclaim. On Chawla's suggestion, Ai lay down on the beach, copying Alan's posture. Ai's performance generated controversy across mainstream media and social media, although scholarly responses have been more sympathetic. Mette Mortensen concedes that Ai's piece decontextualizes and dehistoricizes Alan's fate, but notes that appropriation takes place during any process of formulating icons (2018). Heide Fehrenbach and David Rodogno note that, whatever the moral problematics, representations of suffering or dead children have played a role in humanitarian fundraising for over a century (2015). Carly McLaughlin writes that Ai's image helped propel a child-centered humanitarian response to refugees in England that likened the need for intervention to the *Kindertransport* evacuation of Jewish children from Nazi-controlled territories, but also notes the fallacy of such a basis, since trauma robs children of their childhood (2018).

I am interested in adding the somatics of Ai's performance to these debates. Ai's strategy of shape-matching would at first seem to constitute a demonstration of Julia Kristeva's notion of *abjection*, in which horror derives from the breakdown of the boundaries between self and other. In the classic example, when we see a corpse, we supposedly project our own face

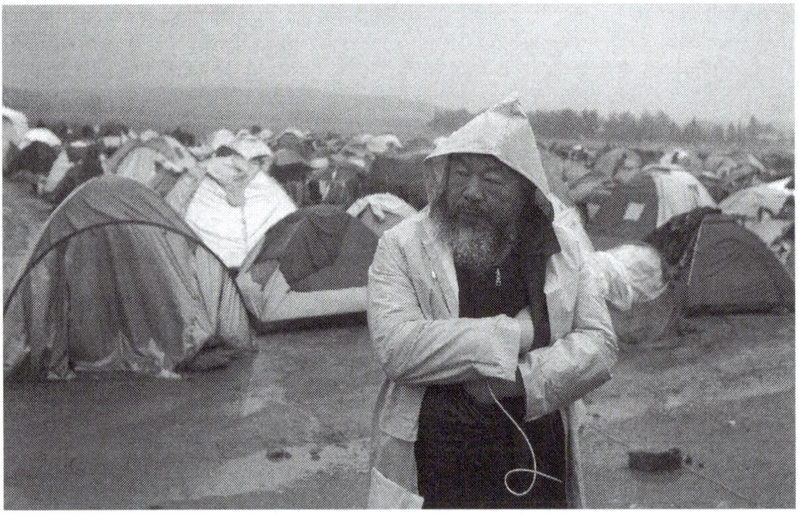

Figure 2.2 Chinese dissident artist Ai Weiwei looks on as he visits a migrant's makeshift camp on the Greek–Macedonian border, near the village of Idomeni. Photo © Stoyan Nenov/Reuters Pictures.

onto the body, and in so doing realize the fact of our mortality (Kristeva 1982). Is this dynamic present here? Does Ai stand in for the child, and do we stand in for Ai? Ai poses with his face towards us, in part to allow us to recognize the artist but also to allow us entrance into the scene. Yet, in most of the images that raked across the world's media, Alan lies with his face *away* from the camera's gaze. This detail is not insignificant. Alan is faceless and therefore anyone. The world has defaced him. His anonymity ensures his universality. He is the lost child, the one who strayed too far into the world of monsters, dreams, and fantasies. He is the child a car hits because no one was looking, the infant who dies unattended in the pool. He is our collective failure, a parent's worst nightmare. We need to see Ai's face in order to enter the portal into the unthinkable.

At the same time, I wonder about the role that shape plays in the experience of horror, and if shape does not offer a better, or at least an additional, way to understand the gut response to death. At the end of my partner's ten-year sickness, when the moment of death finally came, sitting in the presence of her body was overwhelming but not frightening. The body in front of me, that I had attended full time for the previous eighteen months, had fallen asleep for the last time. Beyond the chasm of emotions in that moment, there was a kind of naturalness. However, when a nurse came in and, with movements made efficient through practice, arranged arms and legs, adjusted the head on the pillow, and straightened the sheets, the tableau became disturbing. When a body lies where it falls, we exist in the world of sensation. As the "corpse" becomes a semiotic sign through ritualized posture, distance sets in.

More so than a Kristevan identification with Alan, Ai's performance suggests an attempt at kinesthetic empathy, or relating to another being on a body level. In my acting class, I have my students learn to "step" outside themselves through an empathic shaping sequence based on the old saying, "walking in another's shoes." After dividing into pairs, class members assume roles of A and B. Person A stands normally, while person B tries to match A's posture. I talk them through the process of copying details such as the alignment of the feet, posture, position of the arms, tilt of the head, and rate of breathing. Then, I have person A walk around the room with person B following (they are barefoot, but the action has the same impact as walking in the other person's footwear). Again, I lead the class through a sequence of B matching A's pace, down to specifics such as the sound of footfalls, visual focus, swing of the arms, and break at the wrist. Classes invariably report on the difficulty of walking as another person, of trying to fit into another person's pattern, pace, and breath. However, when we do a "fashion show," with one pair at a time stepping across the room, classes are also struck at the uncanny unison of pairs in motion, regardless of physical differences. As a concluding exercise, I ask each student to embody a real person not present in the room, using a similar progression. At the end of the sequence, I have everyone open their eyes and introduce themselves as their study: "Hi, my name is [the name of the person they were embodying]." Students' voices transform in the new body pattern, and rich conversations follow regarding the emotional states that arise from inhabiting another's posture and locomotion.

Ai's mimicry of Alan would seem to fall under the same sort of experience as my acting exercise. The difference between Kristevan abjection and kinesthetic empathy seems analogous to the relationship between metaphor and simile. For abjection, the observer becomes the object. For kinesthetic empathy, the observer finds elements in common.[18] Shape matching can yield an affective response analogous to "sympathetic resonance," where a vibrating string will cause nearby strings to oscillate on the same frequency. Funny movies are funnier when you watch them with others. Yawns are contagious. Someone standing and holding a baby while swaying back and forth will have an entraining effect on others standing close by. Seeing someone else get kicked in the groin elicits a recoil. Sitting next to a dancer at a dance concert becomes a workout, as you feel your seated companion's muscles twitch in sympathy with the movements onstage. Ai's piece seeks not to evoke horror through the dissolution of self and other but to gain empathy. Assuming another's shape reveals commonalities while preserving differences.

This interpretation of Ai's performance as a shape-driven exercise in kinesthetic empathy rather than abjection falls into line with the artist's self-reflections. At first, Ai tried to identify with Alan mentally: "We [Ai and Chawla] had talked about the image of the boy [Alan], so I had that on my mind," says Ai. However, Ai likened the physicality of lying on the beech to a previous experience, when he visited the site of an 8.0-magnitude earthquake that killed 70,000 people in 2008. Ai recalls,

> When I stood on the earthquake ravel. Under my feet, there were hundreds, thousands of young students [buried beneath] those … buildings. I was standing there and I could feel my body shaking with the wind—you feel death in the wind. You are taken by some kind of emotions that you can only have when you are there. So for me to be in the same position [as Alan], is to suggest our condition can be so far from human concerns in today's politics.
>
> (Chawla 2016)

Rather than seeing himself among the dead, Ai tried to experience the physicality of place, assuming their shape. He made daily pilgrimages to a beach in Lesbos, putting on his jacket to feel what almost a half-million refugees might feel, cold and wet. By matching Alan's shape on the border of the surf, he tried to deepen his empathy.

For an audience watching Ai hold Alan's shape, kinesthetic empathy still applies. Dee Reynolds and Matthew Reason extend the idea of kinesthetic empathy from person-to-person to person-to-art. Drawing on Henri Bergson's definition of the "durational dimension of human experience" as "the embodied mind's capacity to give meaning to each present instant by making recourse to past embodied memories," and related to John Dewey and Maxine Green's theory of artistic-aesthetic engagement, Reynolds and Reason contend that an appreciation of art depends on an embodied response (Reynolds and Reason 2012, p.12). Ai's photographs are not durational, but again, the artist has a knack for somehow implying the passage of time in his work.

Ai's enactment fits within a wave of sympathetic resonance in response to Alan Kurdi's drowning, but, for lack of a better word, his *succeeds* better than others. Still, these interpretations merit mention, as Demir's images caused shock throughout the world. The images of it replayed over media and social media, Alan's body carried the force of a gut punch, an upset akin to a blow to the viscera that the French word *bouleversé* conveys better than English analogs.[19] Artists and citizens responded with an outpouring of modified Alans—an Alan face down in bed, an Alan face down with angel wings and a rose in hand, and so forth, many of which still rend the heart. Yet acts that began to feel like simulacra proliferated as well. Graffiti artist COR (a.k.a. Justus Becker) stretched Alan to 120 meters on the side of a wall along the bank of the Main river in Frankfurt, across from the European Central Bank headquarters, a spatial relationship that implied criticism of Europeanization, globalization, or both. The Finnish treasury flattened, struck, and copied Alan for a box coin set commemorating its nation's centenary with the theme "social justice," which included an image of Alan and a public library on opposite sides of one of the coins. The German NGO Sea-Eye put Alan back in the water, rechristening one of its refugee rescue boats the *Alan Kurdi*. Unfortunately, these gestures engendered backlash. In June 2016, vandals covered the giant Frankfurt Alan with slogans like "Borders protect lives!" (*Grenzen Retten Leben!*), a reference to right-wing groups like Patriotic Europeans Against the Islamization of the Occident (Pegida), and "Fuck antifa" (in English), an allusion to an anti-fascist movement that plays a larger role as bogeyman for right-wing extremism than it perhaps does as a political force ("Aylan Kurdi Graffiti Vandalized in Frankfurt" 2016). In April 2017, the Finnish government recalled its Alan coins following a public outcry (Finns found the violent images inappropriate for their nation's 100th birthday, and Alan's avatar might have stirred memories of the *sotalapset*, when Finland evacuated 70,000 of its children to Sweden during World War II) ("Drowned Asylum Seeker Child" 2017). In September 2019, Matteo Salvini's crusade against refugees included barring Sea-Eye's *Alan Kurdi*, with thirteen Tunisians it had plucked from the sea, from landing in Italy, an action that seems especially grotesque given the cause of Alan's death ("NGO Rescue Ship Barred From Italy" 2019).

None of these outcomes inspires confidence. Particularly in the case of the bridge vandals and the blockade of a refugee vessel, the perpetrators likely perceived themselves as aggrieved victims, heroic knights slaying evil dragons, making bold stands against monstrous forces assuming (to them) frightening shapes. Such acts betray cowardice. They merit disgust, though they also indicate, like a fever, the point at which empathy moves into appropriation. We would do well to interpret these examples as instances of J.L. Austin's conception of speech acts that "misfire," but they also read as acts of monstrosity (Austin 1975, pp.16–17). Again returning to the shape operations at the top of the chapter, the bridge distorts Alan through magnification, the boat through distortion (and magnification), and the coins through multiplication (and distortion).[20] These responses become mis-shapen, and thus monstrous, with a whiff of camp. Ai's performance perhaps succeeds where these others succumb to hatred, since he sought to match Alan's shape instead of changing it, thereby adhering to *mimesis* more strictly.

Timing also plays a role. In 2015, preceding the Alan Kurdi phenomenon, the global community had tuned out the devastation of five years of civil war in Syria and its attendant hundreds of thousands of deaths. In a study of Alan images a year after *India Today* released them into planet-wide consciousness, social psychologists Paul Slovic, Daniel Västfjäll, Arvid Erlandsson, and Robin Gregory comment that the world had been "basically asleep" to Syria's implosion up until that point. By analyzing quantitative indices such as the changes in the number of Google searches for terms like "Syria," "refugees," and "Aylan" (a hundred-fold increase) and donations to the Swedish Red Cross (an eleven-fold rise), Slovic et al. concluded that global levels of empathy for the civil war had returned to their pre-Alan levels within six weeks (2017).

This chronology makes Chawla's images of Ai all the more remarkable, since they appeared in June 2016, four months after the Frankfurt vandalism and well outside the window in which the Alan photographs jarred the world awake. At that point, Alan iconography may have begun to take on an inadvertent tinge of sarcasm. In a classic argument, Homi Bhabha claimed that colonizing powers enforce their will in part through mimicry. Such "figures of farce" reflect "the desire for a reformed, recognizable Other, as *a subject of a difference that is almost the same, but not quite*" (italics in original). Miming becomes a "sign of the inappropriate," which creates additional layers of meaning, and control (Bhabha 1984, p.126). I think here of the scene in Wole Soyinka's *Death and the King's Horseman*, where a colonial administrator and his wife don sacred indigenous funeral garb for a costume party and do not understand the subsequent horror of their "local" servant (Scene Two). As events seem to disappear into the "memory hole" of the present day, the ongoing use of a death-child icon begins to seem lurid.[21] At yet another reminder of Alan's drowning, the metaphorical sleeper groans and rolls over, awash in lotus flower dreams of the latest iPhone or a new kitchen remodel, or more charitably, feels too exhausted from constant political chaos to dwell. The implicit critique in Alan's death threatens nationalists who, already feeding on a right-wing media diet of victimization, turn the tables and interpret multiculturalism as colonizing the majority. Either the Alan-cum-speech-act becomes a belabored punchline, or his near-mimicry a taunt. Thus we become inured to children dying.

I believe Ai's piece succeeds whereas poignant social media posts fade, and the bridge, boat, and coins failed, because of his kinesthetic investment. Ai does not look like Alan and does not try to. He wears dark clothing with long pants and sleeves, rather than colorful shorts and a short-sleeve shirt. He looks like the fleshy, full-grown, late-middle-aged man that he is, rather than a lithe toddler. The frame of the shot is wider, encompassing the ocean, so as to make the reference to Alan clear. Similarly, Ai's body points to the water while the camera's eye is farther behind him, again repeating the story. Demir's photos of Alan are in color whereas Chawla's of Ai appear in black and white. However, Ai's performance does not call for suspension of disbelief. We do not have to forget that we are watching the internationally known artist effect a *statement*. Chawla's pictures allude to Alan, but the boy does not *feel* present. We see not Alan, but rather Ai embodying Alan. True, Ai can claim a connection as a fellow refugee, and in fact one taking a break from making a major film about refugees to perform this impromptu. He carries an unspoken authority. At the same time, "seeing is believing," and Ai's performance carries a Roger Bannister-like force (if someone else can run a four-minute mile, then I can too). If Ai can "get it" by lying in the sand, then others may too. The pathway is open. Ai risks coming across as arrogant by playing the Bodhi Sattva, an enlightened being who has stayed behind to show the rest of us the way, but to be frank, his body of work backs up the claims his body makes on the beach.

On the flip side, Ai's enactment queries our own capacity for empathy. If Ai can relate to the terror of Alan's absence, and by his example we can too, then why don't we? Across his oeuvre, Ai seems concerned about watching the watcher, implicating the unseen participant in moments of destruction. What is *our* stake (and who are the "we" watching Ai play Alan)? Why are we watching? Why are we watching *now*? Although I take Ai's explanation of remembrance at face value, the visual poetics of Ai lying face down by the surf cannot help but recall Émile Zola's single-word indictment of French President Félix François Faure regarding the Dreyfus Affair: "*J'accuse*" (Zola 1898).

Notes

1 So-called "action states" and "action drives" combine two or three, respectively, to model psychological states.

2 Comments like those of the Dutch Party for Freedom leader Geert Wilders should give pause, as in, "The Moroccan scum in Holland … once again not all are scum … but there is a lot of Moroccan scum in Holland who make the streets unsafe, mostly young people … and that should change" ("Far-Right Leader Geert Wilders Calls Moroccan Migrants 'Scum'" 2017).

3 "Obeah" refers to magical practices in slavery and post-slavery Jamaica. Similar traditions exist throughout the Caribbean, although zombies do not figure prominently in vodun.
4 Frank Darabont produced *The Walking Dead* for the AMC network based on a comic book series by Robert Kirkman, Tony Moore, and Charlie Adlard, and Fox Networks Group distributes the series internationally.
5 Although, Season 8 viewership still clocked in at an average of 11.4 million per episode (Otterson 2017). At the time of this writing, the show is in its tenth season.
6 For vivid demographic charts, see Katz (2016).
7 And possibly urban legend. The chicken biting might be from a 1947 film titled *Nightmare Alley*.
8 The show also references the stereotype of the Asian perpetual immigrant. Daryl banters with Glenn (a native English speaker), "You got some balls for a Chinaman." "I'm Korean." "Whatever" (Season 1, Episode 4).
9 A sedentary lifestyle constitutes a risk factor for heart disease on a par with obesity, tobacco use, diabetes, high blood pressure, and elevated cholesterol.
10 The oldest discovered shipwreck lies off the coast of Turkey, a 3,600-year old vessel laden with 1.5 tons of copper ingots.
11 Barnes maintains, however, that refugee search and rescue falls under human rights obligations. Taking a pragmatic stance, he states that improvements to the system should happen at the level of international cooperation, "burden sharing," and policy. The problem is that the forces that create refugee problems also cause retrenchment into isolationism, making cooperation less likely just as it becomes increasingly needed.
12 In this case, the prosecutor made calls for an investigation without evidence, Hall states. At times, smugglers do contact coast guards at moments of disembarkation, knowing that their ships are unseaworthy and expecting rescue ships to pick survivors from the water. At other times, they do not make such calls and simply let the boats sink.
13 Suvendrini Perera (2013) notes that refugee rhetoric positions sea-bound bodies as feminine, troubling the usual construct of hyper-masculine sea captains.
14 Alistair Hardy (1960) first proposed that human evolution might involve aqueous as much as savannah-oriented adaptations. See Morgan (2011) for an articulation of the aquatic ape hypothesis; cf. Lewin and Foley (2004) for a critical reading of the evidence.
15 For more information than you hopefully would ever have cause to know about drowning, see Bierens (2009).
16 I take the liberty of referring to Kurdi with the implied diminutive "Alan," but in Chinese, the surname precedes the given name. "Ai" is Ai Weiwei's "last name," a formality that I acknowledge when referring to the artist.
17 Chawla also presented the images at a related event, The India Art Fair in New Delhi, January 28–31, 2016.
18 In terms of set theory, the difference between union ($\{a = b\}$) and intersection ($\{a \cap b\}$).
19 I am at a loss to find an expression that captures the (meta)physical concussion of the dead Alan. Such as cipher would have to have the right mixture of moral and physical outrage, like the French word for "rape," *viol* (hence "violence," "violation"). Yiddish supersedes all other tongues in expressions that embody

stupefaction, along a spectrum of deprecation, like *verblonshit* (struck to the point of discombobulation), *vermisht* (mixed up), *verklempt* (exhausted), etc., although nothing about Alan Kurdi implies irony. Arabic, which would have been Alan's language heritage, makes room for multiple words for "stun," such as *faja*, *saeaq*, *sarae*, *dhahal*, *fiqdan alsawab*, *dahsh*, *duhk* … perhaps one or more of these words would carry resonance for a native speaker.

20 Perhaps we should forgive the Finns for "finding the line," but a coin, a symbol of institutionalization *sui generis*, does seem an odd canvas for social action and, as *money*, the set literally commodified the death of a child.

21 At risk of appropriating popular culture, Jon Favreau, co-host of the popular, progressive podcast *Pod Save America*, repeatedly uses the phrase "memory hole" to refer to the American public's inability to hold in mind President Donald Trump's offensive statements and scandals, due to the density of their frequency.

References

Aizenberg, Edna. "'I Walked with a Zombie': The Pleasures and Perils of Postcolonial Hybridity." *World Literature Today* 73, no. 3 (1999): 461–6.

Austin, J.L. *How to Do Things with Words*. Cambridge, MA: Harvard UP, 1975.

"Aylan Kurdi Graffiti Vandalized in Frankfurt." *Deutsche Welle*, June 23, 2016.

Bakhtin, Mikhail. "Introduction." In *Rabelais and His World*, 1–58. Bloomington: Indiana UP, 1984.

Barnes, Richard. "Refugee Law at Sea." *International & Comparative Law Quarterly* 53, no. 1 (2004): 47–77.

Bertoni, Steven. "How Jared Kushner Won Trump the White House." *Forbes*, November 22, 2016.

Bhabha, Homi. "Of Mimicry and Man: The Ambivalence of Colonial Discourse." *October* 28 (1984): 125–33.

Bierens, Joost J.L.M., ed. *Drowning: Rescue, Prevention, Treatment*, 2nd ed. Heidelberg: Springer, 2009.

Casdorff, Stephan-Andreas, and Lorenz Maroldt. "'Die Liste' von Banu Cennetoglu: Künstlerin dokumentiert das Sterben von 33.293 Geflüchteten." *Der Tagesspiegel*, September 11, 2017.

Chawla, Rohit. "Artist Ai Weiwei Poses as Aylan Kurdi for *India Today* Magazine." *India Today*, February 1, 2016.

Chemers, Michael. *The Monster in Theatre History: This Thing of Darkness*. London & New York: Routledge, 2018.

Cisneros, J. David. "Contaminated Communities: The Metaphor of 'Immigrant as Pollutant,' in Media Representations of Immigration." *Rhetoric and Public Affairs* 11, no. 4 (2008): 569–601.

Crofts, Penny, and Anthea Vogl. "Dehumanized and Demonized Refugees, Zombies and World War Z." *Law and Humanities* 13, no. 1 (2019): 29–51.

de Zúñiga, Homero Gil, Teresa Correa, and Sebastian Valenzuela. "Selective Exposure to Cable News and Immigration in the US: The Relationship between Fox News, CNN, and Attitudes toward Mexican immigrants." *Journal of Broadcasting & Electronic Media* 56, no. 4 (2012): 597–615.

"Drowned Asylum Seeker Child, Civil War Execution Special Coins Spark Online Fury." *Yle UUTISET*, April 25, 2017.

"Far-Right Leader Geert Wilders Calls Moroccan Migrants 'Scum.'" *The Guardian*, February 18, 2017.

Fehrenbach, Heide, and Davide Rodogno. "'A Horrific Photo of a Drowned Syrian Child': Humanitarian Photography and NGO Media Strategies in Historical Perspective." *International Review of the Red Cross* 97, no. 900 (2015): 1121–55.

Hall, Richard. "What It's Like Aboard an NGO Ship Rescuing Hundreds of Migrants in the Mediterranean." PRI, September 4, 2017.

Hardy, Alistair. "Will Man Be More Aquatic in the Future?" *The New Scientist* 24 (1960): 730–733.

Joseph, Yonette. "In Their Own Words: Marine le Pen and Emmanuel Macron." *The New York Times*, May 5, 2017.

Katz, Josh. "'Duck Dynasty' vs. 'Modern Family': 50 Maps of the U.S. Cultural Divide." *The New York Times*, December 27, 2016.

Kristeva, Julia. *Powers of Horror: An Essay on Abjection*. Translated by Leon S. Rudiez. New York: Columbia UP, 1982.

Lewin, Roger, and Robert Foley. *Principles of Human Evolution*, 2nd ed. London: Blackwell, 2004.

McLaughlin, Carly. "'They Don't Look Like Children': Child Asylum-Seekers, The Dubs Amendment and The Politics of Childhood." *Journal of Ethnic and Migration Studies* 44, no. 11 (2018): 1757–73.

Morgan, Elaine. *The Aquatic Ape Hypothesis: The Most Credible Theory of Human Evolution*. London: Souvenir Press, 2011.

Mortensen, Mette. "Constructing, Confirming, and Contesting Icons: The Alan Kurdi Imagery Appropriated by #humanitywashedashore, Ai Weiwei, and Charlie Hebdo." *Media, Culture & Society* 39, no. 8 (2017): 1142–61.

Murphy, Carole. "Rivers of Blood, Sea of Bodies: An Analysis of Media Coverage of Migration and Trafficking on the High Seas." In *Beasts of the Deep: Sea Creatures and Popular Culture*, edited by Jon Hackett and Séan Harrington, 154–70. Bloomington: Indiana UP, 2018.

"NGO Rescue Ship Barred from Italy Despite New Government." *The Guardian*, September 10, 2019.

Otterson, Joe. "'Walking Dead' Season 8 Premiere Draws Lowest Opening Ratings Since Season 3 (Updated)." *Variety*, October 24, 2017.

Paravisini-Gebert, Lizabeth. "Women Possessed: Eroticism and Exoticism in the Representation of Woman as Zombie." In *Sacred Possessions: Vodou, Santería, Obeah, and the Caribbean*, edited by Margarite Fernandez Olmos and Lizabeth Paravisini-Gebert, 37–58. New Brunswick, NJ: Rutgers UP, 1997.

Perera, Suvendrini. "Oceanic Corpo-Graphies, Refugee Bodies and the Making and Unmaking Waters." *Feminist Review* 103, no. 1 (2013): 58–79.

Quail, Christine. "Nerds, Geeks, and the Hip/Square Dialectic in Contemporary Television." *Television & News Media* 12, no. 5 (2011): 460–82.

Reynolds, Dee, and Matthew Reason, eds. *Kinesthetic Empathy in Creative and Cultural Practices*. Bristol, UK & Chicago, Intellect Books, 2012.

Rhys, Jean. *Wide Sargasso Sea*. London & New York: W.W. Norton & Co., 2016.

Sheller, Mimi. *Consuming the Caribbean: From Arawaks to Zombies*. London & New York: Routledge, 2003.

Slovic, Paul, Daniel Västfjäll, Arvid Erlandsson, and Robin Gregory. "Iconic Photographs and the Ebb and Flow of Empathic Response to Humanitarian Disasters." *PNAS* 4, no. 4 (2017): 640–4.

States, Bert O. "The Dog on the Stage: Theater as Phenomenon." *New Literary History* 14, no. 2 (1983): 373–88.

Ussery, Emily N., Janet E. Fulton, Deborah A. Galuska, Peter T. Katzmarzyk, and Susan A. Carlson. "Joint Prevalence of Sitting Time and Leisure-Time Physical Activity Among US Adults, 2015–2016." *Journal of the American Medical Association (JAMA)* 19 (2018): 2036–8.

Wallace, Rebecca. "Contextualizing the Crisis: The Framing of Syrian Refugees in Canadian Print Media." *Canadian Journal of Political Science/Revue canadienne de science politique* 51, no. 2 (2018): 207–31.

Yaxley, Charlie. "As Mediterranean Sea Arrivals Decline and Death Rates Rise, UNHCR Calls for Strengthening of Search and Rescue." Press Briefing Summary, United Nations High Commissioner for Refugees (UNHCR), July 6, 2018.

Zola, Émile. "Open Letter." *L'Aurore*, January 13, 1898.

3 Space

Revisiting Arendt and a trip to *The Jungle*

Chapter 2 introduced Laban's systems for describing Body, Effort, and Shape, and applied them to representations of refugees. Bodies do not exist in vacuums, however. Chapter 3 explores the ways refugee performance negotiates, and also produces, space. The chapter begins by describing Laban's system of *space harmony*, a method of training spatial awareness through movement visualizations based on Platonic solids. Chapter 3 then links space to personhood by applying Laban's sense of space to Hannah Arendt's concept of *spaces of appearance*. The chapter theorizes the existence of an inverse structure, *spaces of disappearance*, to describe how refugee spaces rob individuals of their sense of personhood. It then combines all of these ideas in a close reading of *The Jungle*, by Joe Robertson and Joe Murphy, an immersive play that places audiences in a restaurant in a refugee camp in Calais that comes from work "the Joes" conducted within temporary geodesic structures within the camp. The project relies on a somatics that first inserts a Western sense of space into a multi-cultural environment, and then recreates a portion of the refugee camp space in Euro-American theatrical buildings. By exchanging spaces, *The Jungle* creates kinesthetic empathy across worlds.

Laban and space

Laban movement analysis takes a formalist, neo-Platonist, approach to space. Movement analysis takes the "kinesphere," or a malleable bubble that a body produces with its inhabitant at the center, as a basic unit. In everyday life, we encounter kinespheres in our mediation of speaking distance (private, conversational, group distances), a topic that an entire branch of communication studies, *proxemics*, investigates. Informally, individuals have varying levels of "aura" or "personality" that we can feel—a skill that performers can develop into "stage presence," a learnable skill that Joseph Roach theorizes in his historical investigation of charisma, *It* (2007). Cultures train their members to use varying amounts of space, based on gender, age, social status, and other factors.[1] On an individual level, some people have presences so large that heads turn when they walk into a room, whereas others have kinespheres small enough to seem invisible.

Space, both onstage and off, proves plastic. An actor can imagine holding a jewel in her hand, and spectators in the theater will look at her palm. Alternatively, skilled performers can make an audience believe that they are standing on the fields of Agincourt just before a battle. An ancient Greek performer could play to an audience of 10,000 in the round, whereas a Fosse dancer can pull us into a back-and-forth motion of her index finger. Likewise, American suburbanites seem to require increasingly vast vehicles in which to drive, whereas commuters in Tokyo endure *oshiya*, who help cram people into overstuffed subway compartments. These differences derive from the modulation of perceptual space. Space is a capacious category, whose expanse exceeds the spatial confines of this book. A fuller treatment would include an explanation of "spatial intent," or the directions in which a person sends their movement intentions. It would also designate "spatial pulls," by which movers can project a sense of reach towards fixed points in their spatial environment. A "hinge" is a clear example, where a dancer perches on his metatarsal arches, bending backward from the knees, hips, and ankles so that his body ends up parallel to the floor. Without a spatial pull to the ceiling (and powerful abdominal muscles), the dancer would fall over.

Space involves psychological factors and physiological work, in addition to Euclidean properties. In practice, these levels interdepend. As Bartenieff cautioned, "the space in which the body moves and the resultant shapes that are made in space ... are determined by intent, preparation, and developing, changing complexity of the movement process producing them" (2002, p.xiii). Nevertheless, analysts describe the body in objective terms. Using physiological language, movement analysts describe the body's movement along three axes: the *sagittal* plane, as when the body bends front or back; the *transverse* plane, around which the spine twists on its vertical axis; and the *coronal* plane, as when the body bends from side to side. References to near, mid, and far distance can also be helpful. These directions are deictic. In other words, a mover takes his kinesphere with him, unlike stage directions, in which stage right is always stage right, regardless of a performer's facing.

Laban analysis goes farther than describing space, and prescribes patterning exercises that heighten a performer's awareness of space. In his system of "choreutics" or "space harmony," Laban designed movement "scales" within five imagined regular solids of increasing complexity: cube, tetrahedron (a pyramid shape), octahedron (two tetrahedrons whose four-side bases attach), dodecahedron (twelve surfaces, each a pentagon), and icosahedron (twenty surfaces, each a triangle). For anyone who has played the role-playing adventure game *Dungeons and Dragons*, the solids will be familiar from the game dice. In space harmony (a.k.a. "choreutics"), a dancer imagines his center at the solid's center, and performs tracing movements along the solid's edges, vertices, or axes.

As an example of using a spatial form as a patterning exercise, space harmony begins with the "dimensional scale." This sequence engrains awareness of the X, Y, and Z axes, with the body as the center. The practitioner steps forward on her right foot in demi-pointe (on the metatarsal arch), reaching her right hand up while pressing her left hand down behind her. Shifting awareness down along the vertical axis, she steps the right foot back, squats on both forced arches, and presses her hands down. To establish the horizontal axis she rises, plants her right foot in front, turned out, crosses her arms in front of her chest, and looks to the right. To feel forward and back, she shifts weight on the right foot and raises her left leg in parallel to the floor, pointing her foot forward, while leaning her torso back into a layout. The final position involves a transition that ends with the mover again on her right foot in a sort of arabesque, her torso facing down, parallel to the floor, her right arm forward, left arm and leg pointing back. She has now established spatial pulls in three linear dimensions. She may reverse the combination to the left, and also perform these movements in a flowing form, much like the difference between block and cursive handwriting (Newlove and Dalby 2004).

Space harmony makes spatial patterning conscious, often in the service of dance training, but we engage in space all the time. We drive, walk through doorways, and avoid other bodies while ice skating. Moreover, like any social act, we perform space, obeying the socially sanctioned cues, distances, and conventions. Children are inexpert at spatial etiquette, but they are small. If a toddler careens into adults standing in line at the bank, her parents may reprimand, but the recipients of the young one's boundlessness might smile indulgently. Drunk people, who are larger than children, lose their spatial inhibitions, a characteristic that makes them either fun or frightening. Space also affects affect. Lovers advertise their relationship through closeness. When someone is upset, we might want to "give him/her some space."

Space harmony takes the performance of space as an object of artistry through a sequence of patterning exercises of increasing complexity. For example, the "octahedral 6-ring" consists of six linear movements that traverse the double pyramid's vertices, ending back at the point of origin. The "A-scale" links the four corners of the body's sagittal, transverse, and coronal plane (or XY, XZ, and YZ planes in geometry) with flowing movements that each connect two points on the icosahedron, without passing through its center. To make these visualizations accessible, movement analysis classrooms sometimes have models of the solids large enough for students to fit into in learning the scales.

Dis-placed persons inhabit different patterns of spaces, which impacts their somatics. They confront vast expanses, such as oceans, deserts, mountain ranges, highways, and fields. Alternatively, they negotiate density, cramming into potentially lethal trucks, storage containers, and cargo holds of ships. They encounter dimensionality in immediate ways, such as the three-dimensionality of geographic features. They huddle inside of makeshift tents within the agoraphobic two-dimensional vastness of camps. Finally, they

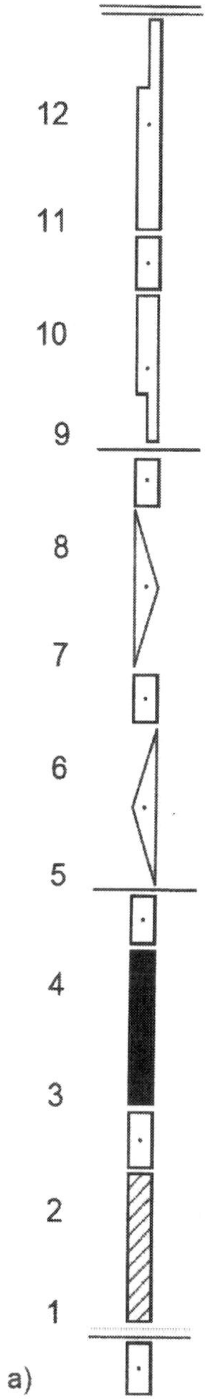

Figure 3.1 The dimensional scale in Laban motif writing. From Charlotte Wile with Ray Cook, *Moving About: Capturing Movement Highlights using Motif Notation*, Author, 2010, © Charlotte Wile. Image courtesy of Dance Notation Bureau.

Note: Chapter 5 explores methods of dance writing, including Labanotation.

squish into soul-crushing one-dimensional lines, awaiting papers, asylum, or deportation. Above all, refugees experience a sense of in-betweenness, of waiting and traveling and never-quite-getting-there, whatever "there" may mean.

Scholars spill ink trying to capture this feeling of floating, and each argot contains a bit of ore that illumes a bit of the sensation of stagnation: *un-place*, *non-place*, *interstitial space*, *borderlands*, *liminality*, and so forth. Anthropologist Marc Augé claims that we all inhabit non-spaces. With mobility as a defining feature, flow systems like highways, online platforms, and other kinds of networks typify what Augé calls "hypermodernity," a state of non-stillness "in the manner of immense parentheses" (1995, p.111). You can never step in the same river twice. The idea of "immense parentheses" seems deeply intuitive. Waiting on a delayed flight, standing in line for a driver's license, staring at the proverbial pot awaiting a boil, feel like references to life rather than acts of living. As an analytic, ideas of non-spaces carry the seeds of their destruction. As Tim Cresswell notes, "if place is the very bedrock of our humanity, as some have claimed, then it cannot have vanished because it is a necessary part of the human condition" (2015, p.85). Space never disappears.

Yet *something* spatial happens in times of stress. Having introduced space harmony, I will ask forbearance for the next two sections of the chapter. In order to show how space harmony connects to refugee somatics, I would like to first invert a philosophical conception of space that impinges on one's sense of humanity, and then to show through a case study an unexpected connection between Hannah Arendt and documentary refugee theater. The resulting exercise will show the relationships, at which Cresswell hints, between space, somatics, and personhood.

Spaces of appearance

Our world confronts a crisis of human flow on a scale we have not seen since the aftermath of World War II, and therefore we may find inspiration in theory from that time. In considering a world faced with fascism and, like today, witness to mass displacement, Hannah Arendt created a critique of politics based on human dignity. Particularly in *The Human Condition* (1959), Arendt distilled her observations. In this critique, she reframes the classical notion of the *vita activa*, or "life of doing," which the weight of Western thought holds inferior to a life of contemplation, for the twentieth-century polis. Arendt characterizes *action* as a concept that corresponds to intuitions like personal agency. For Arendt, action differs from *labour*, or activity that pertains to sustaining life, and *work*, which has to do with making things that would not otherwise exist in nature. For example, foraging for food is labour, whereas fashioning an ax to cut wood is work. Preconditions for action, labour, and work impinge on materiality, rather than on society.

Action exists above the animal-like nature of labour, and the toil of work. Arendt bases action on two ideas. Firstly, action depends on the ability to do something new. Humans have a birthright to the "infinitely improbable" through *natality*, the fact of being born (Arendt 1959, pp. 177–8). Coming into the world stands as an act of originality *sui generis*. Action-from-natality marks perhaps the opposite pole of the Richard Schechner/Victor Turner understanding of performance as "restored behavior." In Arendt's view, as originary beings, humans honor their birth through novelty, in contrast to repeating social scripts. Secondly, action depends on *plurality*, which is to say that freedom only makes sense in the context of other people. A hermit in a cave is neither free nor not-free. Rather, the presence of others provides the basis for the concept of choice to make sense. When natality and plurality combine, action can occur.

Arendt's is a social theory, although the idea of groups contains a paradox. Plurality implies *equality*, which suggests sameness ("If men were not equal, they could neither understand each other and those who came before them nor plan for the future"; pp.155 6). People must have a common denominator for communication to work. At the same time, without *distinction*, individuality would vanish ("If men were not distinct ... they would need neither speech nor action to make themselves understood"; p.156). Through speech and action, individuals emerge into the social realm, an event Arendt likens to a "second birth" (p.157). Humans oscillate between individuality and plurality, moving back and forth between individual and communitarian awareness.

During the times in which people partake in the social, they may create *spaces of appearance*. These spaces require action, but do not depend on physical context. Arendt argues, "The space of appearance comes into being whenever men are together in the manner of speech and action, and therefore predates and precedes all formal constitution of the public realm" (p.178). The idea recalls Matthew: "For where two or three are gathered together in my name, there am I in the midst of them" (18:20). Arendt's spaces exist ephemerally. The polis is fragmentary, exceptional, not fashioned from stone. A group of people engaged in weaving fishing nets does not constitute a space of appearance, but if the group were to reflect and speak to one another about their roles in making the nets, it might be, for as long as the glow of such a conversation lasts. However, spaces of appearance have a precariousness that derives from their potentiality: "Wherever people gather together, it [a space of appearance] is potentially there, but only potentially, not necessarily and not forever" (p.178). Spaces of appearance are soap bubbles. Arendt describes human intercourse as remarkable, and not something that has appeared with regularity since the ancient Greeks.

Spaces of appearance engender traits, like dignity, humanity, or empathy, that carry positive valence—the better angels of our nature. As social mammals, humans self-organize according to hierarchy, which drives survival, reproductive rights, and violence. Arendt's spaces of appearance sound idealistic, in that they emerge when we transcend sociobiological impulse. They evoke an almost Kierkegaardian "leap of faith" across the void of otherness as consciousnesses commune. In spaces of appearance, we witness one another's identities, "where I appear to others as others appear to me, where men exist not merely like other living or inanimate things, but to make their appearance explicitly," as Arendt describes it (p.198–9). The mutual recognition of a shared spark is the *namaste* at the end of a yoga class, or Jill Dolan's "utopian performatives"—glimpses of emergent social justice that audiences feel during performance events. Within spaces of appearance, individuals speak and act as fellow humans. Members of such spaces can try to prolong the experience, but the act of codification kills the vibrancy that makes spaces of appearance joyous. Attempts to extend these moments lead to institutionalization at best, or fascism at worst.

Arendt's ideas have influenced decades of scholarship, though discourses of displaced persons tend to overlook spaces of appearance in favor of Arendt's paradox of stateless people. When people become displaced, they stand denuded of everything except their humanity, which they lose because, bereft of citizenship, they are helpless. Just when humans own nothing but their humanity, they are least able to claim protections, a condition Arendt calls "the paradox of human rights" and Serena Parekh, applying Arendt to Giorgio Agamben, calls "the ontological deprivation of statelessness" (Parekh 2017, pp.82–103). Significant exceptions apply spaces of appearance to immigration politics. In some of these readings, peoples on the move are noncitizens, since they inhabit non-public spaces.[2] For example, Christina Beltrán uses Arendt's spaces of appearance to argue that when immigrants staged a mass demonstration in 2006, they achieved a public consciousness, if not legislative change (2009). Beltrán argues that protests did not bring immigrants out of the shadows, as a reading of Arendt's work on totalitarianism might suggest, but rather created what Michael Warner calls a "counter-public," which is an "ongoing space of encounter" that makes a group self-aware of their subordinate status relative to a dominant society (Warner 2002, p.90). By engaging in discourse in novel action (Beltrán uses the phrase "festive anger"), the immigrant community created a sense of community, raising themselves above animal-level labour.

Discourses about migrants also put Arendt into conversation with theorists like Algerian-French philosopher Jacques Rancière, who argued that majorities do not discount migrants and other subalterns as humans as much as fail to see them (think Ralph Ellison's novel *The Invisible Man*). For instance, Mustafa Dikeç draws from both Arendt and Rancière to characterize migrants as interlopers in public spaces (2013). Similarly, Marieke Borren distills Arendt's formula that since displaced persons are stateless they have no civil rights and therefore no human rights into the phrase "public invisibility" (2008, p.218). For Borren, dignity emerges out of the synthesis of plurality and publicity, and therefore, "stateless people lose all significance as well as their humanity" (p.219). When people vanish, action and speech become irrelevant. Displaced persons lack both "home and mask," and the "politics of in/visibility" uncovers "regimes of obscuring and exposing" (pp.223–5). The interplay between power and gaze does not apply, as invisible people do not have a social presence.

Arendt and Arendt-based critiques enrich theater and performance studies, which have tended to favor theories like Habermas' public sphere (*Öffentlichkeit*), which denotes a shared space where citizens can speak freely so as to influence public opinion and thereby create a sense of "the public." Arendt's critique of "rights in an age of rightlessness" is also helpful because hers is not a system floating in a vacuum. Attending to the world filled with totalitarianism and massacre, Arendt spoke to the cataclysms of the twentieth century. As Ayten Gündogdu shows, an engagement with Arendt serves the moment, since in many ways the 1930s have returned, but also because globalization has created conditions that renew displacement as a scourge. Using Arendt's language as a way of understanding the present, Gündogdu rejects fatalism, but rather sees current paradoxes of the rightless as "challenging political and ethical dilemmas that can be navigated differently, including in ways that bring to view new understandings of the relationships between rights, citizenship, and humanity" (2015, p.5). Gündogdu approaches Arendt like a grammar, with which we may speak of today's wanderer with fluency.

As critical as conversations about distilling the essence of citizenship continue to be, Arendt's spaces of appearance emphasize discourse to the detriment of embodiment. In particular, feminist scholars have had a contentious relationship with Arendt, in part because she flattens bodies into exchangeable units of (potential) social polity. Arendt does reject Christianity's placement of the physical at the bottom of a values hierarchy, though she does not dwell on this point other than to note Thomas Aquinas' recognition of the body's appetites. Likewise, she mentions Karl Marx's description of the role of the body in the creation of wealth. She sets more store by John Locke's axiom that the body is personal property. Following Locke, she contends that the body becomes the "quintessence of all property" because the owner cannot share it, even willingly (p.97). The body is antagonistic to sociability, and if anything, becomes an impediment to spaces of appearance, Arendt reasons. Politics occur in public space, and since the body constitutes privacy *sui generis*, the body occupies a point opposite political life. Moreover, pain causes somatic awareness to involute, creating an awareness "thrown back upon itself."[3] A body in distress withdraws from public life. At best, freedom from pain functions as a precondition for "experiencing the world" (Arendt 1959, p.98). Despite her refutation of Christian Platonism, Arendt returns to speech as the highest good and equates utopic bubbles of humanity with communities of discourse.

Within feminist responses, some scholars make cogent critiques of Arendt that cut to the point. Bonnie Honig observes that Arendt considers the body to possess a "univocally despotic and irresistible character" that would-be humans seek to overcome through performative speech acts (2013, p.234). Arendt would seem to want to avoid talking about corporeality, and gender in particular. In Honig's anthology, Linda M.G. Zerilli suggests Arendt's aversion to exploring gendered embodiment borders on a Freudian sense of taboo. Also, too much physical differentiation precludes the possibility of plurality, and therefore spaces of appearance. Agreeing with Honig, Zerilli characterizes the "Arendtian body" as "grotesque, mute, oral, desiring, engulfing." That kind of body hurls personhood back into nature's cycles—not a goddess-nature of internal fluidity that might suggest a subject-in-process but the mindless regurgitating of *animal laborens* (Zerilli 2010, p.177). Like the ancient Greeks whom Arendt idolizes, speaking of bodies in the plural (that is to say, distinction) not only threatens plurality but raises uncomfortable questions (for both the Greeks and Arendt) about the types of "bodies that matter." On the other hand, Joan McAlister underscores Arendt's insistence on birth as a cornerstone of her theory, an event that could not be more physical (2010, pp.303–04). John Tambornino takes a middle ground, arguing that Arendt held contradictory views of embodiment, and that the body and politics threaten one another. Tambornino calls for a revision of Arendt that "would make the body a concern of political action and a source contributing to natality and individuality," and that also would show that "attention to one's body would be seen as part of thinking and judging" (1999, p.190). The body jams Arendt's philosophical gears, but also stands as a provocation to continue moving the conversation forward.

To repeat Cresswell's critique of theories like Augé's, humanity implies bodies, which implies space. Perhaps we will come to a technological point at which consciousness exists in diffuse networks. For now, refugees are *displaced* persons. That is to say, forces against their control push them from spatial tethers. Movement occurs in space, and therefore the loss of agency in motion is a spatial question, or at least one that involves spatiality. We are therefore at the nexus of the questions this book addresses. What is the relationship between forced movement and dehumanization? What do involuntary movers lose on a somatic level by virtue of unwilling motion? The conditions of movement relate to a person's sense of personhood. Whether a mover travels by train or hidden in the hold of an oil tanker has to inform a person's sense of humanity, and their ability to form spaces of appearance, or …

Spaces of disappearance

If *spaces of appearance* can exist in moments of stasis, then *spaces of disappearance* can occur in times of dislocation. This chapter will posit its own definition of "space of disappearance," what this type of space is and does, and how it contributes to our understanding of displaced persons. The term presently exists, though in architectural discourse rather than in performance theory. George Baird began discussing Arendt in architectural literature in

The Space of Appearance. Baird observes that Arendt intuited the implications of her work in terms of materiality when she wrote

> The whole factual world of human affairs depends for its reality and its continued existence, first, upon the presence of others who have seen and heard and will remember, and second, on the transformation of the intangible into the tangibility of things.
>
> (Arendt, quoted in Baird 1995, p.19, note 31)

For Baird, Arendt's phrase "the tangibility of things" relates to practicalities in the organization of social spaces, such as the layout of streets, highways, and shopping malls.[4] Whereas philosophers speak in terms of "space" in the abstract, architects translate spatial theory into everyday experience.

Ackbar Abbas seems to have been the first to use the phrase "space of disappearance," which he defined as the loss of something not real. Abbas suggests that in the lead-up to China taking back control of Hong Kong in 1997, media created an image of Hong Kong culture that had never existed, as a presentiment of loss (1994). Abbas' space of disappearance is like a virtual image, a projection on a soon-vanishing screen. Jordan H. Carver also uses the phrase "space of disappearance," by which he means secret prisons during the US-led "War on Terror." Carver explores how the design of American covert detention centers helps dehumanize prisoners, and makes close readings of such architectural spaces (2018). Architects like Baird, Abbas, and Carver apply Arendt to the material but, being architects, focus on architecture that contains bodies, rather than on bodies themselves.

Consequently, introducing motion into the conversation on Arendtian bodies, I would like to define a space of disappearance as a space that violates agency, and that comes about through involuntary displacement of the body. Within groups of involuntarily moving bodies—evacuees, migrants, asylum seekers, refugees, and the like—a space of disappearance may manifest. Spaces of disappearance can occur whenever people gather together in extremis—these spaces are, to use Arendt's language, potentially there, but only potentially, not necessarily and not forever. They are there whenever people are together in the manner of speech and action, yet their speech produces no force, and their action has no effect. A space of disappearance is not a space of work or labour, in Arendt's sense, since members need not engage in making or doing anything. More often, like inhabitants in a land of the dead, a disappeared space's members produce nothing. A space of disappearance contains plurality, yet it is not political, since without agency, speech carries no force. Those within such spaces no longer reveal their identities because something blocks them from doing so. Members of spaces of disappearance may also vanish physically and permanently, and are often at heightened risk of doing so, but "disappearance" refers to the erasure of their humanity.

A space of disappearance is more than an oubliette in which to put someone in order to forget about them. The ever-watchful Eye does not espy inhabitants of spaces of disappearance in some Foucauldian Mordor, because there is no humanity left within them to surveil. Spaces of disappearance are not counter-publics, nor are they the absence of society. A space of disappearance is an anti-space, where people exist in bare form yet are incapable of seeing themselves, or being seen, as human. Spaces of disappearance are more than the absence of a space of appearance, and maybe more like an abscess. Rather than a lack, they are a *something*. They are a cancer cell in that they hijack a healthy mechanism of the body politic and turn that pathway into something that can sicken or kill. They are a space of appearance gone awry.

Spaces of disappearance can manifest in several ways, and since they involve bodies in space, time, and energy, movement terms will help describe what scholars often describe in the abstract. For example, spaces of appearance can mutate into spaces of disappearance when bodies fail to locomote. Probably everyone can relate to the feeling of discomfort when a dinner party or some other gathering has gone on too long. Taking this dynamic to an institutional scale, the Soviet Union transformed into a fascist state after the glow of class-consciousness congealed into the horror of Stalinism. Arendt's spaces, like Phelan's definition performance, depend on ephemerality. The line between utopia and dystopia can be a matter of duration. Tension exists between spaces of appearance and institutionalism. The idea of a Heaven of eternal, unchanging bliss is terrifying from this perspective. The "surge" of "uprisings" peaks. Political "movements" subside. "Revolutions" (the noun form of the verb "to revolve") changes direction into "counter-revolutions." Secret police "put down" dissidents. Movements lose momentum. Like a cartoon character, the group has run off the edge of the cliff but hovers in mid-air. Butchers like Stalin, Mao, or Pol Pot gather up their lambs after euphoria's rush has gone stale. Spaces of appearance can feel like oases of disclosure that dot oceans of loneliness. The urge to linger in paradise is understandable, but can result in a ship's crew becoming Lotus Eaters—they let down their guard and become prey.

Segmentation into too many movement initiations can also create a sense of having "stayed too long at the fair," or a staccato sense of stuck-ness. To take a relatable example, cutting up movement is one of the reasons air travel can be grueling. When you fly, you do not just take an airplane but engage in a series of mini-journeys, such as driving to the airport, walking to and standing at check-in, walking to and standing at security, walking through a terminal, standing at a gate, getting on a plane, getting off a plane, walking to and standing at customs, going up an escalator, riding a people mover, taking a tram to another terminal, walking a long distance to another gate only to find your second flight is late, and so on. "One" trip encompasses dozens of stages, with periods of waiting punctuating movement. Similarly, refugees do not just walk or sit in camps but make multi-stage journeys to points of embarkation, go with smugglers to secondary locations, wait in warehouses, wait on beaches, wait on boats, transfer to a second boat, end up back on the beach when different smugglers come on board and turn the boat around, go in trucks, end up as ransom, walk through the desert, and so on. Refugees' and other displaced persons' journeys can comprise scores of stages, spaces that fail to collapse, renewing with each stage of the trek, like an eye that never blinks. When involuntary movers do end up in camps or detention centers, their journeys freeze, states-of-becoming that enter a gravity well of never-arriving that can span from days to decades.[5]

Not every displacement becomes a space of disappearance. Adverse circumstances can create communitas in full register, such as miners trapped together underground, or soldiers who become like siblings and have trouble coming home, or prisoners of war tapping messages to one another through cell walls. Exceptional circumstances can even become the stuff of drama. The hit musical *Come from Away* (2013) dramatized the true experiences of global travelers when the terrorist attacks of September 11, 2001, grounded flights. Air traffic controllers redirected thirty-eight planes to Gander, Newfoundland, due to the small town's pre-transatlantic capacity runway, and the show focuses on hospitality and kindness, and the lifelong bonds the experience forged. Likewise, Patrick Myers' *K2* (1983) explores the drama that arises in the potential violation of trust. Two mountaineers are at 27,000 feet, attempting to summit the world's second-highest peak. At 1250 feet from the ledge, one of the characters breaks his leg and becomes immobilized. What choice will the uninjured climbing partner make? Myers' juxtaposition of movement and immobility leaves the two climbers at a crossroads: will they remain within a space of appearance, which will result in rescue, or will they shift into a space of disappearance, which will likely produce abandonment and death?

Under certain conditions, subaltern spaces can contain the seeds of empowerment. Although we must approach such claims with caution, some roles can carry a thrill, such as speaking truth to power, activism, revolution, counter-culture leadership, avant-garde art, and non-normative roles. Oppression incises boundaries of self and community, provokes creativity, and can—again, with circumspection—lend cachet. To some extent, these archetypes are hegemonic romanticism, like courtly scribes appropriating fictitious Robin Hoods as fallen nobles. By tautology, oppression is oppression. However, living outside of a society's boundaries can create a sense of aliveness, a higher awareness that may not mitigate hardship, hatred, privation, and danger, but can align dissidents with a sense of righteousness. In contrast, spaces of disappearance do not accentuate uniqueness. They are pits of dehumanization.

Spaces of disappearance have boundaries. A camp has a fence. A ship has a hull. Family separation detention centers along the US–Mexican border have cages. Like dancers on a stage, refugees in a disappearing space must avoid falling off the edge. Also like performers, their spaces create alternative worlds which they inhabit for the duration of the performance. Unlike (most) stage events, refugees' performances occur on unmarked platforms, invisible to outsiders. with no wings to which to flee, no crossover space behind the back wall. As in Camus' play *No Exit*, a bounded stage becomes a prison of the soul. Karamazov's prisoner felt free, despite his shackles, but only because the rest of the world languished in mental penitentiaries. In contrast to Gertrude Stein's overused phrase "there's no *there* there," refugees do experience a "there," and cannot leave it. They are fish in a tank. The performance becomes real because of a sense that it will never end.

Spaces can also move. Refugees often disappear when they abscond inside of transport spaces. Such vessels of mobile confinement provide invisibility at border crossings, and degrade an individual's humanity, if not taking their lives. Usually, nation-states consider unauthorized border crossings a crime. As such, smugglers charge as much as the market will bear for their contraband services, and have little regard for the safety of their clients in the pursuit of profit and avoidance of law enforcement. The Spanish word for "human smuggler," *coyote*, perhaps captures the predatory nature of human smuggling best, though opportunists exist everywhere. Smuggling entails packing as much human cargo as possible into hidden spaces, such as the holds of ships, the backs of trucks, the inside of fuel tankers, warehouses, and safehouses. To take examples of trucks, from among dozens from the past twenty years: in 2006, a federal court found a Jamaican American immigrant guilty on fifty-eight counts relating to nineteen immigrants who suffocated to death in the back of his milk truck (Blumenthal 2006). In 2015, Hungarian police arrested three Bulgarians and a Lebanese in connection with a former Slovakian chicken truck, whose driver left seventy-one refugees locked in the hold near the Austrian border. A state employee mowing the grass noticed putrefying liquid seeping out of the back of the truck, in addition to an overpowering odor ("Hungarian Police Arrest Driver of Lorry" 2015). A similar scene occurred along the Bulgarian border with Turkey, with 129 victims ("Refugees Found in Refrigerated Truck in Bulgaria" 2015). We could rehearse analogous types of horrors across types of confined spaces. The point is that refugee spaces can kill, and since people produce space, only their deaths collapse confined spaces.

When refugees come to "rest" in transient communities, these locations become fertile grounds for spaces of disappearance. Refugee camps, detention centers, and other kinds of "processing centers" create temporal bubbles, like an always-delayed flight. Long term, like any immigrant, refugees can become perpetual newcomers. In Europe, migrants tend to cluster in the suburbs or outskirts of cities, a spatial metaphor that makes their status as "outsiders" a geographical reality.

Escapes from spaces of disappearance do not exist. However, repatterning the space within such spaces can function as a form of resistance that reestablishes humanness. In the early stages of my partner's medical journey, in pre-Obamacare Texas, we found ourselves unable to secure health insurance. As a final recourse, we paid a visit to our state Medicaid office. The low-income health provider's spatial semiotics could not have been clearer. We entered the back door of an unmarked warehouse to find cubicles with no reception area. A worker told us to wait on two metal folding chairs on the side of the room. As well-enculturated members of our culture, we understood the spatial semiotics of the conservative region of America to mean, "How dare you? How dare you commit the sin of penury? How dare you impose on the largess of others for your illness? Wait here for hours for an administrative process that you will not understand and that will render judgment against your request." Unwilling to engage in the genre of bureaucratic performance that the space required, my wife pulled out a pack of playing cards. We spread out to play a game, while chatting and laughing. Within moments, an administrator, visibly angry, materialized, and said something along the lines of "What seems to be the problem here?" The problem was that we were not conforming to our roles as supplicants, based on the office's spatial patterning. She had us fill out an application, which she then approved, removing us from her space as quickly as possible.

Prisoners within spaces of disappearance can subvert their fate by subverting spatial performance. On a much larger scale, I believe that during the civil rights movement in America, Dr. Martin Luther King, Jr.'s strategy of "sit-ins" worked in part because they involved people sitting on the floor. His marches drew attention because people walked in the street instead of on the sidewalk. The Selma bus boycott created indelible, incongruous images of empty busses juxtaposed against commuters walking along bus routes. Transgressing spatial patterning requires an insider's knowledge of a culture's conventions of space, and then a deliberate repatterning of that space. When linked to moral imperative as strategy, confounding spatial codes can serve as a powerful protest tactic. Either the dominant society will engage in negotiation, or it will seek to destroy the space that is supposed to suppress its embodied agency, because the deviants have coopted it. The following discussion shows an example of the latter, when the French government leveled a refugee camp because its members tried to turn it into their home.

A Jungle in Calais

The Jungle is a groundbreaking play, born of art as activism, that transforms refugees and audiences through an exchange of space. The title refers to an area that French officials referred to as the Camp de la Lande ("Calais Jungle" or "countryside camp"), though "shanty" perhaps better describes the makeshift sprawl of tents, dirt, garbage, and structures of canvas and corrugated siding. Migrants began assembling in this region, unfit for habitation due to pollution, near the Port of Calais as early as 1999. Given its nature as an eddy in the river of migrants, numbers prove precarious, but the "camp" swelled to around 3000–4000 by 2015.

The Sarkozy administration responded with increasingly violent attempts to clear the area. In February 2016, the French government evicted about 1000 camp residents, a process that produced stone-throwing, tear gas, and fires. Tension between authorities and migrants simmered, and a riot occurred in May 2016. The government built a wall in September 2016, along a highway that served as transit from Calais to England, in an effort to tamp down the flow—the camp had grown to over 7000 by that point. From October to November 2016, the government cleared the camp, bulldozed the plain, and relocated the migrants to facilities throughout northern France and nationwide—a chaotic process that resulted in thousands of missing persons, including unaccompanied children. Multiple uninvestigated reports allege police abuse of migrants, including firing pepper spray at children (Human Rights Watch 2017). Additional eyewitness accounts suggest that right-wing militias wearing police uniforms accounted for some of these attacks, with actual police failing to intervene (Quine 2016). Although horrible, the story of Calais would make for compelling theater.

British playwrights Joe Murphy and Joe Robertson (a.k.a. "the Joes") met as fellow English majors at Oxford University, and made an immersive play based on their experiences living in the camp, where they lived for seven months and built an eleven-meter geodesic dome. I speak with Naomi Webb, the executive director of Good Chance Theatre, the Joes' organization, via video chat. Ms. Webb resembles the personnel at Battery Dance in New York: smart, savvy, and resourceful. A former classmate of Murphy and Robertson, Webb worked with London-based Complicité Theatre, volunteered with Good Chance on related projects, and then joined full time two-and-half years ago. Since I have to know, I first ask her if Murphy and Robertson go by "the Joes" in real life. She says, "everybody calls them that, yes … it's sort of agreed thing that basically whichever Joe you meet first is *the* Joe, and the other one is *the other Joe*. 'Joe,' 'Joe,' and 'Joes'—it's very common" (Webb, 2020). Ms. Webb also confirms the origin story of Good Chance's use of domes as an applied theater strategy.

After having developed a writing partnership, the Joes happened upon Calais during a post-graduation trip to Munich in search of ways to bear witness to the growing refugee crisis. Planning on staying for a day, they tarried for a week, and then came back for seven months. "It was very different from what they'd see on the news," Webb describes. With the material conditions of the camp before them, the Joes bought a geodesic dome second-hand for £10,000, which became a communal performance space. Their name for their space, "Good Chance Theatre," winks at a camp saying that "there might be a good chance to cross the border to the U.K. that night" (Thompson 2017). Webb relates that, having built the structure together with the residents, the Joes then said to the community, "This is your space, what do you want to do here?" Individuals came forward from the globally fractured camp—an Afghani kickboxer, an Iranian kung-fu master, a storyteller, dancers.

The geodesic dome became a beacon. Light, portable, and strong, the space is a Grotowskian "poor theater" *par excellence*. The Calais dome created a safe space for camp members, though it also attracted global theater practitioners. Webb says that the shape served as

> sort of a doorway and a platform for so many artists who were going, "we see this crazy thing that's happening in our world, but we don't know what to do." And what Good Chance did was create a space and a platform that was open to everybody, where everyone was equal and autonomous, that said, "okay, well you're artists … so come."

They did come, including the Young Vic, Knee High, and Royal Court companies. Actors from The Globe brought their production of *Hamlet* to the camp in February 2016, which they performed for about 300 migrants. Glitterati like actor Jude Law and playwright Tom Stoppard paid visits. Good Chance has since established domes in Paris and elsewhere, which act as beacons for over 600 volunteers. London-based companies like Sadler's Wells and The Globe give free tickets to Good Chance refugee company members, as do theaters and museums in Paris.

When they went back to England, the Joes wrote a play based on how camp residents had expressed themselves within the dome, having first solicited opinion on the appropriateness of doing so from people they had spoken to in Calais and who were by then living as refugees in the UK. The National and the Young Vic co-produced the Joes' *The Jungle*, with multiple-award-winning Stephen Daldry and Justin Martin as co-directors. The play recreates the Afghan Café, a bustling spot in the center of the Jungle camp, on the eve of the French bulldozers, and dramatizes the community's anticipation of its own destruction. *The Guardian*'s assessment typifies critical consensus: "this extraordinary play set in the Calais Jungle is vivid and complex in its portrayal of human resilience in the face of humanitarian catastrophe" ("The Jungle Review" 2017). After the sold-out run at the Young Vic, the production moved to the West End in 2017, again to critical exuberance and sold-out houses. The production transferred to St. Ann's Warehouse in Brooklyn in December 2018 to January 2019, and then to the Curran Theatre in San Francisco until May 2019. Critical superlatives from all the runs cluster around words like *heartbreaking*, *throbbing*, *timely*, *vital*, and *devastating*. Still early in its life cycle, the play appears to have touched a nerve. *The Jungle* is set to return to St. Ann's in Brooklyn at the time of this writing, while Good Chance is also set to inaugurate a dome project in Tijuana, Mexico.

The Jungle immerses audiences in the sensoria of the refugee camp, with Miriam Buether's scenic design leading the way. For each of its venues, the piece involves an extended load-in to effect transformation. The performance space itself resembles a Middle Eastern interior space that has collided with a fashion runway. An alley runs across the length of the set, and two narrow ones branch off in either direction. When the actors stand on the walkways, their bodies help establish a tetrahedral X, Y, and Z framework. Audiences sit in fourteen areas of restaurant-style counter-tops, some of which run right up to the platforms, so that the performers' shins cross at eye level. Other audience groupings array behind cut-out windows, above the set, and along elevated benches along the periphery. The walls exhibit a riot of textures, including

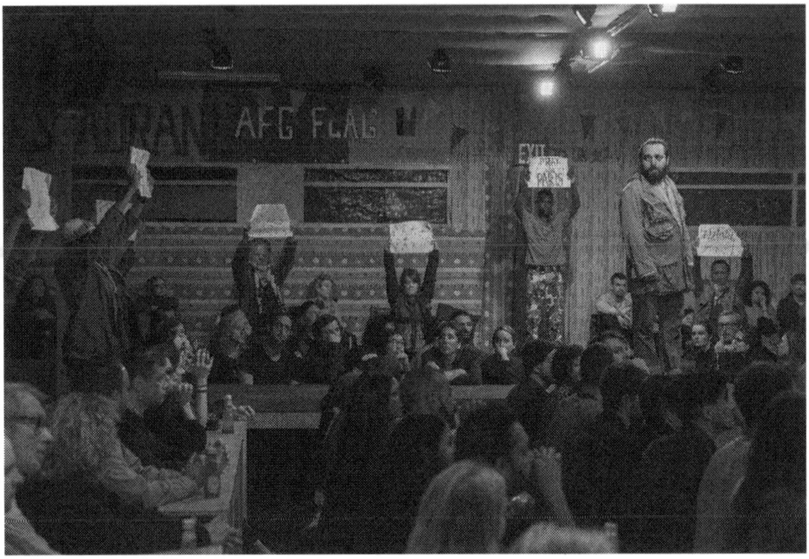

Figure 3.2 The Jungle at St. Ann's Warehouse. Photo © Teddy Wolff.

blue-white-orange herringbone wallpaper, flags, hanging lights, banners, and video screens that play images of refugees, including the dead three-year-old Alan Kurdi. Tristan Shepherd and Duncan McLean designed the videos, John Pfumojena composed music, and Paul Arditti contributed sound design.

The arrangement of the house includes elements for all the senses. Audiences seated on ground level rest their feet on a dirt floor, and there is food. The Afghan Café was a real establishment in the camp. The *Sunday Times* food critic A.A. Gill reviewed the café, giving it four stars for both food and atmosphere (he liked the chicken livers), a plaudit that the Joes worked into one of the scenes (Gill 2016). A line from Gill's review—"When does a place become a home?"—becomes a leitmotif. The *New Yorker* critic noted, "'Immersive theatre' can be a cringe-inducing phrase, redolent of conceptual kookiness and awkward audience-participation gimmicks," but *The Jungle* "is immersive in the true sense. The show does not so much present its story as plunge us directly into it, to astonishing emotional effect" (Schwartz 2019). Actors pour chai tea for audience members, when not including them in dance, music, or other stage business. Paul Arditti's sound design include atmospheric effects like vehicle noise, as well as incidental camp sounds.

Enwrapped within the hospitality of the Café, the play explores the relationship between space and personhood. *The Jungle* opens with an Aristotelian late attack, with an Arendtian disclosure of identity following:

DEREK Right. Can I have everyone's attention, please? I know there have been a lot of rumours going around. People are frightened. I'm going to explain as clearly as I can the facts as we know them. Can you translate that, please?

MOHAMMAD Arabic.

SALAR Pashto.

HELEN Tigrinya.

ALI Farsi.

Translations.

PAULA Salar, I need your information.

SALAR Salar Malikzai. Thirty-two years old. I come from Afghanistan. I've been here eleven months.

DEREK Another eviction notice was posted this morning. This one gives police the authority to clear all the southern half of the Jungle. That includes the school, the mosques, the churches.

HELENE My church!

DEREK Most of the shops …

SALAR The restaurants?

DEREK Yes, Salar, it does include the restaurants. ("One. The Judgement")

The play lacks the traditional clash between protagonist and antagonist. Rather, *The Jungle* vaults the audience into one scene that interrupts the next in which characters attempt to hang on to their humanity, as well as their connection to one another. When Safi intones the play's central question, "When does a place become a home?", or when Kevin says, "The name of this place, our temporary home. It does not feel like a jungle to me," and proposes changing it to "Hope Town" ("Four. The Gold Rush"), or a character declares, "I have been waiting to become a person again," we witness yearnings for a return to a space of appearance.

Critical reception as a whole characterizes *The Jungle* as revelatory. Negative responses, such as they are, describe the growing pains of an evolving work. Nicole Serratore wrote a less-than-glowing review for *Variety* for the St. Ann's iteration, that resolves within a deeper conversation about space. Serratore felt *The Jungle*'s "storytelling comes across as heavy-handed and constructed, substituting atmosphere for dramaturgy" (Serratore 2018). Specifically, the critic did not seem sold on the set, adding, "It's a lot of vivid illusion without emotional impact. The excessively theatricalized production, directed by Daldry and Justin Martin, puts distance between its subject and the audience when it could be collapsing it." The last line about *adding* distance seems fascinating given the proxemics of the performer–audience relationship in the production. How could the performance get any closer to the audience?

Serratore in the above quotation refers to emotional distance. Aesthetic distance (knowing the world of play is not real) exists in tension with suspension of disbelief (choosing to believe that the world of a play is real, at least for the duration of the event). In general, we want to disappear into a work enough to enjoy it, but not so much that we lose connection to reality, and Serratore's disparagement suggests that something is off with this balance.

Serratore adds, "Even with the production design's 'authenticity,' the theatricality of the production keeps pushing reality further away. You are acutely aware you're at a show being acted." Serratore's critique reminds me of an experience I had with my daughter. While attending a conference in Belgrade, we stopped for dinner at a restaurant that had a sign announcing (in English) "Authentic Serbian Food." In Brooklyn, Williamsburg sports an area of souvenir shops that cluster near an upscale Whole Foods grocery store, where tourists can have an authentic hipster experience, so perhaps the critic is expressing a gut-level response against commodification. The idea of having an "authentic" refugee experience might strike some as containing a similar problematic. Serratore might argue that audience members are largely Western citizens with the wherewithal to afford access to the West End, Brooklyn, or San Francisco. For the equivalent of around two to three days' worth of the global median salary (per ticket), audience members can purchase the thrill of *being there*, while salving their consciences by feeling engaged.

A dislocation between the real and the unreal might drive Serratore's sense of distancing. *The Jungle* makes no claim to tell verbatim stories. The writers drew their characters based on their experiences in the camp. The archetypes that emerge correspond to hundreds of people, or composites of the thousands that flowed through Calais. However, by Aristotle's law of mimesis, the migrants in the play transform into "migrants," and the Afghan Café becomes "The Afghan Café." Enclosed in quotations, the sensoria in the play conjure experiences in a physical location that machines have already destroyed, filled with artistic interpretations of people who have since scattered. The play's very intensity highlights disjoint. Yet the ensemble knows from whence it speaks. Although casting changed across venues, the Young Vic production boasted performers from a dozen countries, in addition to England, Wales, and Scotland. Some had been actual residents in the camp. Ammar Haj Ahmad (Safi, the narrator) and Milan Ghobsheh (Omid) had trouble traveling to America for the Brooklyn run because of Donald Trump's "Muslim Ban."

Is this play a misappropriation? I don't believe so. In a television interview, PBS correspondent Jeffrey Brown asks the Joes to explain "why you went, as writers, as artists" to Calais, a question that seems to carry the subtext, "does first-world privilege inflect your activism?" Joe Murphy responds:

> I think the key word there is "artist," and it's probably worth trying to interrogate what that word means. I think an artist is an adventurer, somebody who seeks to try to more deeply understand a situation, who's not necessarily willing to listen at second hand or at third hand often, and wants to explore.
>
> (Murphy and Robertson, interview with Jeffrey Brown, 2019)

Probably all artists have had motorcycle dreams through whichever jungles would transmute them into revolutionaries. The Joes wink that they are wise to this trap. *The Jungle* pokes fun at humanitarian tourism, when a group of Oxbridge idealists, who sound like they have bounded forth from Axminster-carpeted seminar rooms in search of worldly wounds to heal, encounter one another in the camp:

DEREK: Things are going to get really awful. The people here need to organize, politically.
PAULA: Tell me you're from a major NGO.
DEREK: I'm from Reading.
PAULA: Halle-fucking-lujah. Paula.
DEREK: Derek.
SAM: Sam.
BETH: Beth.
NORULLAH: Norullah.
BETH: I think I'm going to build a school.
SAFI: A school?
SAM: Shit. A school is a great idea.
BETH: I think it's the first idea I've ever had.

> *Boxer enters with Helene, playing his banjo and singing. A raucous duet.*
> **Boxer** *and* **Helene**
> 'Now, I'm king of the swingers
> Oh, the Jungle VIP
> I've reached the top and had to stop
> And that's what's bothering me!
> Oh, oobee doo
> I wanna be like you
> I wanna walk like you
> Talk like you
> You'll see it's true
> An ape like me
> Can learn to be human too!'
> *Helene pushes him away in a fit of giggles, and he finds the other volunteers.* ("Three. The Arrival")

The staccato greetings among the aid workers echo the rapid-fire introductions of language groups at the start of the play, although the volunteers, far from home, rejoice in their homogeneity rather than diversity. Paula's exclamation "Halle-fucking-lujah," suggests a moment of relief from the constant inversion of representation—she's tired of being in the minority, despite the fact that she brings the power latent in her Western identity with her into the camp.

The song that Boxer and Helene sing comes from the 1967 animated Disney movie *The Jungle Book*, based on Rudyard Kipling's 1894 cycle of law-of-the-jungle fables by the same name. In the Disney movie, orangutans have kidnapped the boy-child Mowgli and be-bop their wish to act like (white) men before Baloo the Bear rescues him. The catchy Sherman brothers song flirts with racism on two levels. In the Disney adaptation, when the primates turn into a jazz band, the number equates black Americans with apes, and the orangutans' song-and-dance antics mimic a minstrelsy-inflected breakdown. Secondly, the apes' desire to ape the ways of humans recalls rationalizations for Empire, that less-than-human "natives" yearn to be like the Colonials, so Western domination counts as stewardship. By having Boxer and Helene sing a song from the Disney adaption of Kipling's *Jungle Book* in *The Jungle*, a play about the Calais "Jungle," the Joes remind Westerners of the racist resonances that good-doers may inadvertently harbor, for want of self-reflection, whether the characters are in on the joke or not.

The Joes evade misappropriation, while also avoiding sentiments of *noblesse oblige*. Webb relates that the Joes, the Good Chance associates, and the directorial staff consulted with refugees throughout refugee communities in England about the stories they wanted to tell during the workshop process—and *if* they should tell them—in addition to including three refugees in the original cast. "I think that the reason that doesn't ever feel uncomfortable is because we don't go in and go, 'Right, this is our theater, and we're doing this, and we're here to teach you about our lives.' It genuinely is an open space for everyone," Webb relates. For its current project, curators manage Good Chance domes in three-week cycles, always with cultural inclusion at the fore.

Rather, *The Jungle* creates kinesthetic empathy through an exchange of space. The choice of a geodesic dome as a controlling metaphor permeates Good Chance, both on a creative and on an organizational level. Ms. Webb notes that although the company could now afford to hire workers with cranes to erect domes, they continue to rely on human power, since a non-mechanical approach requires coordinating the efforts of thirty to forty people. The task establishes ensemble, while showing that group effort can solve well-defined problems. Six-sided figures organize the company's website. As a logo, the only brand that seems as clear is New York's Circle in the Square Theatre (the logo is a circle in a square). The structures also connect Good Chance to other performance venues, in both space and time. The polyhedral domes recall Elizabethan polygonal theater buildings, such as Shakespeare's twenty-sided Globe (itself originally on the "wrong" side of the Thames River), and the Parisian dome echoes I.M. Pei's iconic triangle-and-rhombus pyramid at the Louvre. Apropos, the architect, author, and scientist Buckminster Fuller (1895–1983) invented geodesic domes in response to *housing*. Because geodesics maximize the ratio of volume-to-surface area, they are the most energy-efficient structure, in addition to their strength, so the geometry of Good Chance's domes as "home" conjoin artistry and mission.

Geodesics are also Platonic forms, a touchstone of Western thought. Geometers have studied regular solids since ancient Greece. Astronomer Johannes Kepler embedded solids as a model for predicting planetary orbits in

Mysterium Cosmographicum (1596) and studied dodecahedrons in *Harmonices Mundi* (1599). In Harmonices Mundi ("The Music of the World") Kepler sought to establish quasi-mystical correspondences among mathematics, music, and planetary orbits. Laban drew from the same well. Geodesics are variants of icosahedrons (twenty-sided figures). A performer could practice Laban's A-scales inside one of the Good Chance domes. Moreover, domes collect information across contexts: radio telescopes, which do not need line-of-sight, often have geodesic protective shells, such as MIT's Haystack Observatory; the secretive National Security Agency's project "Echelon" uses geodesic housing to contain mysterious apparatus; and archaeologists use geometric housing to project digs.[6] In all these ways, the Joes juxtapose patterns of space, creating interference patterns of culturally specific somatics.

Conversely, *The Jungle* brings the refugee camp into theatrical spaces. The theater buildings in which *The Jungle* appears have their own histories of space. The Young Vic (an offshoot of the Old Vic, which itself owns 200 years of history) rests atop the ruins of a bakery, in which a bomb killed fifty-four people who were taking shelter there during World War II, and so refugees haunt that theater as well. Calais echoes this history. In addition to the Siege of Calais in 1558, a climactic moment in the Hundred Years War, the Siege of Calais in 1940 resulted in German supremacy in France, and precipitated the Anglo-French retreat to Dunkirk and narrow escape across the Channel, an itinerary that present-day migrants seek to follow.

The Brooklyn venue was originally the Church of St. Ann and the Holy Trinity, a Gothic Revival structure whose red brick walls, rounded arched windows, and matching doorways flatter the cobblestone street beyond its wide sidewalks. The Brooklyn Bridge disappears just past the theater's roof, with metal webbing and Gothic lancets leading towards Manhattan just over the river, a one-time ethnic suburb of New York, in the European tradition of excluding outsiders. Replace Syrians, other Middle-Easterners, and Africans with Jews and African Americans, and the Brooklyn suburbs held not so different a vantage of racial distance, before gentrification made the borough a hipster paradise. San Francisco's Curran Theatre carries its own spatial resonances. The organization began when a Stanford-educated concert pianist helped the New York-based Shubert family empire establish a West Coast presence, which has different at times housed the San Francisco Opera and San Francisco Light Opera. The building reflects a certain California trait of building history that was never there. Paint makes the ceiling look like wood (an industrialist affectation). Carpeting covers marble in the main lobby. A green curtain hangs in front of a gold one, perhaps a reference to the ore that would bring fertility to an arid land.

For *The Jungle*'s audiences, the immersive strategies scramble Western theatrical conventions. The audience sits on dirt while the performers walk on wood. The audience can eat during the show instead of beforehand. Instead of going to a restaurant before the play, the set is a restaurant. The audience sits on the "stage," while the performers pass along raised aisles.

No front focus exists, and therefore the usual stage directions (stage right, upstage center, etc.) do not apply. The theater space does not divide into "the stage" and "the house"—everything is the house, forcing everyone, again, to ask, "When does a place become a home?" Inside this jumble of spatial patterning, the characters struggle to extricate themselves from a space of disappearance. More accurately, they acknowledge the unlikelihood of making it to England, and therefore to the kind of personhood that asylum bestows. Rather, they try to transform their space of disappearance into a place of belonging. The play takes *that* struggle as its object of dramatization, to make the camp a space of appearance through a transformation of spatial relationships, and so brings audiences, performers, and characters together as people.

Notes

1 Ray Birdwhistell founded kinesics as an academic field. Although culturally problematic at this point, his works (e.g. 1972) remain touchstones.
2 Greatly simplifying, Arendt's public sphere consists of a space of appearance + a common world, a contextualizing *Umwelt* different from nature, and possesses artificiality, spatiality, and public vs. private interests.
3 Elaine Scarry (1985) makes a similar argument, positioning pain as a basis of identity.
4 Baird (1995, pp.305–47) provides a history of the interweaving between philosophy and architecture.
5 Spaces like refugee camps have engendered an entire body of discourse. For the purpose of this argument, camps are another stage of the journey, stuck like a broken gear or a movie stuck on a frame.
6 According to documents that NSA whistle-blower Edward Snowden leaked, a facility in Ft. Mead, Maryland, coordinated a global cell phone spying effort from geodesic "radome" buildings, which contained satellite apparatuses.

References

Abbas, Ackbar. "Building on Disappearance: Hong Kong Architecture and the City." *Public Culture* 6, no. 3 (1994): 441–64.

Arendt, Hannah. *The Human Condition*. Garden City, NY: Doubleday & Co., 1959.

Augé, Marc. *Non-Places: Introduction to an Anthropology of Supermodernity*. Translated by John Howe. London & New York: Verso, 1995.

Baird, George. *The Space of Appearance*. Cambridge, MA & London: The MIT Press, 1995.

Bartenieff, Irmgard. *Body Movement: Coping with the Environment*. New York & London: Routledge, 2002.

Beltrán, Cristina. "Going Public: Hannah Arendt, Immigrant Action, and the Space of Appearance." *Political Theory* 37, no. 5 (2009): 595–622.

Birdwhistell, Ray. *Kinesics and Context: Essays on Body Motion Communication*. New York: Ballantine Books, 1972.

Blumenthal, Ralph. "Truck Driver Found Guilty in Deaths of 19 Illegal Immigrants in Texas in 2003." *The New York Times*, November 5, 2006.

Borren, Marieke. "Towards an Arendtian Politics of In/Visibility: On Stateless Refugees and Undocumented Aliens." *Ethical Perspectives: Journal of the European Ethics Network* 15, no. 2 (2008): 213–37.

Carver, Jordan H. *Spaces of Disappearance: The Architecture of Extraordinary Rendition.* New York: Terreform, 2018.

Cresswell, Tim. *Place: An Introduction.* London: Wiley Blackwell, 2015.

Dikeç, Mustafa. "Beginners and Equals: Political Subjectivity in Arendt and Rancière." *Transactions of the Institute of British Geographers* 38, no. 1 (2013): 78–90.

Gill, A.A. "Table Talk: AA Gill Reviews a Refugee Camp Cafe in Calais's The Jungle." *The Sunday Times*, February 28, 2016.

Gündogdu, Ayten. *Rightlessness in an Age of Rights: Hannah Arendt and the Contemporary Struggles of Migrants.* London & New York: Oxford UP, 2015.

Honig, Bonnie. "Toward an Agonistic Feminism: Hannah Arendt and the Politics of Identity." In *Feminists Theorize the Political*, edited by Judith Butler and Joan W. Scott, 233–54. New York: Routledge, 2013.

Human Rights Watch. *"Like Living in Hell": Police Abuses against Child and Adult Migrants in Calais.* July 25, 2017.

"Hungarian Police Arrest Driver of Lorry That Had 71 Dead Migrants Inside." *The Guardian*, August 28, 2015.

"The Jungle Review—Devastating Yet Uplifting Story of the Migrant Crisis." *The Guardian*, December 17, 2017.

McAlister, Joan Faber. "Natality Vs. Mortality: Gender and Embodiment in Hannah Arendt's Political Philosophy." In *The Functions of Argument and Social Context: Selected Papers from the 16th Biennial Conference on Argumentation*, edited by Dennis Gouran, 300–6. Washington, DC: National Communication Association, 2010.

Murphy, Joe, and Joe Robertson. Interview with Jeffrey Brown. PBS NewsHour, May 13, 2019.

Newlove, Jean, and John Dalby. *Laban for All.* New York & London: Routledge, 2004.

Parekh, Serena. *Refugees and the Ethics of Forced Displacement.* New York & London: Routledge, 2017.

Quine, Oscar. "Calais Jungle Refugees Targeted by Armed Far-Right Militia in Brutal Campaign of Violence." *The Independent*, February 12, 2016.

"Refugees Found in Refrigerated Truck in Bulgaria." Al-Jazeera, November 1, 2015.

Roach, Joseph. *It.* Ann Arbor: University of Michigan Press, 2007.

Scarry, Elaine. *The Body in Pain: The Making and Unmaking of the World.* New York & London: Oxford UP, 1985.

Schwartz, Alexandra. "'The Jungle': A Play That Conjures Life Inside a Refugee Camp." *The New Yorker*, January 3, 2019.

Serratore, Nicole. "Off Broadway Review: 'The Jungle.'" *Variety*, December 9, 2018.

Tambornino, John. "Locating the Body: Corporeality and Politics in Hannah Arendt." *The Journal of Political Philosophy* 7, no. 2 (1999): 172–90.

Thompson, Isobel. "The Jungle: A Reminder that Everyone Deserves a Good Chance." *Vanity Fair*, December 30, 2017.

Warner, Michael. *Publics and Counterpublics.* New York: Zone Books, 2002.

Webb, Naomi. Personal interview with the author, March 4, 2020.

Zerilli, Linda M. G. "The Arendtian Body." In *Feminist Interpretations of Hannah Arendt*, edited by Bonnie Honig, 167–94. University Park, PA: Penn State Press, 2010.

4 Trace forms

The non-hero's journey

Chapter 3 combined Laban's use of space with Hannah Arendt's understanding of the relationship between space and personhood to conduct a reading of *The Jungle*. Chapter 4 continues with space, but from a choreographic perspective, and applies it to refugee storytelling. In particular, the chapter takes refugee performance into narratology by introducing a pair of terms that refer to the perception of body pathways through space: "floor pattern" and "trace forms." The chapter will show how, as refugees travel through space, the afterimages of their trajectories help establish the performative identities they inhabit, as well as the character arcs that stage performances about refugees follow. The chapter begins with an explanation of floor pattern and trace form, which fall under Laban's discussion of the "kinesphere" but have application in dance composition. The chapter then makes a twist on Joseph Campbell's classic notion of the "hero's journey" by defining the "non-hero's journey" as a trace form in which a narrative arc fulfills the structural requirements of a hero's tale, yet the protagonist does not enjoy the accolades of a hero's return.

With the construct of the non-hero's journey in hand, the chapter explores the use of trace forms and floor patterns in two case studies. The first, *Iftu's Story*, involves a close reading of my own solo "text and movement" solo performance as part of a dance festival at the Alvin Ailey studios in New York, in which I use my own simultaneously speaking and dancing body to retrace the journey of an Ethiopian teenager, with all of the problematics such a project entails. The piece used floor pattern and trace forms as a spatial reinforcement for storytelling. The second involves a pair of tales from al-Hakawati, a multi-nation storytelling project that collected traditional folktales Syrian refugees told one another during their refugee flight. The reading shows the striking ways in which refugees became characters in their own myths. Theorizing from these stories, the chapter suggests that the Syrian storytellers inhabit a two-dimensional floor pattern, whereas their tales function as three-dimensional trace form projections of their experiences. In sum, floor pattern and trace forms provide a kinetic way of describing character arc in refugee performance.

The moving body in space

The previous chapter explained how Rudolf von Laban used the word "kinesphere" to describe the space around a human body that observers perceive. To fill in some of these dynamics, and to develop vocabulary for the following discussions, "arcing" refers to when a distal point of the body (like a hand) moves along the surface of the performer's kinesphere. "Spoking" happens when a body part traces a line between two points within the kinesphere, like a spoke that runs from the hub to the rim in a bicycle wheel. When a body locomotes through space, it leaves behind additional traces. As Valerie Preston-Dunlop specifies, a *trace form* refers to "The dancers' pathways tracing shapes in space, as living architecture." "Trace" refers to content, whereas "form" indicates direction in one (linear), two (planar), or three (plastic) dimensions (Preston-Dunlop 1995, p.305). A trace form is the path that a body part takes through space in three (or four) dimensions. If a body could leave a mark through space as it travels, the resulting smear leaves behind a record of its trajectory. Although trace forms travel through all dimensions, within dance composition (the study of choreography), speaking more informally of floor pattern versus trace forms can be helpful. In studio, *floor pattern* refers to the tracings on the ground as an observer would see them from overhead, like the "X"s and "O"s on a coach's chalkboard in athletics.

Floor pattern and trace forms form part of a choreographer's toolbox. Floor patterns afford artistry, like the configurations a marching band makes during a football halftime show, or Hollywood choreographer Busby Berkeley's montages of assembly line, bathing-suit clad, interchangeable women that seemed to suit post-War, patriarchal America. Much of social dance, from line dancing to "figures" in folk dance, *is* floor pattern. Trace forms provide pathways through space, like a baseball pitcher's curveball. A rhythmic gymnast twirling her ribbon on the end of a pole in precise patterns has achieved virtuosity in trace forms, as has a Polynesian dancer who can cause a length of skirt tassel to travel from the floor to his hand with a flick of his hips.

We encounter trace forms and floor patterns in everyday life. Traffic follows (or is supposed to follow) floor patterns. Sports "plays," military "maneuvers," and crowd movement are floor patterns. Control towers guide airplanes to the runway via trace forms. In a game of catch, the ball travels through the air in a parabola. Boxing matches involve flowing heads, bodies, and hands. Above all, trace forms and floor patterns establish relationships. As Ciane Fernandez explains, kinesphere changes in the presence of others (who can co-create kinespheric environments), so by necessity, "[a]n exploration of Kinesphere consists of interacting in public environments," Fernandez writes (2015, p.201). Solo bodies can and do establish pathways in space-time, but when more than one body moves in shared space, they influence one another's kinesphere and their combined trace forms and floor patterns make larger, more complex patterns.

For this reason, floor pattern serves as a useful visual metaphor for story structure. Aristotle's ever-reproduced plotline is a line. Freytag bent Aristotle's curve along three vertices to form a triangle. Screenplays take Aristotle's graph and give it timecodes and/or page numbers for when plot points should occur, much like a Cartesian graph. Experimental storytelling still has a geometry. *Écriture feminine* wends its way in circles. An absurdist play like *Waiting for Godot* displays ebbs and flow, meandering lines, and few sharp angles, but still has a shape, perhaps a spiral that loops back on itself yet still maintains a sense of forwardness, despite its title. "Non-linear" movies prove surprisingly easy to follow, since audiences perceive the underlying XY template and subconsciously rearrange the plot pieces into sequence. Storytellers have employed flashbacks and foreshadowing for as long as they have plied their craft.

Floor pattern is so powerful a structuring device that it creates a story whether one exists or not. During a graduate school dance composition seminar, my friend Julie performed a short solo. Julie traveled around the room, making spirals, level changes, and shape choices around the other class members, who sat in the center of her pathway. She traversed the perimeter of the studio, eventually finishing back where she started. At that point, we launched into a discussion about what Julie's dance meant. Julie started laughing as we interrupted one another in our eagerness to praise the embodiment of *autobiography*, the sense of *journey*, the *change* that her dance represented. At this point Julie was in hysterics. We finally asked her what her piece was "about." She answered, "I was making a map of Texas on the floor." With this caveat in mind, the following primordial story structure is a floor pattern that also happens to follow a circle.

Rescuing the hero[1]

"The hero's journey" refers to a narrative structure in which a hero undertakes a quest, overcomes challenges, and returns home triumphant and transformed. Like refugees and dancers, heroes are bodies in motion. Refugees resemble heroes in that both are unwilling protagonists who obey a call, undertake a journey, confront both internal and external obstacles, and grow as a result of their journey. However, refugees do not enjoy the hero's triumphant return. Heroes enjoy the status of hero, whereas reactionary forces vilify refugees as pollution. Why? What accounts for this difference?

The hero's journey has become the organizing spine for movies, novels, and other entertainments. Joseph Campbell established the definitive template for the hero's journey in *The Hero with a Thousand Faces* (2008 [1949]), in part based on work by previous thinkers. For example, Otto Rank, one of Freud's students, noted the "intimacy" between dream and myth, and argued that hero journeys lend themselves to psychoanalytic interpretation. Rank felt that myths function as "mass dreams" of the collective consciousness from which they spring (2004 [1922], p.6). Anthropologist Lord Raglan felt that because heroes tend to be royal, hero myths must emerge from ritual drama. Raglan

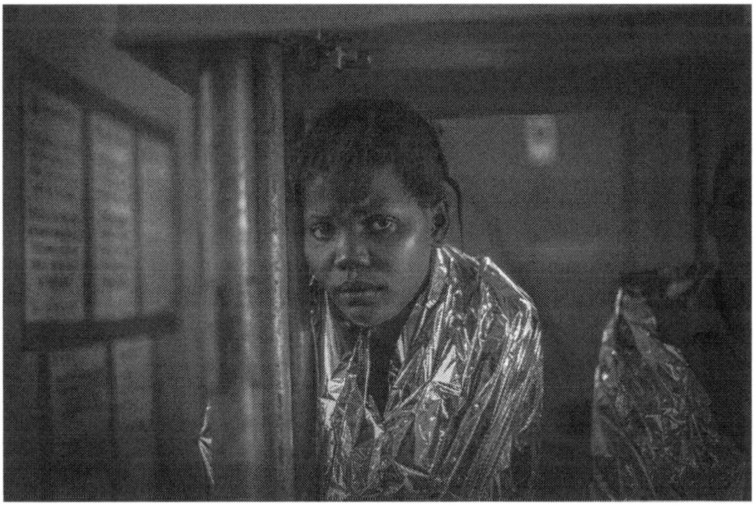

Figure 4.1 A West African woman aboard the refugee rescue ship the *Vos Hestia* moments after being rescued from an overcrowded vessel launched from the Libyan coastal town of Zabratha. International waters, the Mediterranean. Photo © Louis Leeson.

suggested that so-called "monomyths" started when kings, chiefs, or their actor-priests played the hero's role in semi-sacred enactments, for the good of their communities (see especially Raglan 2003, chapter XXV, "The Royal Hero"). Taking a functional analysis, Vladimir Propp identified thirty-one elements of the hero myth. For example, heroes always leave home (Element XI). Also, some type of ordeal "prepares the way for his receiving either a magical agent or helper" (Element XII) (Propp 2003 [1968], pp.39–40). In these systems, the journey of the hero is a psychic voyage, a royal prerogative/shamanic ritual, or a folkloric template. Subsequent interpretations have extended the idea of a hero "monomyth."[2]

Nevertheless, Joseph Campbell's *The Hero with a Thousand Faces* has proven the most influential guide. Campbell, a comparative literature scholar, set out the hero's journey as a composite blueprint, which he calls "the destiny of Everyman" (Campbell 2008, p.28). By using the word "Everyman," Campbell indicates universality rather than seeking to imply that heroes are in some way "of the people"—for Campbell, they are not. Not every tale takes all elements of the hero myth, any more than diners order every item on a menu. In its totality, Campbell's hero journey divides into three sections, with substructure within each triad. In the first stage, which Campbell calls "separation" or "departure," the hero receives a call—some kind of sign that he is, in fact, a hero—refuses this call, receives aid, and then crosses into darkness. In the "trials and victories of initiation," the hero encounters the dangerousness of the gods, regains the bliss of infancy, relives the agony of Oedipus, atones with a father-like character, undergoes an apotheosis into divinity, and receives a magical gift. In the final part of the cycle, the hero faces resistance to return, effects a magic escape, receives assistance in a second escape, returns to the normal world, achieves mastery of two worlds, and is finally able to live in peace (Campbell 2008, pp.28–9). In simpler terms, the hero's journey involves undertaking a physical journey following a break in normalcy, making friends along the way, overcoming external and internal challenges, and returning home. *The Hero with a Thousand Faces* has become an organizing system for crafting stories, in addition to understanding myth.[3]

Virtually all movies involve a main character who leaves following a break in stasis, confronts inner and outer challenges, and returns victorious. In the *Wizard of Oz* (1939), a tornado takes Dorothy (Judy Garland) away from Kansas to the Land of Oz, where she makes friends, defeats the Wicked Witch of the West, and makes up for a missed balloon by clicking her ruby heels together. In the sci-fi thriller *The Matrix* (1999), Neo (Keanu Reeves) moves his body for the first time once Morpheus (Laurence Fishburne) frees him from a water tank (machines have imprisoned humans in virtual reality and are using their bodies to make electricity). Neo takes a pill and slides down a rabbit-hole, defeats Agent Smith (Hugo Weaving), and eventually accepts his role as *The One* (in the final scene, Neo is back in the Matrix, but flying this time). In the *Harry Potter* series (2001–9), Harry (Daniel Radcliffe) takes a magical train to Hogwarts with his friends Ron (Rupert Grint) and Hermione (Emma Watson) at the start of each year, accrues knowledge and power while breaking school rules, and goes home for summer vacation to await the next nefarious step of the vile wizard Voldemort. In each of these examples, the hero undergoes a transposition to an unknown place, filled with danger and adventure, prevails, and then goes home.

Campbell popularized myth not only within literary criticism but among the general public, with successful projects such as his PBS television series in the late 1980s, *The Power of Myth*. Nevertheless, Campbell's work lends itself to criticism. As Robert Segal notes, Campbell is "an uncompromising world ecumenist," and "lopsidedly universalistic" (1999, pp.135, 140). Although theorists attempt to draw generalities from instances, Segal notes that Campbell, "in his search for similarities … brazenly ignores lingering differences" (p.140). In a period of the scholarly pendulum that seeks to include silent voices, restore lost power, and debunk universal narratives, Campbell's Ur-theory has fared about as one might expect. Elleke Boehmer, to take one of many examples of feminist critique of Campbell, shows how the male-hero monomyth perpetuates patriarchal power in postcolonial Africa. She writes, "Narratives … give form to and legitimate the process of postcolonial and national coming-into-being. Stories codify national reality and space, and allow emergent national identities to be performed" (2005, p.66). By creating a "syntax" of leadership biography, only those (men) whose praise-songs include treks from the countryside to the city may become presidents and prime ministers, Boehmer argues. Whereas the motherland is female, her steward is male.

For all its gendered, colonial, and probably racial problems, let us assume that the hero myth drives many stories. Let us therefore explore its null-inverse, the refugee that undertakes a hero's journey without accompanying paeans. At risk of universalizing the "non-hero," or flattening refugee experiences into a victim trope, many displaced persons do answer the summons to journey, overcome challenges, and achieve self-discoveries, yet receive none of the hero's accolades at the end of their quests. I speak with Louis Leeson, a photojournalist who covers the refugee crisis. Leeson gives an eloquent rendition of a refugee journey that typifies one category of refugee arc, so his summary merits quoting at length:

> The stories were not dissimilar. She [the woman in Figure 4.1] would have traveled years from somewhere like Sierra Leone or Senegal. She would had to have gone through Mali and Niger, through the desert, at each of these points having to wait for months to find enough money or to find the correct network of people smugglers who will often abuse these people, steal their money, ring their families to extort more money. So, just to have gotten from wherever her hometown might have been and to have gotten to that port in Sabratha in Libya, that journey alone would have taken years.
>
> And, harsh as those conditions are in the [rescue] boat, they will be the first scenario in which they would have been given any sort of human care and attention. Along that journey, it's just exploitation, the whole way through. And when you get on board that ship, it's the first time for a lot of people they can actually breathe, and cramped as the conditions are, people are there to care for them, and for their human rights …
>
> And what makes it doubly hard in those situations is they think—those people on board those ships—think they are crossing the sea to a land that's going to welcome with open arms, and the awful reality back then, as it is now, is that it's probably no worse time to be a refugee in Europe. The attitudes of the politicians, much of our electorates are turned against them. So, it might be the first bit of human kindness they receive, and then the forty-eight hours that it takes to travel from Libya to the southern coast of Italy, it might be the only bit they get, because once they get out, they're straight into a detention center. Often those detention centers are run by gangs themselves. Italy has a very questionable way of allocating the spaces that become detention centers. And a lot of those people end up on the streets selling drugs, or selling their bodies. The very best most people can expect is to get a very low-paid job somewhere, and not many of them manage that. So, it's very difficult.
>
> (Leeson 2020)

In Campbell's monomyth, the idealized hero is a white man who goes somewhere, resolves inner demons, beats the bad guy, and gets the girl. Fade to black.

Except when he isn't, and he doesn't …

Iftu's Story

In October 2019, I presented *Iftu's Story*, a seven-minute "text and movement" solo as part of the American Dance Guild Festival at the Alvin Ailey Citigroup Theater in New York. The festival theme, "Shaping the Now—Dance in Uncertain Times," foregrounded works that broached the political. The Guild itself (a dance education association) gave lifetime achievement awards to dance educator Jody Gottfried Arnhold, modern dance pioneer Gus Solomons, Jr., and African choreographer and director Abdel R. Salaam. My solo involved me speaking a first-person account of a fifteen-year-old Ethiopian refugee, named Iftu, while dancing. The premise of the work raises issues of translation and appropriation, though the audience received the work with enthusiasm. The case study provides a way of fleshing out the idea of a "non-hero's journey," based on floor pattern and trace form, while highlighting some of the ethics in trying to perform in the place of an "other." In particular, the work exemplifies a problem in kinesthetic empathy that I call "dancing with an accent," or to what degree a person can embody the movements of another.

"Text and movement" is a sub-genre of performance in which one or more people speak on stage while dancing. Greek drama followed this pattern, and musical theater involves the blending of acting, dancing, and singing, the so-called "triple threat." Although modern dance occasionally incorporates spoken text, relatively few practitioners work in text and movement as an evening-length solo form; examples include some of Bill T. Jones' work, as well as that of New York-based Claire Porter and Ara Fitzgerald. My explorations with evening-length work include *The Erl King* (2003), an original piece in which I investigated Eurasian mythology, military history, and German Romanticism to create a character piece about the ghost of a World War I German cavalry officer, based on Goethe's classic ghost poem "Erlkönig." *K.Lear* (2007), involved playing Act III of Shakespeare's *King Lear* (the "storm scene") in its entirety while dancing in a straitjacket. I gave each of the characters a distinctive dialect and movement quality and interpreted them as personalities batting for psychic control. *Beowulf is Min Nama …* (2009) required two years to learn Old English, master Anglo-Saxon poetics, assimilate Medieval English social history, and prepare a modern English translation of the last third of the Beowulf epic for supertitle projections for an eighty-minute recitation of 600 lines of the epic in its original dialect while dancing. As well as providing the satisfaction of achieving performance challenges, these projects allowed me to explore how movement and speech can interweave, at times supporting, contrasting, or operating independently of one another.

In this account, fifteen-year-old "Iftu Omar" (a pseudonym) relates his flight from Ethiopia to the United Nations High Commissioner for Refugees ("Iftu Omar's Journey" n.d.) An ordeal, Omar's experience fulfills the formal requirements of Campbell's hero template. I will signpost Campbell's categories in the following summary, as a rhetorical strategy *ad absurdum* in service to the questioning of the hero monomyth that follows. In Aristotelean fashion, Omar begins his account late into his story, "My nightmare began when I arrived in Obock, Djibouti." A port city on the Gulf of Aden, Djibouti is about 900 kilometers from Addis Ababa, a significant journey in itself. Of the given circumstances, Omar only says that he left home following his father's murder (*The Call*). He had arranged to meet with smugglers in Djibouti who would help him across the Gulf into Yemen. Upon arriving in Obock, Omar made contact (*Receives Aid*), and the smuggler took him to "others like me,"— which is to say, other refugees heading towards Yemen. "In total we were 57. Among us were one woman and two children." Omar states that, "naively," he felt that his impression of the smugglers' small boat was wrong, and that they would all fit aboard.

To put fifty-seven in a boat that could fit "twenty to thirty," the smugglers made the passengers sit in such a way as "to save space." Omar sat in a squat position, weight forward, his legs pressed against his chest (*Bliss of Infancy*), with horrific echoes of the Middle Passage. Omar heard the engine turn on, and then off. The smuggler shouted, "You have to stay here," and jumped overboard (*Dangerousness of the Gods*). At this point, Omar began to fear. Numb, starved for air, and lacking food and water, Omar and the others stayed in the boat overnight (*Crossing into Darkness*). When the smuggler returned with another man and another boat, they did something unexpected (one of many Aristotelean reversals in the story): "They pulled our boat back to Djibouti's shore." After two days on the beach with no food or water, Omar began to understand the stakes of his journey: "I was afraid. I was at an unknown place with unknown people, and I did not know for how long I would remain here." He also began to suffer the privations of vision quest: "I was unable to carry my own weight. I was exhausted" (*Apotheosis into Divinity*). The smugglers turned out to be human traffickers. They took Omar to another location by truck. After they had tortured him for fifteen days, Omar gave them his mother's cell phone number. She paid a ransom (*Magical Gift*) and they released him into the wilderness (*Magic Escape*). Along with three others, Omar trekked through a desert, until he stumbled upon a mosque (*Second Escape*). After three days, Omar relocated to a refugee center (*Resistance to Return*). At the time of his narrative, he was awaiting status determination: "I am recovering from my journey. I am looking towards a better future, free from fear and persecution." Omar's story ends at this point.

The Iftu Omar piece offers insights into trace forms. Structurally, Omar's first-person narrative burgeons with hero tropes. A teenager, Omar sets out at the right age for a coming-of-age quest. Heroes may traverse any medium, but the sea evokes classical poems like the *Iliad*, the *Odyssey*, or Christ's journeys by boat with his disciples. Above all, Omar's journey is episodic, pulsing between motion and stasis. His experience is fluid, but locations function as "states of exception," to use Giorgio Agamben's term (Agamben 2005). By constraining the movement of Omar and the other refugees, the smugglers make the dock, the ship, and the beach bubbles of power that lend a sense of semi-permanence for those within them. Omar had to wait on the beach, wait in a boat on the water in a contorted/fetal position, and then wait on the beach again, with dangerous passages in between each stage, like Odysseus's adventures. The appearance of the mosque after a trek through the desert seems a *deus ex machina*, or a story from the Torah, New Testament, or the Qur'an.

Significantly, Omar's story finishes with him waiting in a refugee camp, with no possibility of physical or narrative motion, even though Campbell's cycle is not complete. A refugee camp is a way station, a shadow of Utopia (lit. "no-place"). In his classic study of performance in a Laotian camp, Dwight Conquergood notes that "Refugee camps are liminal zones where people displaced by trauma and crisis—usually war or famine—must try to regroup and salvage what is left of their lives," or, more concisely, "Their world has been shattered" (1988, p.180). The sense of un-place and un-identity would seem to go hand in hand. Speaking in terms of camps, Adam Ramadan notes: "Refugee status is an embodiment of … liminal temporality, not a normal life to be lived but an enduring struggle for survival and return to a time and place of meaning" (2013, p.73). As Ramadan observes, refugees have slipped not just out of political and geographical space but also out of time. Omar did not get a hero's journey but dropped out of the song.

On a choreographic level, I made use of floor pattern to chart Omar's non-hero's journey. Following the advice of text and movement specialist Claire Porter, who was gracious in watching a rehearsal run of the piece, I sharpened stage location. As a prelude, I made looping, space-consuming floor patterns that took up the entire stage space, signifying an omniscient narrator voice. I opened with, "Normally, we associate movement with joy" and went on to explain essentially the same concept of "involuntary motion" as in this book. I stopped downstage left to talk about Iftu. Indulging in a Brechtian moment, I allowed the audience to watch me become the boy by turning to face upstage and walking from the far upstage left to right. Putting on a knit hat in this moment, as well as a light cue from a "special" (i.e. a follow-spot) to heavy sidelight and the start of music (ambient port sounds), reinforced the work that floor pattern did to shift into the middle of the dance. The dance concluded with me returning to the downstage left "narrator's place" (and also taking off my hat, a shift in light cue, and the end of the music), and finished telling the story as myself—explaining Iftu's torture, his mother's payment of the ransom, and his indeterminate status.

The middle section constituted me as Omar, telling his story. Use of stage space matched shifts in setting. As Omar, I traveled to downstage right and pointed offstage to "put" the smuggler's docked boat there. For the sections

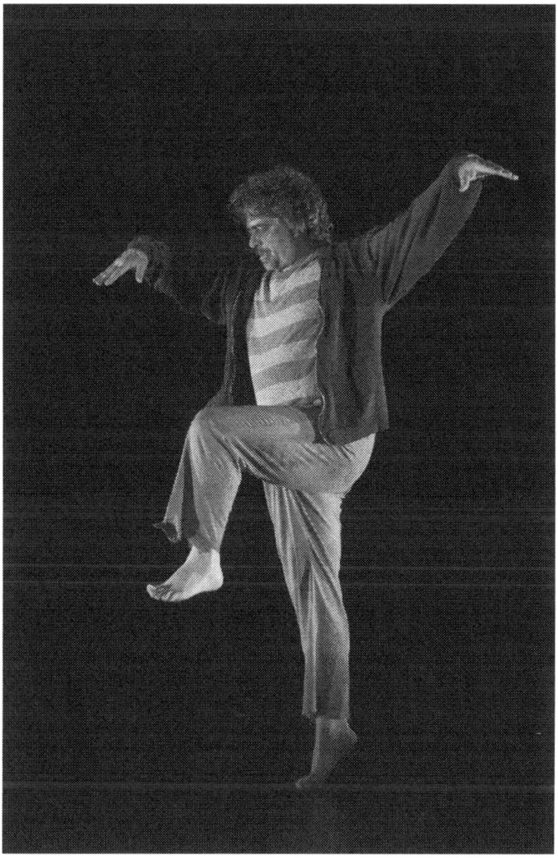

Figure 4.2 The author at American Dance Guild Festival at Ailey Citigroup Theatre, New York City. Photo © Yi-Chun Wu.

with Omar waiting on the boat offshore, I performed right of center stage. When the boat started moving towards open sea, I stamped my feet to imitate the boat engine, and traveled from stage right to left. Later, I gave ocean waves a rapid zig-zag pattern that traversed the entire stage. I indicated the sole woman passenger's fear of getting lost at sea, and therefore her decision to leave the ship, by rushing back and forth to points along the stage perimeter, using moments of suspension at each change of direction.

Whereas I relied on floor pattern to support shifts in narrative voice and changes of location within the story, I used trace forms to interweave my commentary with the given text, and also to help mediate an oscillation between literalism and abstraction. Some trace forms reinforced realism. For example, as I spoke Omar's opening lines, "My nightmare began when I arrived in Obock, Djibouti," I traced a line with my outstretched hand from house right to house left, with a far visual distance, leaving behind a horizontal arc. Likewise, when the boat engines started, I executed a jump from two feet to two feet, stamping my soles on the ground, mimicking the sound and motion of pistons. At other times, I leaned into abstractions. As a motif for "smuggler," I made a snaking motion, starting with a strong ("impulse") movement initiation at the head and allowing the curve to travel down my spine, one vertebra at a time ("sequential" movement). I hoped that the afterimage of the sinewy gesture would convey a sense of slipperiness in the unnamed smuggler character, who turned out to be party to a successful plot to kidnap Omar for ransom.

I finished the piece by opening up the floor pattern, echoing the introduction's pathways, while saying, "So, those of us who have the freedom to move, yet all too often remain still, have the moral obligation to open our hearts to those who would be still but yet are forced to move ..." I then took a slow walk backward from downstage left to upstage left, while completing the line, "... otherwise, we will have truly built a 'Wall,'" and waited for the lights to fade. The reference to Donald Trump's call for a physical border to keep out racialized others across the US–Mexican border drew an audible gasp from the audience, which they followed with sustained cheers and applause. Having found the piece emotionally intense, strangers across race, age, and gender later embraced me in the lobby. I had a sense that the audience was "with" me at every moment of the dance, and attribute the clarifying the narrative to floor pattern, which allowed them to "follow" my performance.

I wish that I could have found Omar, whoever and wherever he is. The United Nations High Commissioner for Refugees (UNHCR) considers *status determination* to be "the legal or administrative process by which governments or UNHCR determine whether a person seeking international protection is considered a refugee under international, regional or national law" ("Refugee Status Determination" n.d.). Omar's movements ended with the end of his story, as far as I know. Waiting in a camp, he is not an Ethiopian national, or an "internally displaced person" (a refugee within his national borders), or a victim of trafficking, or even a "refugee." The Omar at the end of the story is still waiting for international bureaucracies to tell him what he is. "Iftu Omar" is not even the speaker's real name. The UNHCR page footnotes, "***Name changed for protection reasons**" (bold in original). Or, at least it did, as Omar's story no longer appears on the UNHCR webpage at all. When clicking on the link in my browser as I edit this chapter, an error message appears: "This site can't be reached." I can't help but marvel at the unintended aptness of these words. Omar has vanished again. The non-hero does not return home, does not enjoy accolades, and does not reintegrate into society. Omar's destination, along with his identity, stays out of reach. The last third of Campbell's hero's journey remains unfulfilled.

Perhaps unidirectionality disqualifies Omar from hero status. A refugee flight is a linear (though not necessarily straight) floor pattern, whereas a hero's journey is circular (e.g., *The Hobbit, or There and Back Again*). ABA patterns seem heightened. For example, all able-bodied adult Muslims must undertake the *Hajj* ("to intend to journey") once in their lifetimes. However, Hajjis do not remain in Mecca. Generally, they go home. A pilgrimage differs from an exodus in having a second half. There's no place like home. For the audience, the hero's return ends the story, and the story has to end for the everyday world to resume. Once heroes cross the threshold back into their own worlds, the listeners can reenter theirs. Campbell writes that the hero's shift back into society links into larger cycles. The returning protagonist's reintegration into society "is indispensable to the continuous circulation of spiritual energy" (Campbell 2008, p.29). Repatriation must occur, lest the narrative remain in dreamtime. Familiarity creates a sense of safety ("tell it again …" says the child, which isn't possible if the story never concludes). In Victor Turner's understanding of liminality as a break, Omar has dropped through the crack into a pit. He has sailed over the edge of the world.

Moreover, whose story is Omar's? How can a middle-aged, American, white academic play "Iftu Omar," without his knowledge, in an ethically responsible way? To take one of many identity factors at stake (coloniality, age, social class, etc.), E. Patrick Johnson claims that representations of blackness intertwines with appropriation. Johnson writes that "blackness is not always self-constituting," and that "'blackness' does not belong to any one individual or group. Rather, individuals or groups appropriate this complex and nuanced racial signifier to circumscribe its boundaries or to exclude other individuals or groups" (2003, pp.2–3). My impersonation of a black African youth might seem problematic, but so is my assemblage of whiteness, which, as a member of American society, I necessarily perform as "not-black." Similar figure/ground binaries follow for the rest of Omar's identity factors.

Beyond these problematics, finding my truths in Omar's story raises a larger somatic concern. To echo Chapter 2's discussion of Ai Weiwei's enactment of Alan Kurdi, how much can I "get" someone else's embodiment? As a dancer, I want to believe that movement is universal, that people can connect through kinesthetic empathy. As an actor, I know that I can play characters with differing given circumstances. Actors have to be able to impersonate, otherwise acting could not exist. Yet I have doubts. I can learn the steps in West African dance technique, for instance, yet I will not have grown up in a West African language culture. Nuances of food, family, history, spirituality, climate, pace of life, and countless intangible factors escape my history. In the same way that non-native speakers speak with an accent, I feel that non-native bodies will always "dance with an accent." In a dance history seminar, I showed my class a video of a woman who we read as Caucasian performing *bharatanatyma*, or Indian classical dance/drama, in full costume and stage conditions. Her performance demonstrates mastery of the steps and rhythms, but something about the patterning of her spine and turns screams "ballet training" to us. Her facial performance does not quite have the nuances that the form demands. She dances with an accent.

I can follow Omar's steps, so to speak, but probably not the way that he steps. The last I saw of Omar was a newspaper article with an image of him and his mother, presumably after his return. They stand in a relaxed half-embrace. He is wearing a jacket. Both glowing, they seem happy, despite Omar's tribulations. I remember resisting the urge to take away the "grass is always greener" or "there's no place like home" homily that the photo appeared to suggest. Like the UNHCR story, the image appears to have vanished from cyberspace as well, or perhaps I need to take better notes. Either way, Omar's path, which is to say his floor pattern, diverged from mine.

Al-Hakawati

The following two case studies come from a storytelling project that emerged from the horror of civil war in Syria. A brief history: the "Arab Spring" wave of anti-government movements in the early 2000s reached Syria relatively late. In March 2011, a group of fifteen adolescents, aged ten to fifteen, spray-painted slogans like "Freedom," "Down with the regime," and "Next it's your turn, doctor!" (a reference to Syrian leader, Bashar al-Assad's pre-political profession) on a high school wall in Daraa, a small town near the Jordanian border. Police arrested, held, and tortured the boys. Bashar al-Assad responded to subsequent outrage in Daraa, Aleppo, and Damascus with violence, which solidified opposition to his government. During 2012, rebel factions took control over northern cities like Aleppo, plunging the country into chaos.

In 2013, outside fighters entered the fray, including Iranian-backed Hezbollah and the Islamic Revolutionary Guard Corps. In the ensuing fracas, ISIS declared a caliphate with its headquarters in Raqaa, on the northeast bank of the Euphrates River, and eventually took control over about one-third of the country. ISIS's entrée, in turn, triggered US intervention in its "War on Terror," but Syria's growing humanitarian catastrophe could not rouse an increasingly nativist America. At the same time, Russia, a long-time ally of al-Assad, intervened, taking the view that reestablishing state control was the only way to end the violence. Israel also mounted periodic attacks at weapons headed towards the Palestinian territories, and with so many players, the fact that regional war did not erupt seems miraculous. During 2016–18, allied forces steadily pushed back ISIS, while al-Assad's forces, with support in the form of Russian air strikes, pushed back the rebels. By the end of 2018, some semblance of *status quo ante* settled, with President Trump declaring, with his usual graciousness, "We have defeated ISIS in Syria, my only reason for being there during the Trump Presidency" (Donald J. Trump, tweet, Dec. 19, 2018). President Trump's baffling deference to Russian interests has allowed Assad's ally to regain control, and therefore some measure of stability, at the cost of human rights abuses.

The costs of the conflict are difficult to hold in one's mind. Death tolls range from 300,000 to 600,000. The UN estimates that the first five years of conflict took 400,000 lives, about 2% of the pre-war population.[4] Somewhere between 7000 and 20,000 children died, and al-Assad (as well as rebel forces) used chemical weapons. One government chemical attack in 2013 killed 1000 civilians ("Attacks on Ghouta" 2013). The war caused hundreds of billions of dollars in physical damage. According to the UN report, the violence sent about half of Syria's population into motion. As of 2018, 13.1 million Syrians remain in need; 5.6 million had crossed the border, mostly to Turkey and Lebanon; 6.6 million are still internally displaced; and almost three million are in difficult-to-reach areas ("Syria Emergency" 2018). Physically, the conflict created a gash in Syria's consciousness that might never heal.

The causes, effects, and lessons of the Syrian catastrophe will provoke debate for decades to come. The following case studies derive from a project that collected folktales Syrian refugees told one another during their flight from the war. Al-Hakawati began with funding from the Swedish Postcode Lottery. The name comes from *al-Halqa*, which translates as "storyteller's circle." This circle is perhaps the original form of theater and the most widespread, the word referring to the shape that audiences spontaneously form around a solo performer in a public place. The principle collaborators included the Arab Education Forum (Jordan), the Arab Resource Center for Popular Arts – Al Jana (Lebanon), Al Balad Theater (Jordan), and Fabula Storytelling (Sweden). Paul Mattar of Al Jana led six Syrian researchers who interfaced with Syrian refugees in Lebanon and Syria. Ethnography entails complicated ethical negotiations in any circumstance, though the researchers found the refugees eager to share their folktales. The age of participants ranged from thirty to fifty, from which the ethnographers concluded, "the older generation no longer tells, and the younger ones no longer listen" (Abu Risha 2015, p.6). Mattar's team collected 250 folktales, a corpus that Mattar winnowed down to fifty-five.

Mattar then turned the project over to member of the Jordanian literati Zulaikha Abu Risha. Risha began by hosting a residency in Amman in 2014, which included storytellers from the Palestinian territories, Lebanon, Syria, and Sweden. Based on how the folktales played in oral performance, Risha curated the collection from fifty-five, thirty-four, twenty-eight, and finally fifteen. At that point, the project produced the collection as the dual-language Arabic and English *Timeless Tales*, with Serene Huleileh translating and Jack Lynch editing. Performers Nimer Salamun and May Skaf recorded the stories, and *Timeless Tales* served as a source text for storytelling performances by Fabula in Sweden, Al Balad in Jordan, and Al Jana in Lebanon.

The project involves multiple levels of transposition: from refugees' telling of traditional folktales, to those a team of ethnographers recorded, to a subset that a team leader selected, to a further distillation by a poet, linguistic translation, and then performance in storytelling festivals for the benefit of audiences who bring their interpretations to the tales, and the inclusion of this case study in the present book. A skeptic could enumerate the problematics of such an undertaking, but I would point out the enthusiasm with which the Syrian refugees shared their stories. Also, sharing folktales honors them, as well as keeping them alive. For the purposes of this study, the project is remarkable in its overlay of the narrative arcs between its characters and audiences. I will later argue that the violence of the war blasted refugee storytellers into the world of their myths. The refugees occupy a two-dimensional floor pattern, whereas their corresponding stories form trace forms in a (at least) three-dimensional story space.

"The Lemon Fruit"

One of the stories involves a lemon. In refugee Samir Amer's rendition, a poor man named Faheem learns that the King has announced that anyone needing a job should come to the palace. Faheem's wife encourages him to go, but Faheem, recalling ancient laws of hospitality, worries that he cannot afford a present for his host. Along the way, he buys a single lemon, which, after some confusion, makes its way to the King's hands. The gift strikes the King: the fruit turns out to be remarkably tasty, but more importantly, the King cannot believe that "a poor needy person should think of bringing a present to a King" (Abu Risha 2015, p.71). The penury of the gift makes the gesture meaningful. The King invites Faheem to table for rice, and insists the peasant should serve the roast turkey. After demure denials, Faheem divides the main dish in the following way: he gives the King the turkey's head, the breast to himself, the wings on the King's children's plates, the legs on the plates of the King's advisors, and the back on the plate of the King's wife. Following the meal, the King betrays his curiosity and asked how Faheem had made his decisions. Faheem responds,

> Oh wise King! The head is for the head, and you are our elder and decisionmaker.
>
> The breast is for your people, who love you from the bottom of their hearts ... just as I do! The wings are for your children because they make you fly with happiness! Your ministers are your legs because they help you move things around. Your wife is your back, your support, and in your absence she protects you!
>
> (pp.71–2)

Impressed, the King bestows money and gifts upon Faheem, and makes him his counselor.

Later, Faheem's wife tells the wife of their neighbor, the greedy merchant Naeem, about her family's good fortune. Sensing opportunity, Naeem presents himself at court dressed as a peasant and bearing an entire bag of lemons. Once again at table, Naeem gives the King the turkey's breast and serves himself the head, when the sovereign interrupts. Naeem explains, "Oh wise King, I gave you the biggest portion, the breast, and I gave myself the head which doesn't contain anything that's edible." The King explodes,

> I was just testing you and found that you are neither clever nor sharp. Do you think I need food or drink that you give me the bird's breast? What I need in my kingdom are shrewd people who use their heads! You brought me a bag full of lemons—what use do I have for it? It's obvious that you are imitating the one who preceded you [Faheem] but it's clear that you are nowhere near as clever as he is.
>
> (p.73)

As monarch, the king can take whatever he wants, but only the wise can give him their wisdom. He needs neither someone to give him food nor lemons, but cleverness. The King at first threatens to cut off Naeem's head, and probably some versions of the folktale end this way. In this telling, the King sends the greedy merchant from the palace (and, by implication, the kingdom, or at least respectability). Amer's rendition ends with the formula: Faheem "became so rich that neither he nor his children nor his grandchildren would ever want for anything ever again." Happily ever after?

The valence of the protagonist at first seems odd. A refugee audience would be able to relate to Faheem as a man in need. At the same time, Faheem flees from financial need rather than persecution. He needs work, which would seem to play into right-wing tropes of refugees as economic migrants, taking advantage of the naively generous welfare systems in Western nations. Faheem wins a coveted position through his cleverness, yet his aplomb makes his conniving worse (i.e., refugees are cleverer than "we" are). The gossip between Faheem's wife and the wife of the (native) merchant plays on the merchant's greed, and resultant ruin, so the story acts as an object lesson against the dangers of rumor. Yet the tale begins and ends with the intersection of movement and money. Populist leaders draw this connection, so is the resonance for Syrian refugees in the audience of this tale a form of reappropriation of a painful trope?

The story seems to contain a wink in that the initial gift of a lemon comes across as ironic. Faheem's choice of a single fruit touches the king, eliciting an "it's the thought that counts" response. The gift is out of the ordinary, a relic of a past ethos. Its allusion to laws of hospitality in the desert strikes even the characters of the folktale as anachronistic. These codes are antediluvian, which forms the gesture's charm. Who brings a present to a job interview? Naeem overreacts with an entire bag of lemons, because most people in the world of the tale no longer possess fluency in the old codes. He miscues by virtue of his membership in modernity, in addition to avarice.

Naeem also comes across as tone-deaf to what he *should* read as a resonant gesture. Lemon juice appears in recipes across the region, and historically served as a preservative. However, lemons also count for more than garnish. The fruit symbolizes a history of cultivation that goes back to Islam's Golden (like the color of lemons) Age. The love of citrus broke earth across the Arab world in the seventh century. The name of the fruit comes from

Arabic (*laimun*), and as Toby Sonneman notes, lemon trees figured as *sine qua non* elements in palace gardens across Arabian, Persian, and Indic architecture (2012, pp.24–9). As a sign of domesticity, the importance of courtyard garden spaces is difficult to overstate. Latiff and Yaman stress the social function of courtyard gardens in Arabic domestic architecture regionally, and especially in Syria (2017). From citrus groves flanking al-Alhambra to the kitchen garden of a merchant's courtyard, cultivation serves as a sign of the cultivated. We might go as far as saying that planting a lemon tree is tantamount to establishing a home. The refugee relief organization Lemon Tree Trust echoes this theme. Focusing on Middle Eastern refugees, their activities have included: distributing 1250 "Crisis Garden Response Kits" in Iraq and Syria; hosting garden competitions, such as one in the Kurdistan region of Iraq with 1000 entries; graywater reclamation; and distributing over 91,000 trees and plants to the region ("Field Notes" 2018). Beyond the tangible impact the Lemon Tree Trust's activities have, the group emphasizes the mental healing that greenery provides, planting the hope of homes for those who have lost their domiciles to war.

Nevertheless, "The Lemon Fruit" seems pessimistic. A story about an out-of-work commoner who becomes the King's advisor reads like the exception that proves the rule. How many other supplicants passed through the King's door, or did not win an audience? What are the chances of standing in an employment queue in the morning, and through dint of cleverness walking out with multigenerational financial security by the evening? Such tales make for popular stories but tend to conserve power structures. Thus, Charles Dickens' novels of plucky urchins and encounters with the underclass proved wildly popular, but, if anything, reaffirmed England's class distinctions. Similarly, the American myth of a (European) immigrant arriving on Ellis Island with only a suitcase and achieving untold riches through sheer force of brio displayed an unlikely outcome for the vast majority of the tired, poor, huddled masses that shuffled into tenements, and proved a sleeping draught against pressure for vested interests to ameliorate working conditions or raise wages, or for workers to revolt. Faheem cast his lot with the official channels. He worked within the system—following protocol to absurdity—and his gamble paid off. Are Syrian refugee audiences to conclude that they too should wait in line, wait for the hearing date, avoid smugglers, obey the rules, and if they do so, they might be the one in a million that ends up as the King's counselor? A call to undertake Jeffers' bureaucratic performance, a doomed path for the overwhelming majority, would seem to be the inescapable takeaway. The lemon tree casts its shadow from its story space onto the flat world of its storyteller's circle.

"Iben Kanawat and Iben Atil"

The final case study also comes from the *Timeless Tales* collection, though it follows a different trace form as its arc. The story of "Iben Kanawat and Iben Atil" is short enough to include in its entirety:

Iben (the son of) Kanawat met Iben (the son of) Atil on the road between the two villages, and the latter borrowed 1000 liras from the former, promising to repay him as soon as possible. A month passed by and Iben Atil was nowhere to be seen. When Iben Kanawat went to pay him a visit and demanded his 1000 liras, Iben Atil denied ever borrowing that amount. Iben Kanawat then went to Abu Assaf the judge, and told him the story of how he had loaned Iben Atil 1000 liras under a tree between Kanawat and Atil and how the latter had denied ever taking the money! The judge then ordered his bailiff to bring Iben Atil to stand before him, and asked him if he had, in fact, borrowed 1000 liras from Iben Kanawat. This he denied, so the judge asked Iben Kanawat:

Do you remember the exact location where he borrowed the money from you? He answered "yes," so he told him:

Go get me a stone from that place so I can believe you!

He then ordered Iben Atil to wait. It was a hot summer, and the weather that day was scorching, so after an hour had elapsed the judge started pretending to be sleepy, yawning and stretching his arms, and Iben Atil naturally caught the contagion and felt sleepy as well. The judge then suddenly asked him:

Is the place where he went far from here?

And Iben Atil answered:

Not very far!

So you think he would have reached it by now?

Yes, yes, he must have reached it!

And then the judge said:

Go get the 1000 liras, and don't waste any more of my time!

And when Iben Kanawat came back he told the Judge:

Judge … here is the stone!

And the Judge answered:

And here are your 1000 liras, no more and no less.

(pp.12–13)

Although brief, the story contains density. As in "The Lemon Fruit," the story centers around money and therefore the conflict between tropes of economic migrants versus humanitarian perceptions of displaced persons. The story takes care to specify that Iben Kanawat loaned Iben Atil 1000 liras underneath of a tree, "on the road between the two villages." The conflict plays out in a liminal space, a narrative "borderland," in Gloria Anzalduá's term that denotes the experience of straddling two citizenships, having presence in both but full membership in neither (1987). By definition, refugees exist beyond the borders of their homes. In happening on the road between two villages, the story becomes a proxy for refugee flight. A refugee's home is the road, a generic tree the only signpost between villages.

The story of the two Ibens offers additional symbolism. First, the presence of a judge as the arbiter of the tale recalls Alison Jeffers' argument that the refugee system compels asylum seekers to undertake what she calls "bureaucratic performance," a role for which they ordinarily have neither the resources nor the supporting documentation. Second, the inclusion of a stone seems symbolic. Without taking recourse to cultural simplification, stones would seem to mark the boundary between life and death within Islam. Following older Semitic models, early Islamic cultures adopted stoning as a method of capital punishment that fell in line (*hadd*) with religious law (*sharia*), especially for sexual crimes like adultery. Alternatively, the golden Dome of the Rock (Qubbat al-Sakhrah), which rests atop the Judaic Second Temple in Jerusalem, functions as the third holiest site in Islam. Faithful Muslims believe that Allah's prophet Mohammed leaped from the seventh-century mosque's "foundation stone" (*al-Sakhrah al-Musharrafah*) into heaven. Islamic tradition also ascribes the rock as the place where God created Adam, and also where Abraham nearly sacrificed his son, Isaac. The role of rocks (or at least certain rocks) as gateways between the worlds of life and death imparts added weight to the judge's decision regarding the Ibens' financial transaction. Status determination hearings can have similar mortal stakes for refugees, whose verdicts can return supplicants to the threat of death in their home countries or grant them passport to seek a new life elsewhere.

Finally, the story illustrates *inshallah*, an Arabic expression that, like many cultural idioms, proves difficult to translate. Literally "God willing," *inshallah* expresses hope, but also a sense of empathy through shared humility. Since Allah predetermines events, an overdeveloped sense of control over outcomes smacks of arrogance, if not idolatry (Jandt 2010, p.134). God decides the future, not individuals. For example, "Ghaith," a Syrian law student at the University of Damascus who hoped to become a judge, fled Syria in 2014, after witnessing the death of his neighbor from a car bomb. Amid a grueling, multi-nation refugee experience, Ghaith came close to losing the will to live. His brother's wife, Noor, messaged him, "God is generous … All will be well soon, *inshallah*" (Schmidle 2015). Noor offers God's supremacy as a consolation. She does not actually mean "all will be well soon" (although one may always hope), but rather, to adapt a phrase from another context, "what will be will be." An outsider, particularly from a Calvinist/cult-of-the-individual culture, may view *inshallah* (favorably) as stoicism or (cynically) as learned helplessness. Either way, the two Ibens place their fate in the hands of the judge. On the one hand, this act depicts them as law-abiding, and therefore eager to stay within citizenship. At the same time, this transference of power reflects the sense of helplessness that refugees may feel. Refugees have made a leap of faith in fleeing. From that point, their fate is not their own.

The al-Hakawati project involves stories of ancient provenance that relate to the present plight of Syrian refugees. Granted, multiple curators have sifted a pool of tales, bringing filters to their task. Still, the relevance of legend to the present moment lends the sense that the bombs of Damascus have blown the Syrian storytellers into the world of their myths. They have become the characters in their stories. Maybe dimensionality serves as a way to understand this process. The refugee storytellers follow floor pattern paths across the two-dimensional Flatland.[5] They trudge through deserts, sail on ships along the surface of water, ride in vehicles. Meanwhile, their tales are trace forms, higher-dimensional etchings in the collective. During the telling of tales, all involved ascend into multidimensional myth. With nothing left but the possessions they carry, storytellers and story listeners leave behind traces in the floor patterns of time.

Notes

1 Thanks to Andrew Eglinton for this turn of the phrase.
2 Other important works include Calvert Watkins' study of dragon slayers (1995) and Thomas Carlyle's application of hero myth to the idea of "Great Men" in history (1841).
3 Screenwriting books that take Campbell as point of departure abound, such as Booker (2004). Combined with Aristotle's plot structure as set out in the *Poetics*, movies are prescribed to the point where software can suggest page numbers on which plot points should occur.
4 Given the chaotic conditions, estimates vary. Aid organizations may not have access to all areas, rebel groups might inflate numbers, and the Syrian government likely underreports causalities. Whatever the final tally, the destruction is difficult to overstate.
5 For a helpful entrée into the mind-bending subject of hyperdimensionality, see Edwin Abbott Abbott's satirical Victorian novella *Flatland* (1884).

References

Abbott, Edwin Abbott. *Flatland*. London: Seeley & Co., 1884.
Abu Risha, Zulaikha, ed. *Timeless Tales: Folktales Told by Syrian Refugees*. Translated by Serene Huleileh. Revised by Jack Lynch. Stockholm: Cultural Heritage without Borders; Amman: The Arab Education Forum; and Beirut: Al-Jana Center, 2015.
Agamben, Giorgio. *State of Exception*. Translated by Kevin Attell. Chicago & London: University of Chicago Press, 2005.
Anzaldúa, Gloria. *Borderlands: La Frontera*. San Francisco: Aunt Lute Books, 1987.
"Attacks on Ghouta, Analysis of Alleged Use of Chemical Weapons in Syria." *Human Rights Watch*, September 10, 2013.
Boehmer, Elleke. *Stories of Women: Gender and Narrative in the Postcolonial Nation*. Manchester & New York: Manchester UP, 2005.
Booker, Christopher. *The Seven Basic Plots: Why We Tell Stories*. New York: Continuum, 2004.
Campbell, Joseph. *The Hero with a Thousand Faces*, 3rd ed. Novato, CA: New World Library, 2008.
Carlyle, Thomas. *On Heroes, Hero Worship and the Heroic in History*. 1841.
Conquergood, Dwight. "Health Theatre in a Hmong Refugee Camp: Performance, Communication, and Culture," *TDR* 32, no. 3 (1988): 174–208.
Fernandez, Ciane. *The Moving Researcher: Laban/Bartenieff Movement Analysis in Performing Arts Education and Creative Arts Therapies*. London & Philadelphia: Jessica Kingsley Publishers, 2015.
"Field Notes No. 4: Impact Report 2018." *Lemon Tree Trust*, 2018.

"Iftu Omar's Journey, Yemen." United Nations High Commissioner for Refugees (UNHCR), "Stories." web page (defunct), n.d.

Jandt, Fred E. *An Introduction to Intercultural Communication: Identities in a Global Community*. Los Angeles: Sage, 2010.

Johnson, E. Patrick. *Appropriating Blackness: Performance and the Politics of Authenticity*. Durham, NC & London: Duke UP, 2003.

Latiff, Zainab Binti Abdul, and Maheran Binti Mohd Yaman. "In Search of Contemporary Garden Typologies in Moroccan and Syrian Courtyard Gardens." *Advanced Science Letters* 23, no. 7 (2017): 6223–6.

Leeson, Louis. Personal interview with the author, March 11, 2020.

Preston-Dunlop, Valerie. *Dance Words*. London & New York: Routledge, 1995.

Propp, Vladimir. *Morphology of the Folktale*, 2nd ed. Edited by Louis A. Wagner. Translated by Laurence Scott. Austin, TX: University of Austin Press, 2003 [1968].

Raglan, Lord. *The Hero: A Study in Tradition, Myth and Drama*. New York: Mineola, 2003.

Ramadan, Adam. "Spatialising the Refugee Camp." *Transactions of the Institute of British Geographers* 38, no. 1 (2013): 65–77.

Rank, Otto. *The Myth of the Birth of the Hero*. Translated by Gregory C. Richter and E. James Lieberman. Baltimore & London: The Johns Hopkins UP, 2004 [1922].

"Refugee Status Determination." United Nations High Commissioner for Refugees (UNHCR), web page, n.d.

Schmidle, Nicholas. "Ten Borders: One Refugee's Epic Escape from Syria." *The New Yorker*, October 19, 2015.

Segal, Robert A. *Theorizing about Myth*. Amherst: University of Massachusetts Press, 1999.

Sonneman, Toby. *Lemon: A Global History*. London: Reaktion Books, 2012.

"Syria Emergency." United Nations High Commissioner for Refugees (UNHCR), web page, statistics updated April 19, 2018.

Watkins, Calvert. *How to Kill a Dragon: Aspects of Indo-European Poetics*. New York & London: Oxford UP, 1995.

5 Labanotation

Writing and/on/of refugee bodies

This book's final chapter explores writing about the body within the context of refugee politics. How might we write about bodies in involuntary motion in a responsible way? What assumptions does inscribing movement into syllabaries make? Chapter 5 first explores the ways movers record motion. In particular, it introduces Labanotation, a method of documenting movement using a complex symbol system, suggesting that "motif writing" might be a better metaphor than "close reading" for writing about bodies. The chapter then discusses the resonances that occur when bodies wear clothing adorned with text. First, it considers an image of Melania Trump's tour of a detention center in McAllen, Texas, for children of separated families, during which she wore a Zara jacket bearing the words "I really don't care, do U?" Then, it discusses an image of an African refugee sitting on a patrol ship in the harbor of Malta's capital city Valletta, wearing a shirt that said "Being Human." The chapter ends with a call for all of us to choose words with care.

Writing movement

Allied fields in performance have switched places in how they talk about their subjects. As a self-perceived poor stepchild of the academic arts, dance at times takes its cues from older siblings. Following theater's encounter with semiotics at the start of the 1980s, dance studies followed. Susan Leigh Foster's *Reading Dancing* establishes a rubric for parsing the poetics of kinetic information (1986). Although specific to choreography, Foster's matrix applies to any body in space, time, and energy. Taking inspiration from semiotician Charles Sanders Peirce, Foster posits a five-component analytic: a "frame" that demarcates a performance event; a "mode of representation" that connects embodiment to the larger world; a "style" that differentiates the piece within a genre category; the "vocabulary" of movement choices; and a "syntax" that governs the relationships between movements (p.59). As semiotics, these categories filter through individual experiences. Individual spectators "weave together" inter- and intra-textual references to "establish the harmonies, tensions, and counterpoints that give the dance both its meaning and its energy" (p.97). Foster moved on to other subjects in dance and culture, but her early work on dance semiotics remains influential.

Similarly, Mark Franko developed robust argumentation for linkages between bodies and books in his study of Baroque dance notation—manuals that contain floor patterns, musical counts, and descriptions of steps. For Franko, an overhead image of a dance becomes "the page" and the dancer's body "a cipher on the page" (2011, pp.323–4). Franko then reads Baroque dancing bodies as an alphabet, both on and off the dance floor. For Baroque dance masters, dance "figures" (a floor pattern of a dance) figured as a figurative term that linked body, writing, and dance. As Mark Franko notes, "the choreographic figure presented bodies as physical metaphors of written characters of symbolic designs" (Franko 1993, p.15). As Chapter 4 mentioned, manuals could represent dances on the page as sequences of footprints atop musical counts, or as geometric patterns, because dances *were* these shapes, as were bodies. Like most social dances, reels, galliards, gigues, pavanes, and the like traced floor patterns, which lent themselves to lines, curves, and other two-dimensional pathways, as well as social metaphors and, for Franko, semiotic signs.

Foster's and Franko's works have become classics. However, for dance, an embodied art form, to continue maintaining a text-based model seems odd. Granted, connecting dance to dominant academic trends opens access to larger scholarly worlds. For example, dance theorists like Janet Lansdale built cogent arguments for intertextuality as a methodology in movement (e.g., 2010). In general, though, dancers have spilled institutional blood in arguing for the validity of embodied intelligence. The idea of dancers arguing that dance is of-a-text and not of-a-body feels inane. At the same time, theater, (the art of language), and performance studies (a field built on the idea of the speech act) have embraced corporeality. Perhaps Dwight Conquergood's shot across the bow epitomizes performance theorists' cooling *affair d'amour* with language: "Only middle-class academics could blithely assume that all the world is a text because reading and writing are central to their everyday lives" (2002, p.147). Moving towards where dancers have been all along, theater and performance scholars suddenly cannot get enough of embodied cognition.[1]

On a praxis level, systems of dance writing have not gained the same level of recognition as those in other performance genres. In most cases, choreographers make dances for dancers in person, and only in person, with all participants present. Compare this work requirement to classical music, for instance, where instrumentalists learn their parts on their own and then devote a handful of rehearsals (if at all) to putting the sections together. Whereas instrumentalists have sheet music, and theater practitioners can order scripts online, dance has no comparable *widely used* writing-based template. As choreographers know, dancers do not write down their movement even when asked. Rather, they remember astounding amounts of material in their bodies.

Yet dancers have made symbol systems with which to record movement. Again, social dance lent itself to instruction manuals. Dozens of primers proliferated, such as John Playford's *The Dancing Master* (1651), which inscribed English country dances, or Thoinot Arbeau's *Orchesographie* (1589), which did the same for the poses and curtseys of French aristocrats. Following dancing masters' ad hoc means of documentation, the institutionalization of dance led to more sophisticated systems of notation. Louis XIV established the Académie Royale de Dance in 1661, and one of its members, Pierre Beauchamp, devised a notation system. Raoul-Auger Feuillet codified so-called Beauchamp-Feuillet notation in his *Choréographie, ou l'art de d'écreire la danse* (1700). Beauchamp-Feuillet symbols involve arcs and meaning-carrying end-points along vertical bars, and presume a shared movement vocabulary that courtiers would have learned from their tutors

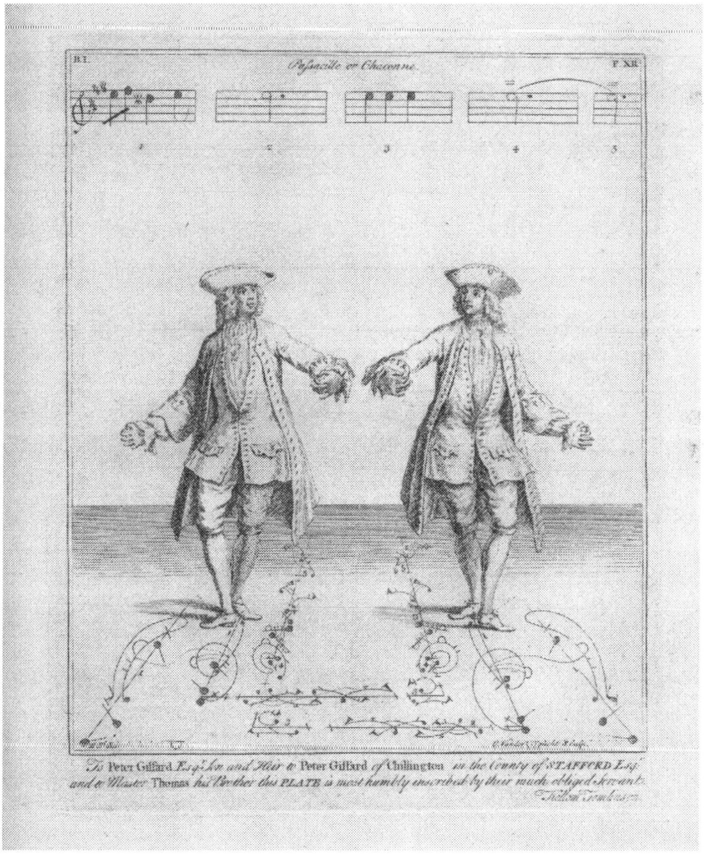

Figure 5.1 "Passacille or Chacone" (1735). Image courtesy of Jerome Robbins Dance Division, The New York Public Library Digital Collections.

(or, in England, Tudors). Joan and Rudolf Benesh created Benesh Movement Notation for the Royal Academy of Dance in London, a horizontal analog to Western sheet music.[2] Other systems exist, and the above examples represent only those that have emerged out of Western movement practice.

Of all codified systems for movement writing, Labanotation carries the most descriptive power. Laban developed an initial symbol system, which his followers filled out. These students, including Ann Hutchinson Guest, founded the Dance Notation Bureau in New York in 1940, which today holds the largest repository of "Labanotated" works in the world. Resembling a musical staff turned vertically, a movement score can log the location, direction, movement quality, and duration of any body part. A notator could, for example, capture the positions of every refugee on board a rescue ship, their facings and points of contact, the positions of their fingers and the direction of their eyes, and then "reconstruct" an identical tableau on another set of bodies. As one would expect, the process is tedious, time-consuming, and expensive, but notating serves as a way to record masterworks, and also copyright them. Labanotation includes "shorthand" methods (e.g., "motif writing" and "effort-shape description") when a notator does not need to render a full-blown, "structured" score.

Labanotation also serves as a visual example of how any method of rendering bodies' movements relies on assumptions. In her standard text on Labanotation, Ann Hutchinson Guest writes, "The particular purposes of the choreographer or the need of the researcher will dictate the form of description and the method of analysis selected" (2005, p.12). Guest means that Labanotation contains a robust suite of tools, much like that which Adobe Creative Suite provides graphic designers. However, Guest's words ring true on a deeper level: the categories with which we parse the world reflect what we expect to see. Labanotation assumes a linear, mechanical view of time. It presupposes that dances should follow the same choreography with each performance (otherwise, why record them?), and that the "dance" exists separately than the performance event—a probably unresolvable philosophical debate to which I will only allude here. We might also add the power dynamics of seeing versus being seen (can we speak of a Foucauldian "choreographic gaze?"). We could also probe the specific assumptions about the choice of tools. In the same way that a Phillips-head screwdriver implies the existence of Phillips-head screws, the presence of a notation symbol for an "action stroke" (one complete action) requires the notator to formulate presumptions as to what constitutes an action.

In other words, we find what we are looking for. If the reader will permit a lighthearted example before turning to difficult case studies, the following flourish ranks on a par with Johnson's stone-kicking refutation of Berkeley, and maybe also forms one of the best critiques of Kantian transcendental schemas. In A.A. Milne's Winnie the Pooh stories, the inhabitants of Pooh Corner become fixated with the idea of finding "heffalumps" after Christopher Robin mentions one in passing. Aside from a sense that such creatures resemble elephants, Pooh is the only character who encounters one, and then only in his imagination. As he falls asleep, he hears a fearsome heffalump say, "Very good honey this, I don't know when I've tasted better" (Milne 2009, p.65). When Pooh and his friends go hunting for heffalumps, they don't know what they look like, but if they look hard enough, they are bound to find one. Academics fall into this same trap (including, and maybe especially, this academic).

Heffalumps or no, competency in Labanotation requires intensive training in graduate-certificate-level programs, plus years of experience. Here, I would like to appropriate the idea of *motif writing* as a heuristic, with which to replace language-biased phrases like "close reading" or "visual poetics." As Guest explains,

> It is not enough just to learn the set structured patterns handed down by teachers. The gist of an action, the idea or motivation behind it, its kinetic "sense," can be recorded in Motif Notation. This form of description has its place not only in certain types of choreography, but also in dance education where freedom for exploration and improvisation on a basic movement idea or theme is desired.
>
> (2005, p.7)

Motif writing is a simpler symbol system method than full-on structure writing, one that practitioners can use in studio as a creative process rather than a mode of documentation. Here, I would like to take the spirit of motif writing, as a tool of analysis that allows others to get the "gist of an action," or a "kinetic 'sense'" of an argument.

In scholarly jargon, "heuristic" often indicates an informal argument. A heuristic is a rough, hasty jot, a way to articulate theory in the same way that a sketch relates to the finished oil painting. However, "heuristic" means "find" or "discover" (from the Greek, εὑρίσκω), which suggests an auto-didactical pedagogy. Although not the most efficient method (from an instructor's perspective), sometimes students have to experiment for themselves in order to learn. Dance studios incorporate heuristics all the time. In most dance classes, the teacher shows a bit of movement, which the students then practice for themselves, knowing that they do not have to make their mastery of the movement perfect on the first try. Effective dance instructors allow students time to master complex movement phrases. At first dancers absorb the general sketch, and then they fill in details with each iteration of the instructor presenting the phrase. The teacher may offer time for class members to try the movement on their own, ask questions, and help one another. In this way, dancers progress from embodying the "gist" of a sequence to being able to perform it "full out." In the same way, a motif writing approach to case studies invites improvisation, rather than a quality of pronouncement. Since we are speaking here of clothing, I would invite the reader to "try on" the following motif ideas—pun intended.

Garments encode their own semiotics. Given their nearness to the body, articles of clothing occupy an ontological position somewhere between the animate and the inanimate, like props (see Sofer 2003). Coming from a body culture perspective, Fred Davis takes a similarly syntactical approach to clothing as Susan Foster does with choreography. Davis attributes to wearable items traits like context dependency, relationships between signifiers and signifieds, vocabulary, syntax, and individual interpretation. He also leaves open the possibility of duality of states, that perhaps clothes "make a clear reference to who we are and wish to be taken as while alternatively or simultaneously evoking an aura that 'merely suggests' more than it can (or intends to) state precisely?" (2013, p.3). For Davis, clothes show others not only who a person is, but who or what they want to be. The adage "dress for success" applies. As a prop, a utilitarian object, and a form of performance, clothing fashions identity.

Whereas clothing communicates, the presence of text on clothing on bodies creates additional reverberations. For example, Cornwell notes that the lowly tee-shirt can function as a "wearable diary," and its ciphers, symbols, and graphics can connote spirituality, life cycle events, trophies, and mating signals (1990). Although sometimes a shirt is just a shirt (we will hear this argument later), clothing can signal desire for membership in groups. A heavy metal tee-shirt functions as a temporary "tie sign," to use Goffman's term, whereas a red hat that spells "MAGA" ("Make America Great Again") might indicate not only a political preference but a polemical stance on race, immigration, and grievance based on a perceived split between "elites" and "lower" cultural classes in America (Goffman 2017, pp.188–238). Or, as Muggleton argues, individuals fashion their identities through a process of mosaic participation in group memberships, which they signal, in part, through fashion choices (2002).

At the same time, we should approach motif writing on clothes on bodies with caution. Foster, Davis, and Cornwell all highlight the context-dependency of "reading" bodies and their accouterments. We should be on the lookout for irony, for example, or the possibility that wearers do not know what they want, or that they do not have singular messages to send out into the world. We all have garments that clash with one another, materially and metaphorically. Also, as with any form of communication, receivers take away differing interpretations based on their own life experiences, expectations, moods, just as senders of information may be more or less conscious of the meanings that they broadcast. Still, as an improvisation, let us assume that words on clothing spell out what the wearer wants to say. Alternatively, if they miscue (and they do), this disconnect can be instructive too. In the following first study, the implications of these assumptions are horrifying, and in the second they are heart-rending.

"I really don't care, do u?"

On May 7, 2018, then-US Attorney General Jeff Sessions announced a change to American immigration policy regarding asylum seekers at the US–Mexican border. US border agents would adopt a "zero-tolerance policy," which included separating children from their families. Homeland Security Secretary Kirstjen Nielsen tweeted, "We do not have a policy of separating families at the border. Period," and also, "This misreporting by [Congressional] Members, press & advocacy groups must stop. It is irresponsible and unproductive" (Sec. Kirstjen Nielsen@SecNielsen, tweet, June 17, 2018). In fact, the administration had begun considering this policy as early as March 2017, and may have been separating children from their parents by October 2017. By the end of May 2018, agents had separated approximately 2000 children, some infants, from their parents, at times keeping them in cages.

The images of boys (the administration did not release images of girls) in detention, juxtaposed with the administration's dissembling, as well as reports of alleged abuse of children in detention centers, raised a firestorm. The administration later admitted to the policy, although a report by the Office of the Inspector General in the US Department of Health and Human Services found that the number of children was closer to 3000, that the policy might have resulted in the detention of thousands more, and that poor record-keeping prior to court-mandated accounting means that the government does not know how many children it separated from their families (Office of Inspector General 2019). The Office of Refugee Settlement processed over 4500 reports of sexual assault against separated children from 2014 to 2018, and admitted to seeing an increase in incidents beginning with the family separation policy (Haag 2019). The revelations of sexual abuse, which additional evidence corroborated, fueled public outrage.[3] Donald Trump signed an executive order ending family separation on June 20, 2018, although government activity on this front remains murky.

On June 21, 2018, First Lady Melania Trump made an unannounced visit to two detention facilities, the Ursula Border Patrol Processing Center and the Upbring New Hope Children's Shelter, in McAllen, Texas. McAllen borders Mexico in the southernmost part of Texas, about an hour's drive west of Brownsville/South Padre Island and the Gulf of Mexico. Ms. Trump herself is an immigrant from Slovenia—and an example of "chain migration" (her parents, Viktor and Amalija Knavs, converted their green cards into US citizenship on August 9, 2018), a means of entry which her husband has demonized, at least for immigrants of color. She seems to have initiated the trip out of concern for the separated children, perhaps wanting to get a view of them for herself. However, departing from Washington, DC, Ms. Trump arrived at Andrews Air Force Base wearing a $39 green Zara jacket with white lettering that said, "I really don't care, do u?" She took off the jacket while on the plane and wore a different one during her tour, but put the Zara coat back on during her return flight to McAllen, where, as journalist Rebecca Jennings noted, the temperature read 81° F (about 27° C) (Jennings 2018). The jacket created a maelstrom. Did the text suggest that the First Lady, speaking for herself or for her husband's administration, did not care about detained children?

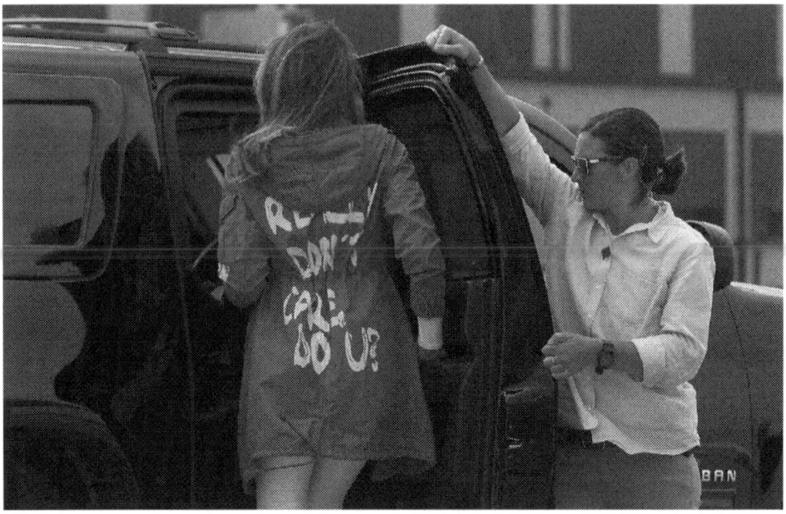

Figure 5.2 US First Lady Melania Trump arrives back at Joint Base Andrews, Washington, DC, from Texas wearing "I really don't care, do U?" jacket. Photo © Kevin Lamarque/Reuters Pictures.

Ms. Trump's response evolved. At first, the First Lady's communications director, Stephanie Grisham, told the press that the jacket possessed no meaning—"There was no hidden message. After today's important visit to Texas, I hope this isn't what the media is going to choose to focus on"—and lobbed out a Twitter hashtag, "#ItsJustAJacket" (Rogers 2018). By the end of the day, Donald Trump had intervened, tweeting, "I really don't care, do u?" written on the back of Melania's jacket, refers to the Fake News Media. Melania has learned how dishonest they are, and she truly no longer cares!" (Donald J. Trump @realDonaldTrump, tweet, June 21, 2018). In a sit-down interview with NBC News on October 13, 2018, Ms. Trump adapted her messaging to match her husband's. She said, "it's obvious I didn't wear the jacket for the children. I wore the jacket to go on the plane and off the plane. And it was for the people and for the left-wing media who are criticizing me. And I wanna show them that I don't care. You could criticize whatever you wanna say, but it will not stop me to do what I feel is right." She meant no subtext by her initial choice, but put it back on when she saw how the media became "obsessed about it" ("Transcript: ABC News" 2018). A victim of the vapidity of the press, she meant the jacket as a riposte to journalists, according to her later comments.

As any performer knows, props and costumes can take on lives of their own once in front of an audience. Despite her former career in fashion, though, Ms. Trump already had accrued a track record of sartorial tone-deafness. In May 2017, the First Lady wore a $51,500 Dolce & Gabbana to the G7

Conference in Sicily, where leaders of the world's seven largest industrialized nations discussed inequality, migration, and hunger. In August 2017, she put on four-inch stiletto Manolo Blahnik BB pumps to visit victims of Hurricane Harvey in Houston. In October 2018, she donned a colonial-style white pith helmet to take a safari in Nairobi, and recreated the ensemble of the Nazi-villain Belloq from *Raiders of the Lost Ark* when she toured Egypt's pyramids. Perhaps these snafus come out of a career of curating photo-shoot themes. Perhaps Ms. Trump adheres to her husband's philosophy that all publicity is good publicity. Maybe she identifies with a Millennial sense of disaffection. In the case of the "I really don't care, do u?" jacket, as the First Lady is a former model, employing a ten-member design team, making a diplomatic foray to the Texas–Mexico border in the midst of the administration's child separation debacle, the contention that no one reflected on optics is either disingenuous or disturbing.

Everything about this photograph calls attention to the Zara jacket's text. Ms. Trump faces away from the camera, about to get into an SUV, which will in turn move her on her journey. We do not see her face, which turns towards the vehicle's interior. One hand rests on the inside of the door. The background is blurry, which helps the eye move from right to left across the frame, following Ms. Trump into the car. A second figure holds the door open while looking at Ms. Trump, inviting us to do the same. The jacket itself is a military-themed woman's garment, US Army green with a high waist and fitted cuffs, which seems like a bizarre conceit since her husband *is* the Commander in Chief of the American armed forces. The frame cuts from the bottom of the jacket down, so the text itself takes up most of the jacket's back. The font mimics brushstrokes, whose informality matches the hip ennui of its message. Ms. Trump's hair spills down around her oversized hood, which in turn blocks the top word "really," further contributing to a sense of casualness.

On a compositional level, the jacket calls attention to a woman's back. Ms. Trump faces away, making her retreat into the car at the moment when the writing on the jacket is on full display. We see no skin except for a small part of her right hand. Clothes, hair, and car envelop the First Lady. While the coat might serve as a metaphor for the bubble in which Ms. Trump enwraps herself, an emphasis on the back body of a celebrity also marks a shift from normal representational focus. The body's front features the organs of sense, secondary sexual characteristics, and the face. The back body remains underexplored, even in art and on stage. One exception to frontedness is Man Ray's photograph *Violin d'Ingres* (1924), which features a seated woman whose nude back reveals violin f-stops. A jibe at nineteenth-century painter Jean-Aguste-Dominique Ingres, who rendered keyhole-perspective, Orientalist scenes of (white) women lounging on one another in Turkish baths, Ray's photograph debunks objectification. If a woman is an instrument, then a player plays her, can tune her, own her, put her back in a case when he is done playing, etc. Especially in live performance, the back often proves an undiscovered country, and the bareness of a woman's back, absent front features, poses a complex pose to parse.[4] The writing on Ms. Trump's back reobjectifies her gender even as it cloaks her skin. Ms. Trump is a placard, a billboard. She literally bears a message.

As Ms. Trump moves towards the car, another woman stands to the right in the frame. She is presumably part of the First Lady's security detail, but lacks the suit, earpiece, and firearm strap of the Secret Service. Rather, she sports an untucked button-down shirt with rolled-up sleeves, hair pulled back into a practical bun, and a sports watch on one wrist with a thick bracelet on the other. Her square hands do not so much hold the car door open for Ms. Trump as grip it, as if gaining purchase to rip the metal off its hinges. She has rings on the middle fingers of each hand and simple stud earrings. Even through her sunglasses, the woman's eyes bore into Ms. Trump's upper back (further calling attention to the jacket's writing). With eyes fixed on her charge, the guard's own back lies exposed. Focus diverted from scanning her surrounds, and a dress shirt that broadcasts a lack of body armor or (obvious) weapon, she plays the part of a living shield.

The two figures provide contrast in gender tropes. Even facing away and wearing a jacket, Ms. Trump transmits the sense of possessing the more fragile features. The guard, facing front, comes across as mesomorphic, casually capable, exuding strength. The guard's hands seem like potential weapons, and although the First Lady's hands are not visible in this image, we might picture them forming a counterpoint. We see none of Ms. Trump's skin, but the guard's forearms, hands, neck, and face are exposed. Ms. Trump walks bundled up in long sleeves and jacket, while the guard has rolled up her sleeves and moved her hair off the back of her neck in the Texas summer sun. Whereas we see the guard's face and not Ms. Trump's, the guard is the anonymous one. She seems to disappear in plain sight. Relaxed yet primed for action should the need arise, she "gives focus" to the First Lady, like a conscientious scene partner. We see the First Lady protected—someone is literally "watching her back"—which makes us watch too, and think of those who are most unprotected and about whom she perhaps does not really care. Ms. Trump claims to have undertaken the trip out of a sense of outrage. Yet, fairly or unfairly, the sum total of these details communicates privilege. One woman lives inside a shell, not even looking at the hands that hold open a door for her. The other resides out in the open, capable, willing to take a bullet. She does seem to care.

What Melania Trump fails to articulate, and why none of this analysis is objectifying, is that the corporeality of public figures becomes public property. As Joseph Roach suggests, celebrities possess two bodies, the "body natural, which decays and dies, and the body cinematic, which does neither" (2007, p.36). On a material level, a jacket is just a jacket. In Texas in late June, you can catch a cold indoors from the air conditioning, as well as on an airplane. That Melania Trump would want a jacket is reasonable. However, the cinematic "Melania Trump" stood in as proxy for Donald Trump's administration. Ms. Trump was not (only) covering her natural body with her jacket, but also wearing the mantel of executive authority. Ms. Trump used her body as a caption. In the context of Mr. Trump's anti-immigrant rhetoric throughout the 2016 campaign, how could the act of bearing that text at a children's detention center *not* read politically?

The jacket incident separated public attention from the children, who were already conspicuous in their absence. To some extent, history has made US administrations wise to the power of images. Eddie Adams' 1968 picture of Vietnamese General Nguyễn Ngọc Loan shooting handcuffed prisoner Nguyễn Văn Lém in the head at point-blank range, or Nick Ut's 1972 photograph of nine-year-old Phan Thị Kim Phúc running naked from her burning village, with napalm roasting her back and emitting a silent, Edvard Munch-like scream, as well as front-page pictures of American coming home in body bags, probably turned public opinion against the Vietnam War more than any policy analysis. Likewise, Alan Diaz's 2000 photograph of six-year-old Elián González, clinging to his uncle in a closet while facing US Immigration agents dressed in battle gear and brandishing tactical firearms, electrified the post-2000 election context in a way reasoned debate never would. Learning from this history, the US government takes pains to control images. Moreover, Donald Trump is a "television" president, more versed in reality TV ratings than policy. The absence of images of children in cement and steel cages, toddlers facing magistrates, or deaths of these children is not accidental.

The US Department of Homeland Security made sure to remove separated children from public view, understanding the visceral recoil such images would engender. The "family" detention centers thus become spaces of disappearance in Carver's sense of physical structures that make people vanish. However, Ms. Trump's visit created a space of disappearance within the media's discourse. They had become virtual children, absent referents of the open question the Zara jacket raised. Is Ms. Trump for or against family separation? Is her husband's administration telling the truth? Does Ms. Trump have influence over her husband's policy? Who is doing the not-caring? Ms. Trump? MAGA voters? We see the back of Ms. Trump's head, so we cannot read her expression. She enters into the darkness of an empty vehicle, and so will vanish from our sight, like the children have. We see images of Ms. Trump on the *runway* (in the sense of both tarmac and modeling show), but exactly zero shots of her inside the facilities with children in cages. Following Ms. Trump's cinematic body, the media obsessed not over frightened children, who had traveled thousands of miles and now did not know where their parents were, but over words on a jacket.

In Chapter 3, Arendt viewed the body as the ultimate form of privacy and therefore antithetical to the political. Yet the body of the First Lady acted as a messenger, bearing text. Furthermore, Ms. Trump's corporeality replaced that of the children in public consciousness. As pundits, celebrities, and politicians chimed in on social media, the children retreated a step further from view, whatever noise their voices would have made drowned out. Opponents of Donald Trump added the jacket to a burgeoning column of grievances, a horrifying capstone to a politics of bigotry, whereas MAGA supporters read the jacket in terms of Mr. Trump's refrain of "fake news." A probably well-intentioned mission to see children in distress, Ms. Trump's visit furthered the disappearance of the migrant children's humanity. Tragically, whatever her feelings, the Zara jacket expressed how millions of Americans, particularly Mr. Trump's political base, did feel about immigrant children.

The separated children represent a disappearing act on at least three levels. They had traveled hundreds of miles, and in some cases thousands, to the US–Mexican border. Then, US officials separated them from their families and put them in cages. Finally, Ms. Trump's appearance sundered their (already hidden) corporeal existence from immigration debates in the United States. Ms. Trump wrote the children out of public existence. These young people exemplify Arendt's paradox of the rightless in need of rights. For Arendt, stateless peoples are humans in essential form, and therefore most in need of protections and least able to achieve them. What happens when those people are invisible children? Is the idea of degree of disempowerment sensible? These beings are: (a) minors, (b) displaced persons, (c) hailed as criminals, (d) invisible, and (e) replaced by an argument over a coat.

At the time of this writing, the following children have died apart from their families, while in US detention centers:

Darlyn Cristabel Cordova-Valle (age 10)
Jakelin Caal Maquin (age 7)
Felipe Gomez Alonzo (age 8)
Juan de León Gutiérrez (age 16)
Wilmer Josué Ramírez Vásquez (age 2)
Carlos Gregorio Hernández Vásquez (age 16)
Mariee Juárez (age 20 months)

Moreover, a US human rights group, Physicians for Human Rights, has issued a report in which the family separation policy, still in effect despite its official termination and having now separated over 5500 children, constitutes a form of torture (Washington 2020).

Yes, we really do care.

"Being Human"

The water between Sliema and Valletta is blue. The baking sun glistens off the Old City's ramparts, which approach along with the chug of the ferry's engine. Malta peels back in layers: European Union leader, Templar redoubt, Arabic outpost, and cradle of civilization. Later that night, I sit at an outdoor café with my daughter (you can enjoy homemade pasta throughout the island) a few days before yet another conference that summer. A man speaks into his cell phone what sounds like Hebrew with an Italian accent. Lines of tattoo-sporting tourists amble down the alley. Crusader castles loom in evening spotlight. An island about 150 kilometers south of Sicily's coast, Malta's ruins go back 6000 years, predating the pyramids of Egypt. A member of the European Union, Malta held the EU's presidency from January to June 2017, and its capital city, Valletta, enjoyed recognition as the European Capital of Culture (ECoC) for 2018 (awarded in 2012).

In a climate similar to that of Greece or Israel, stony hills rise and fall, with Mediterranean vistas never far from view. As an island nation in the middle of the "middle sea," Malta also serves as a point of nexus for refugees who take the gambit of water. The United Nations High Commissioner for Refugees reported in 2018 that there were approximately 10,000 people "of concern" living on the island, the highest per capita population of refugees in any country other than Sweden. Of the 1839 applicants Malta granted protection status in 2017, roughly two-thirds come from Africa (62.7%) and most of the rest from Asia (Martin 2018). These numbers include those who are lucky enough to reach land. The gorgeous waters around the island are a highway of death.

In 2014, Maltese photojournalist Darrin Zammit Lupi served as photographer for the NGO Migrant Offshore Aid Station (MOAS) during rescue operations for refugees caught at sea. At one point, Lupi witnessed the recovery of the bodies of twenty-nine of 600 asylum seekers from Libya on a boat off the shore of Lampedusa, an island scarp midway between Malta and Tunisia. These refugees died of asphyxiation while in the hold of the fishing boat, whereas the smugglers might have stabbed and jettisoned sixty more as the refugees attempted escape from the hold—rescuers tallied 131 missing, including a newborn infant (Lupi 2016).

In July 2014, Lupi positioned himself on a Maritime Squadron Base along with other photojournalists, rather than out on a pier, in anticipation of a boat carrying the recovered bodies of twenty-five asylum seekers. Lupi was cooling his heels, as "it wasn't worth risking leaving our vantage point and then possibly missing the moment when the bodies would start to be brought out. It also gave me a different angle from the norm for pictures of arrivals" (Lupi 2014). When the boat did arrive, Lupi photographed a group of seven refugees sitting on an Armed Forces of Malta (AFM) patrol boat in the squadron's base in one of Valletta's harbors, of a total of eighty-three the Maltese freighter rescued. They all appear to be young black men, looking in different directions, making a complex visual tracing. A man in sunglasses looks forward and down, as well as a middle row of three and another man in sunglasses at the bottom. A man in shirtsleeves looks in the opposite direction, in addition to the focal point of the image: a man in a yellow tee-shirt that reads on the back, "Being Human," as he looks over his left shoulder. The photo almost catches the profile of the figure's face, and an eighth man, also in a yellow shirt, remains mostly hidden behind piping below and slightly to the left. We see the upper torsos of these men only, caught amid the landscape of the ship's pipes, stairs, deck, chains, ropes looped around stanchions, and the seawater at the top of the frame.

The photograph reveals little backstory to the *mise-en-scène*. Do these men know one another? Do they all come from the same place, or even the same

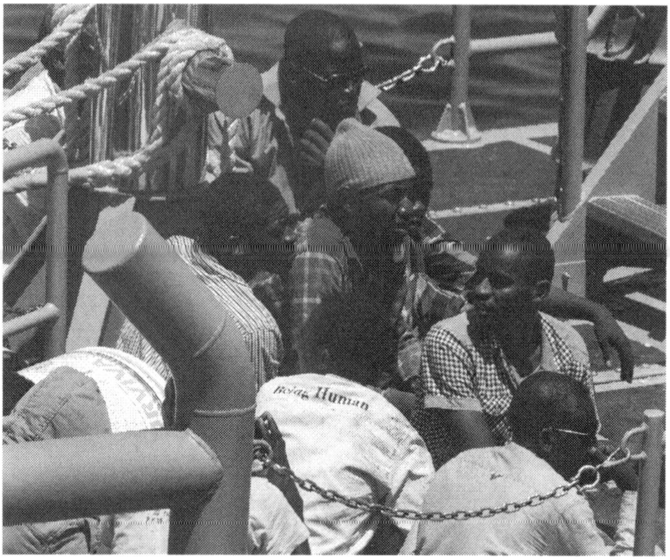

Figure 5.3 "Being Human." African migrants sit on the deck of an Armed Forces of Malta (AFM) patrol boat after arriving at the AFM Maritime Squadron base in Valletta's Marsamxett Harbour, Malta. Photo © Darrin Zammit Lupi.

country? What language(s) do they speak? Did these men know those who died? Where were they intending to go? What did they mean to each other? Should we read anything into the absence of women? Had they formed a space of appearance, before segmentation, duration, and violence robbed them of their humanity? At least in this moment, the men on the boat appear calm, expectant. They look like they are looking around, taking in information. One man rests his chin on his hand, another drapes his arms, his hand limp.

A man in a blue and white thin-striped shirt juts his chin out, but others look out, wear sunglasses, do nothing. "Being Human" clashes against the photo's context, like the shirt's yellow against the other colors of the frame. Being human is the last thing any of these men are doing. Mr. Lupi responds to my email, "With regard to your query, I'm afraid I know nothing about the man you're referring to. The wording on his shirt caught my eye, but that's pretty much about it" (Personal communication, Apr. 3, 2019). Like in so many images, what we see is all we can know of these histories, these journeys. The wording does catch the eye, though. "Being Human" seems like a provocation, or a question, a demand, a complaint, or a thousand other things. Or perhaps it's just a shirt.

This picture's poetics leech humanity. The presence of black bodies compressed on a ship's deck, with chains and tether bounding the frame, cannot help but evoke the Middle Passage. We see this group packed into a small section of the deck. Are there more bodies out of frame on deck? Below in the hold? Boats are spartan, but this nautical landscape looks sere. The ship's struts, spars, and steps sheen with gun-metal. Thick painted pipes end. Rivets lie exposed. Even the seawater with its briny toxins proves inhospitable to human life. Apart from the ropes, the materials around the men are all inorganic. The men array themselves like coral, or perhaps mirror the juxtaposing angles and levels of the ship. They fill in voids on the deck space, and cannot dissemble what they have become: cargo.

Without detracting from the seriousness of the passengers' plight, the arrangement of bodies has strong compositional elements. In particular, all of the men adopt visual foci that extend beyond the frame, and none of them look at the same target. The effect is too panoramic for a stage tableau, more like a sculpture. In Malta's principle harbor, there is much to see. They might be taking in the historic stone walls and garrisons of Valletta on one side of the water, and fashionable neighborhoods, like Sliema, with hotels and nightlife on the other, as well as other boats, docks, and onlookers. Maybe they saw an old artillery bunker from which the locals launch fireworks on saints' days, which in the Catholic calendar is nearly every day. Whatever they notice, the men's multi-focus lends the image a sense of divergence. As refugees, they will disperse. Physically, they form a human mass. Visually, they have already become a diaspora.

The men also seem closed off from one another. The bodies do not evince physical tension, even huddled together (what choice do they have?). The man at the top who rests his chin on his hand bears a resemblance to Rodin's *The Thinker*. His sunglasses hide whatever hints we might glean as to what he might be thinking, as do sunglasses on at least two of the other men. Each man looks like he is pulling into himself, a direction that clashes with the outward force of their eyes, an assemblage of notes that together sound a dissonant chord. The picture suggests a sense of waiting, of playing the part of objects rather than subjects. The figure who lays a languid hand over a bar could be at home watching TV. The Thinker hunkers forward. The man on the left does not notice that the back of his collar is rumpled, but his jutting chin suggests that he is trying to project his presence past the physical limitation of his movement. Their posture of waiting, unable to move, belies the irony that they are moving—first as the boat came in from the open sea, and now rocking back and forth in the harbor water's gentle lapping. A ladder appears on the right that they cannot ascend. Chains on either side block exits from the ship. Maybe they wonder, "What will happen to me next?" For the moment, they have no choices, there are no actions to take.

Colors, shapes, and angles draw the eye to the bottom-center figure, who (like Ms. Trump) faces away from the lens and also bears a message on his back. However, he inhabits the opposite pole of power than the First Lady of the United States. Waiting in a watery cage, his shirt's text, "Being Human" (also like Ms. Trump's garb) arrests the attention with possible ironies. In terms of provenance, the phrase "Being Human" seems to be a meme in Anglophile nations, which may have originated with a television show in England and Canada titled *Being Human*, about a werewolf, vampire, and ghost who live as roommates.[5] Maybe the man is a fan of the show. Maybe he just liked the shirt, or grabbed the first garment he could find. Nevertheless, an activist interpretation feels inevitable, regardless of the wearer's intent. The words (in English) almost require that we read them as a human demanding his right to have rights. Lupi states that by centering his camera on the man with this shirt, he would be "making a small statement of sorts. At times it is good to remember that we are talking about human beings taking dangerous journeys because there are no options to take safer routes" (Lupi 2016). The image's serendipity is remarkable. That this garment, amid dozens of other bodies on one boat in the ocean, would connect with a Reuters photographer had the same chance as a castaway heaving a note into the sea. The man is the note, the ship the bottle.

The expression "Being Human" seems to carry resonance in Malta locally. The Maltese art space Blitz mounted an exhibition of emerging artists around the theme "Being Human" in September 2013. An MP of Malta's Nationalist Party, Charlo' Bonnici, penned an op-ed titled "On Being Human," calling for greater protections for children and other vulnerable members of society, in June 2014 (Bonnici 2014). The Malta Contemporary Art Museum presented "I Am the Body of a Human" by Andrew Birk in October–November 2017. The Maltese Society of Arts featured twenty-four artists in an exhibit titled "Human Matter" (the reviewer titled his essay, "Being Human … the Way Forward") in November 2017 (French 2017). And, American philosopher Eva Kittay presented a talk, "The Moral Significance of Being Human," for the President's Foundation for the Wellbeing of Society, University of Malta, and US Embassy, at the University of Malta in Valletta in May 2018. The Maltese appear to take an enduring interest in the philosophical, aesthetic, and moral aspects of "being human."

On a language level, the expression "Being Human" embraces the ambiguity of English. The shirt does not make an existential claim (*I am Human*), or a statement of emergence (*Becoming Human*), or an imperative (*Be Human!*). A derivative of "to be," the grammar of "being" is slippery. "Being" can be a linking verb (e.g., *she is being paranoid*). On the other hand, it can behave like a gerund (e.g., *I'm just being*), or a post-modifier—a sort of after-adjective (e.g., *the plant was prickly, being a cactus*). Being can also help build passive constructions (e.g., *this article is being written*). "Being Human" seems to defy grammatical category. The phrase hints that "human" is not something intrinsic (in the way that *oranges are orange*), or something that you do (like *riding a bike*), but a kind of a state. "Being Human" has a transience (similar to *being sad, being airborne*). The usage seems active, but it does not suggest specific actions, emotions, or qualities. The phrase sounds definitional, but of what? Above all, "Being Human" is ironic, almost a joke, like Magritte's "*Ceci n'est pas une pipe*." This man is a displaced person, stripped of statehood and naked of rights at the moment of greatest need. Waiting on the deck of a Maltese boat, he stands (or rather, sits) in for Arendt's paradox.

Like the unseen children in government facilities in Texas, these refugees form a space of disappearance. Not one of them even looks at another in the group. They do not disclose their identities. Their bodies have become freight. In fact, we do not see anything of their bodies below mid-torso. Without indicators of motion, not even signs of breathing, we cannot gauge time. The men might have been floating in this bubble on the ship for minutes, hours, days, months, or years. The juxtaposition of a hat, sunglasses, long sleeves, and open shirts make the season unclear, if seasons have meaning anymore on the limitless sheet of blue and gray. Dancers are poets of motion, who distill the physical to its essence, but these men have reached the epitome of impoverishment since they own only their bodies, in Arendt's view. They are movers without agency, inhabiting a timeless circle, reduced to the level of *animal laborens* with no labour to do. Malta will let them disembark, or it will not, *inshallah*. They will stay on the ship, go to a camp, perhaps on the southern coast an hour's drive from the capital, or they will go somewhere else, maybe return to their points of origin.

The "Being Human" man performs for a global audience without, in the moment of performance, realizing his role. He is a mover, fulfilling Peggy Phelan's condition that performance disappears. A human who has vanished into a space of disappearance, he hovers inside a gerund, never arriving. His movements are non-volitional. His journey continues to segment. The bubble never collapses. He is surrounded by others, but he is alone. His body's awareness involutes. He is no longer the author of his own folktale, and the writing of his shirt marks the last entry he made on his notation score. He is a human being without humanity, as layers of society slough off into the sea. He is a dancer on a vanishing stage not of his choosing. Whatever "Being Human" is, it is not enough.

Notes

1 Aside from the volume of articles, books, and anthologies relating to cognitive science, perhaps a humanizing moment demonstrates the interest in embodiment. During a Performance Studies International conference in Calgary, a linguist from UC-Berkeley gave a riveting keynote lecture in which he shone with his joy at having happened upon choreography as a theoretical lens for problems in the philosophy of language.

2 Marie Rambert's use of Benesh notation played a role in the Joffrey Ballet's reconstruction of Vaslav Nijinksy's lost masterpiece, *The Rite of Spring*, for example.

3 US Congressman Ted Deutch (D-FL), released three documents to the House Judiciary Committee: Office of Refugee Resettlement, Health and Human Services, "Sexual Assaults by Date of Incident, FY2015-18," NadUAC-001213; "Sexual Assaults, FY2015-18," NadUAC-001214; "Sexual Assault Policy," NadUAC-001217.

4 The day after writing this sentence, I saw Henri Matisse's painting *La Coiffure* (1901) at the National Gallery of Art in Washington, DC, which features a seated

nude woman's back. The female form forms an important and well-critiqued feature of Western art, but the signification of backspace still seems underexplored.

5 *Being Human* aired for five seasons on the BBC (2001–13), as well as four seasons on Canadian television (2011–14).

References

Bonnici, Charlo'. "On Being Human." *The Malta Independent*, Sunday ed., June 22, 2014.

Conquergood, Dwight. "Performance Studies: Interventions and Radical Research." *The Drama Review* 46, no. 2.(2002): 145–56.

Cornwell, T. Bettina. "T-Shirts as Wearable Diary: An Examination of Artifact Consumption and Garnering Related to Life Events." *NA—Advances in Consumer Research* 17 (1990): 375–9.

Davis, Fred. *Fashion, Culture, and Identity*. Chicago: University of Chicago Press, 2013.

Foster, Susan Leigh. *Reading Dancing: Bodies and Subjects in Contemporary American Dance*. Berkeley: University of California Press, 1986.

Franko, Mark. *Bodies as Text: Ideologies of the Baroque Body*. Cambridge, UK: Cambridge UP, 1993.

Franko, Mark. "Writing for the Body: Notation, Reconstruction, and Reinvention in Dance." Common Knowledge 17, no. 2 (2011): 321–34.

French, Iggy. "Being Human … The Way Forward." *The Times of Malta*, November 5, 2017.

Goffman, Erving. *Relations in Public: Microstudies of the Public Order*. London & New York: Routledge, 2017.

Guest, Ann Hutchinson. *Labanotation: The System of Analyzing and Recording Movement*, 4th ed. New York & London: Routledge, 2005.

Haag, Matthew. "Thousands of Immigrant Children Said They Were Sexually Abused in U.S. Detention Centers, Report Says." *The New York Times*, February 27, 2019.

Jennings, Rebecca. "Melania Trump Wears 'I Really Don't Care, Do U?'." Vox, June 28, 2018.

Lansdale, Janet. "A Tapestry of Intertexts: Dance Analysis for the Twenty-First Century." In *The Routledge Dance Studies Reader*, edited by Alexandra Carter and Janet O'Shea, 158–67. London & New York: Routledge, 2010.

Lupi, Darrin Zammit. "Islelanders: A Photographic Project." Website, 2014.

Lupi, Zammit. "Being Human." *The Daily Star*, June 16, 2016.

Martin, Ivan. "Malta One of Main Refugee Countries." *The Times of Malta*, June 20, 2018.

Milne, A.A. *Winnie the Pooh*. New York: Penguin Books, 2009.

Muggleton, David. *Inside Subculture: The Postmodern Meaning of Style*. Oxford & New York: Berg, 2002.

Office of Inspector General. "Separated Children Placed in Office of Refugee Resettlement." Care Report OEI-BL-18-00511. US Department of Health & Human Services, January 2019.

Roach, Joseph. *It*. Ann Arbor: University of Michigan Press, 2007.

Rogers, Katie. "Melania Trump Wore a Jacket Saying 'I Really Don't Care' on Her Way to Texas Shelters." *The New York Times*, June 21, 2018.

Sofer, Andrew. *The Stage Life of Props*. Ann Arbor: University of Michigan Press, 2003.

"Transcript: ABC News Chief National Affairs Correspondent Tom Llamas Interviews First Lady." ABC News, October 13, 2018.

Washington, John. "Family Separations at the Border Constitute Torture, New Report Claims." *The Intercept*, February 25, 2020.

Epilogue

Is stillness a right?

This book has explored ways that movement studies can inform mobility and refugee studies. Through an exploration of movement initiation, body, space, trace form, and dance notation, hopefully the chapters have highlighted the physics of refugee somatics, and how non-refugees can sensitize their perceptions, allowing for the possibility of kinesthetic empathy. Movement analysis, dance, and somatics are vast endeavors, as are the manifestations of refugee narratives. Perhaps the preceding case studies will give at least some indication of possibilities for future scholarly improvisations.

The introduction hinted at a paradox inherent in using movement to understand a movement phenomenon, to which this coda returns. Movement practitioners live for movement, and interpret the world in terms of the body's potentiality for traveling through space, time, and energy. Yet displacement is the proximate cause of mass-scale suffering in our moment. As I was finishing the initial draft of this manuscript, the Dance Studies Association (DSA), the leading academic organization for dance, dance history, and movement studies released a "Statement on the Inviolability of Movement as a Right" that exemplifies this dissonance. Addressing the global refugee crisis, the DSA wrote:

> As scholars and artists in dance we investigate, theorize, and practice movement in all its expansive meanings and possibilities. Therefore, this statement expresses our deep concern for those moving across borders who seek safety from violence, slavery, military occupation and poverty resulting from colonialism, disaster capitalism, and trans-border exploitative economic policies.[1]

The organization concluded with the proclamation, "We stand in solidarity with the inviolable right and freedom to move," and, as such, "We regard the possibility of shifting in space, and the altering of our physical and social conditions of being, as a basic tenet of our political existence and a connective thread across species as we strive to live in greater harmony with the planet and each other." Since movement is an "inviolable right," and expresses "expansive meanings and possibilities," the pain of refugee performance derives from forces extrinsic to movement, such as "colonialism, disaster capitalism, and trans-border exploitative economic policies," the statement claims. The manifesto ends with an emphasis on indigenous rights, and the incarceration of children along the US–Mexico border.[2] Recalling dance anthropologist Judith Lynn Hanna's linkage between movement and emotion, the statement signs off, "So Moved, The Dance Studies Association."

The DSA's statement calls for empathy with displaced persons, but the email blast feels directed at the organization's membership more than to the world at large, or to refugees. Movement is an inherent good, so, *ipso facto*, anything negative must come from powers that pervert movement, inhibit movement expression, or in some way relate to oppressive practices. For instance, the US government's policy of caging children along the border, which this book has also explored, illustrates an example of arrested movement. The statement expresses solidarity with displaced persons as fellow movers, but beyond this opening of spirit, what is the call to action? More movement? Refugees *are* on the move. Isn't that the problem?

As a mover myself, I applaud the DSA leadership's courage in grappling with the demon of unwilling movement, in an explicit, public way. Having talked about motion for the preceding pages, however, a more productive approach may lie in making a meditation on its inverse. Is stillness a basic human right? If so, from where does this privilege emerge? How would we ensure the right to not move? What obligations does stillness impose upon movers? If stillness is not a human right, why not?

Within mobility studies, stillness has emerged as an inevitable sub-specialty. As Tim Cresswell quips, "Usually, it does not take long for the academically inclined to start to explore the seeming opposite of what is currently fashionable" (2012, p. 648). At first, mobility scholars posited instances of "immobility" and "stuck-ness" as pathological. Antitheses of mobility, stagnant situations effuse senselessness. Going against the grain, David Bissell and Gillian Fuller, in their anthology *Stillness in a Mobile World*, argue for a consideration of stillness within motion as part of their field's methodology. They write, "a topology of stillness haunts the space of flows" (2011, p.4). For Bissell and Fuller, stillness acts as a kind of "other," and the "containers" in which the hegemonic moving majority place moments of stillness illuminate the codes by which cultures perform. Once we start to look, we may see non-motion everywhere, "*Stillness punctuates the flow of all things*: a queuer in line at the bank; a moment of focus; a passenger in the departure lounge; a suspension before a sneeze"—something we typically consider, "more or less, as an aberration and thus a problem to be dealt with" (p.3; italics in original). Woe to a motorist who does not accelerate fast enough after the light turns green. Street performers enact "living statues," with hats on the ground as receptacles (containers) for coins (arrested value).

As actions that confound everyday convention, acts of stillness can serve as vehicles for social protest. Whereas marches provide the format for protest *sui generis*, stillness can prove devastating. To refer again to Martin Luther

King, Jr., his tactics of sit-ins and bus boycotts stilled motion to energize movements. Similarly, an anonymous "tank man" created a defining moment in the history of the Twentieth Century consciousness by standing in front of a row of tanks in Tiananmen Square, China, in 1989, as part of a pro-democracy student uprising. A David vs. Goliath moment, the protester's stillness riveted (fixed into immobility) the world's consciousness.

Bissell and Fuller's insistence on the presence of stillness in motion harks back, at least in general terms, to ancient Buddhist precepts that the world of sensoria functions as illusion and pain (*maya*). Detaching from the incessance of the ever-shifting material heightens consciousness. Taking this premise to its logical conclusion, enlightenment comes when the seeker breaks away from the world of change, thereby severing the cycle of reincarnation, and joins with the universal. Stillness scholars likely do not tend to characterize their work as spiritual, but they would probably offer that glimpses into stillness yield a "deeper" insight into human interchange. Things that move require precision in their description, of course, but such objects of study appear out in the open for all to see. Coming to the world with a presumption of locomotion, movement scholars must take an extra step to theorize about things that do *not* move.

For his part, Rudolf von Laban did not believe that stillness exists, or if it does, that an absence of motion is something to fear. At most, Laban felt that points of recuperation provide a breath before the next movement. Stillness is not a stationary state but one of dynamic tension. Laban wrote, "Stillness is a dimensional balancing of the body mass around the centre of gravity. Movement is a diagonal lifting-out from this state of equilibrium." Like breath, "Every movement has its *beginning in stillness*, a journey leading to a new stillness, with this second stillness being its conclusion" (McCaw 2011, p.169; italics in original). Today, movement analysts use terminology like "dynamic stillness" or "dynamic pause" as placeholders for null movement. At such moments, spatial pulls exert equal force, and therefore dynamic tension, like negotiating a game of tug-of-war. What we perceive as stillness is opposing forces humming in balance.

In his definition of moments of recuperation masquerading as stillness, Laban was searching for ways to express the nature of physical tension, and the metaphysical nothingness from and into which motion exits and enters. An artist-bohemian, Laban sought more colorful ways to convey these same thoughts. During a 1939 speech, Laban poeticized this process of fall and recovery with the phrase "stillness and stir," which probably captures his meaning more than mechanical descriptions (Laban 1984, pp.68–70). For a prelude to one of his dance films, *Dance is Life*, Laban wrote an unmistakable formula: "Dance is Life, stillness is death!" (McCaw 2011, p.169). Dancers of all times may not express themselves quite that baldly, but many would probably go along with the gist of Laban's sentiment.

International law favors motion over stillness also. Treaty touchstones focus on movement. Article 13 of the Universal Declaration of Human

Rights (1948), which the Dance Studies Association statement echoes, states:

1 Everyone has the right to freedom of movement and residence within the borders of each state.
2 Everyone has the right to leave any country, including his own, and to return to his country. (13.1–2)

These points seem plain enough, and Article 13 serves as a guiding principle for international treaty. The language of the Universal Declaration reflects the ebullience of the cessation of global conflict, and therefore puts forth its principles in absolutist terms. Political scientist Joseph Carens makes a case for the argument that freedom entails freedom of movement, and therefore open borders, even if such a policy so goes against the will of the majority (2013). Conversely, without the ability to move across borders at will, we cannot have true freedom of movement and therefore freedom. Inequities arise when some people have more freedom of movement than others. In general, to my knowledge, language that enshrines *stillness* as a basic human right in widely adopted international treaty *does not exist*.

In practice, countries impose restrictions on movement, both *de facto* and *de jure*, which is not the same thing as defending stillness as a right. Within a state, persons may not move wherever they please, for many reasons, such as, though not limited to:

- Safety (you can't drive on the wrong side of the road)
- Private property ("No Trespassing")
- Public spaces ("Do not tread on the grass")
- Gender (at the time of this writing, bathrooms are a bizarrely contentious issue around transgender identity)
- Race (segregation in Jim Crow America or Apartheid South Africa)
- Military (the Berlin Wall, entry to military installations requiring passes)
- Age (minors cannot enter bars)
- Self-quarantine (I am making my final edits to this manuscript at home, as a novel coronavirus, COVID-19, paralyzes the world)

As creatures of habit, most people stick to the pathways they know, so that large cities become small neighborhoods. For movement across borders, states impose restrictions on length of stay, documentation, and the process of crossing. Citizens comply with restrictions, but chafe against them whenever possible. Motorists speed. Teenagers sneak into abandoned houses. Activists impose their presence on avenues of flow.

In anything, authorities use stillness as punishment. That is to say, society takes away freedom of movement as a punitive response to a defined crime. Misbehaving children get "time-outs" or disciplining parents might send children to their room, to sit until their fey madness passes. I am also old enough to remember a teacher making me sit in a corner, facing the walls, for some infraction of classroom etiquette. Police arrest suspects, which to say, they arrest their motion with handcuffs, locked police vehicles, and then cells. Social mores can make people with "arrested" development feel less than human. Stephen Hawking's mind was "trapped" in a body with ALS, his body "confined" to a wheelchair. Victorian wards placed patients, who were essentially inmates, in straitjackets. In contemporary jurisprudence, terms of immobility atone for transgression.

In some cases, stillness can signify virtuosity. To say that someone or something is "arresting" means that a quality the thing or person possesses stills something in us, forces us to stop, and makes us unable to turn away. In live performance, standing still probably counts as the most difficult skill to execute (walking ranks second, running third). In *An Actor Prepares*, Stanislavski described his fictional director's ability to simply sit:

> he rose quickly, walked up to the stage in a business-like way, and sat down heavily in an arm-chair to rest, as if he were at home. He neither did nor tried to do anything, yet his simple sitting posture was striking. We watched him, and wanted to know what was going on inside of him. He smiled. So did we. He looked thoughtful, and we were eager to know what was passing through his mind. He looked at something, and we felt we must see what it was that had attracted his attention.
>
> (1967, p.33)

Stanislavski's teaching on this point works, although like Laban, Stanislavski's hero isn't really still when he sits. In a studio class for non-theater majors one semester, I asked who had the greatest stage fright. A student raised her hand, terrified. I walked with her out of earshot of the class, and asked her to stand in front of the class and do nothing but count the number of bad haircuts she saw. We walked back to the group, at which point she stood for a full two minutes in silence, scanning the room and giggling, to the astonishment of the others. As powerful as these moments seem to an audience, who cannot comprehend the "stillness" of the performer, the performer is a-whirr with activity, albeit internal.

Bringing stillness to inner landscapes belongs within the purview of spirituality. For example, the second verse of the Yoga Sutras of Patanjali states, "Yoga is the reduction of vibrations of the mindstuff."[3] The ancient yogis believed that brain activity amounted to waves, and that the eight limbs of yoga practice could lower their amplitude, like un-throwing a pebble in a pool. The word for "vibration," *vritti*, also means twist or revolution, as in a twisted *asana*, or posture. To lower the vibrations of the mindstuff resembles a process of untwisting or unfurling. Furthermore, death does not result in stillness, since mortal demise does not release us from the cycle of reincarnation. Rather, enlightenment (*samahdi*) allows us to look past the illusion of change (*maya*) and achieve union (*yoga*) with God. One who achieves enlightenment transcends dimensions and so can see all things at once.

In non-spiritual milieus, motion and stillness function as relative qualities and therefore depend on time, culture, and context. Freedom of movement would seem self-evident to a pre-agricultural nomadic tribe. Except for a natural barrier, what would stop a group of gatherer-hunters from ambling about? They might not understand the concept of "freedom of movement" any more than Native Americans could grasp what European settlers meant by "owning" land. Conversely, would we expect thanks from a medieval peasant, or a Russian serf up until 1861, were we to put them on a horse in the middle of the steppe and tell them they were "free?" Where would they go? Is an odometer reading an accurate gauge of liberation? Movement signifies differently depending on context.

Coming back to the original question—*is stillness a right?*—a right to stillness begs a prior conversation about *place*. Where does one go, versus where would one stay? Moreover, "place" need not only map onto physical topography. The case studies in this book have involved *involuntary* motion. A refugee might have yearned to visit some of the countries she had to pass through, but *not in that way*. The physical expulsion from a place signifies an affront, but the violation also, and maybe first, occurs as a psychic violence.

Stillness as it relates to citizenship ends when home becomes a place a person can no longer stay, whether due to an explosion, a threat, or an emotional hurt, an earthquake, mudslide, or climate change. In her classic meditation on early modern drama, Una Chaudhuri denominates "geopathology" as problem of place in which "the figure of home and ideal of belonging are shot through with otherness" (1997, p. 53). In the same way that the process of "hailing" imposes, names, and frames someone as an other—that icy feeling in the gut when someone behind you casts a slur, whether you turn around or not—a force that makes a place pathological to its inhabitant forces its recipient into motion. This slight against tranquility serves as the hero's call to action, but produces outcasts. "Internally displaced persons" probably do experience a sense of displacement of their insides. "Displaced persons" lack a place and, untethered to location, feel like they are flailing.

Consequently, whether stillness is a right depends on the question, "Does a person have a place?" If so, then yes, an outsider can usurp the settlers. However, if people cannot lay claim to ownership of place (a position most humans, for most of our past prior to agriculture-based civilization, embodied), then no, no such right exists, since the notion of stillness itself becomes nonsensical. Does a jellyfish have a right not to float through the water? Can a cloud stop its drift? Furthermore, if stillness does not hold meaning, then movement does not mean anything either. Mystics would claim that stillness and motion emerge from within, a falsity whose vindication results in enlightenment.

As a mover, I value movement. The sense of frozenness and decay in nursing homes repulsed me as a child, an ageism against which I still struggle, probably not unconnected to a difficulty with sitting all day in school or feeling like I would explode during long car rides. Humanity's carving up of the earth into parcels to fight over feels repugnant to me as well, the geometry of asphalt, housing plots, parking lots, and fixity abhorrent. Again, I am not trying to romanticize nomadic cultures. Our wandering ancestors may very well have fought tribe against tribe for access to the fullest fruit and the best fishing spots, struggled for control within groups, desecrated caves sacred to other assemblages, and found ways to banish, exclude, and murder.

However, "history" (the record of settled peoples) does seem to reflect a consistent story of settled peoples grinding out the itinerant. Modern-day unwilling wanderers must shoulder the weight of ten thousand years of opprobrium that the settled have laden onto nomadic peoples, in addition to the proximate horrors that propelled their flight. Refugees are not their motion. They are bodies in motion whose choreography includes an often, but not always, unsuccessful search for refuge. They are unwilling dancers, performing on stages not of their choosing. They are also human.

Notes

1 Given the fluidity of the online universe, the DSA statement in its entirety reads as follows:

January 24, 2020

Statement on the Inviolability of Movement as a Right

As scholars and artists in dance we investigate, theorize, and practice movement in all its expansive meanings and possibilities. Therefore, this statement expresses our deep concern for those moving across borders who seek safety from violence, slavery, military occupation and poverty resulting from colonialism, disaster capitalism, and trans-border exploitative economic policies. These policies have violent outcomes for people whose movements are conducted to survive conditions of precarity; these policies disproportionately harm and destroy populations made vulnerable through ongoing conditions of coloniality and imperialism, including Indigenous peoples, people of color, children, women, queer and trans persons, and others. As a field, we also point out the serious implications for artists and scholars—especially those who are stateless or from underdeveloped countries—who travel to share their work, to research, and to learn, and whose ability to travel freely has been curtailed by travel bans and xenophobic policies.

As such, we extend our support to all those affected by these policies around the world, including artists, students, faculty, and staff in our field and beyond.

We stand in solidarity with the inviolable right and freedom to move.

We move to live, to survive, to thrive, to connect, to exchange, to celebrate, to mourn, to protest, to escape. Movement conducted in respectful relationship to earth and Indigenous peoples and caretakers of land—as well as other-than-human beings inhabiting the land—is an imperative of our existence as a species, and one that must never be compromised.

We regard the possibility of shifting in space, and the altering of our physical and social conditions of being, as a basic tenet of our political existence and a connective thread across species as we strive to live in greater harmony with the planet and each other.

Furthermore, we demand that governments across the world recognize the inviolability and even sacredness of willful and respectful bodily, spiritual, and intellectual movement, reminding authorities (and each other) that nation-state "borders" have been arbitrarily set on native or tribal lands across this entire continent, and beyond.

Moreover, as a professional association rooted in colonial histories and Eurocentric paradigms, we commit to overturning the historical racism, homophobia and transphobia, ableism, and discourses and practices of appropriation in the field of dance studies, by recognizing, underscoring, and supporting the many forms of internal and external movement as an inviolable human right.

Thus, we join The Council of the Native American and Indigenous Studies Association statement issued on August 5th 2019, which in turn echoed an Open Letter by Maya scholars (May 31, 2019) directed at the governments of the United States, Mexico, and Guatemala. These statements called for an end to violence and disappearance of Native American and Indigenous people, and for formal investigations and accountability, as well as acts of reparation by the states involved in the many violations of the right to movement as self-determination at these borders.

We join the UC Davis Asian American Studies statement on DACA from September 2017, condemning "the Trump administration's decision to revoke the Deferred Action for Childhood Arrivals (DACA), the anti- Muslim/Arab/African travel ban," and plans to further militarize and segment the U.S.–Mexico border.

Lastly, we echo the American Anthropological Association statement of June 19, 2018, which states that "the recent order to separate nearly 2,000 immigrant children from their parents now delves deep into the realm of cruel, malicious, and inhumane. The American Anthropological Association resolutely rejects the decision to hold children hostage as an outright mean-spirited political ploy that will have repercussions well into the future on both sides of the border."

So Moved,
The Dance Studies Association
Board of Directors
Melissa Blanco Borelli, President Anne Flynn
Anusha Kedhar
Joanna Dee Das
Sherril Dodds
Jacqueline Shea Murphy
Janet O'Shea
Takiyah Nur Amin
Victoria Fortuna
Imani Kai Johnson
Jasmine Johnson
Royona Mitra
Prarthana Purkayastha
Sarah Wilbur
Meiver De la Cruz
Emily Wilcox

Melissa Melpignano
Irvin Manuel Gonzalez
Lizzie Leopold, Executive Director
lleopold@dancestudiesassociation.org

2 Although not explicitly stated, the DSA here is making the argument that South American governments' persecution of native peoples, and the Trump administration's retreat from regional assistance, generates refugees, including so-called annual "migrant caravans."

3 *Yogas chittas vritti nirodha.*

References

Bissell, David, and Gillian Fuller, eds. *Stillness in a Mobile World*. London & New York: Routledge, 2011.

Carens, Joseph A. *The Ethics of Immigration*. Oxford and New York: Oxford UP, 2013.

Chaudhuri, Una. *Staging Place: The Geography of Modern Drama*. Ann Arbor: University of Michigan Press, 1997.

Cresswell, Tim. "Mobilities II: Still." *Progress in Human Geography* 36, no. 5 (2012): 645–53.

Laban, Rudolf. *A Vision of Dynamic Space*. Compiled by Lisa Ullmann. London: Falmer Press in association with Laban Archives, 1984.

McCaw, Dick, ed. *The Laban Sourcebook*. New York & London: Routledge, 2011.

Stanislavski, Constantin. *An Actor Prepares*. Translated by Elizabeth Reynolds Hapgood. New York: Methuen, 1967.

Index